Nietzsche:
Truth and
Redemption

Critique of the Postmodernist Nietzsche

Ted Sadler

THE ATHLONE PRESS
London & Atlantic Highlands, NJ

First published 1995 by
The Athlone Press
1 Park Drive, London NW11 7SG
and 165 First Avenue,
Atlantic Highlands, NJ 07716

British Library Cataloguing in Publication Data
*A catalogue record for this book is available
from the British Library*

ISBN 0 485 11471 2

Library of Congress Cataloging-in-Publication Data

Sadler, Ted, 1952-
      Nietzsche : truth and redemption / Ted Sadler.
            p.   cm.
      Includes bibliographical references and index.
      ISBN 0-485-11471-2
      1. Nietzsche, Friedrich Wilhelm, 1844-1900.
      2. Nietzsche, Friedrich Wilhelm, 1844-1900–Influence.
      3. Heidegger, Martin, 1889-1976.   I. Title.
      B3317.S23   1995   94-46838
      193–dc20   CIP

Typeset by Saxon Graphics Ltd, Derby
Printed and bound in Great Britain by
the University Press, Cambridge

Nietzsche: Truth and Redemption

To Veronica

There is perhaps nothing about the so-called cultured, the believers in 'modern ideas', that arouses so much disgust as their lack of shame, the self-satisfied insolence of eye and hand with which they touch, lick and fumble with everything; and it is possible that more relative nobility of taste and reverential tact is to be discovered today among the people, among the lower orders and especially among peasants, than among the newspaper-reading demi-monde of the spirit, the cultured.
(*Beyond Good and Evil*, no. 263)

Contents

Preface

The present study attempts an alternative to the subjectivist interpretation of Nietzsche popularized by those whom I call the 'postmodernist commentators'. What I hope to show is that Nietzsche's critique of 'men of modern ideas' applies also to their contemporary descendents, and that, contrary to what recently has become orthodox opinion, Nietzsche is a resolute spokesman for philosophy and truth. If Nietzsche emerges as less timely and familiar than he is commonly taken to be, but more challenging and thoughtworthy, my aim will have been achieved.

I am grateful to the publishers for permission to use parts of a previously published article 'The Postmodernist Politicization of Nietzsche', from Paul Patton (ed.), *Nietzsche: Feminism and Political Theory*, Routledge, London, 1993.

Note on References and Method of Citation

Wherever possible, Nietzsche is cited according to the *Nietzsche Werke, Kritische Gesamtausgabe*, edited by Giorgio Colli and Mazzino Montinari, Berlin, Walter de Gruyter, 1967ff, abbreviated **KGW**. A few texts are only available in the old edition of *Nietzsche Werke*, edited by Otto Crusius and Wilhelm Nestle, Kröner Verlag, Leipzig, 1913, abbreviated **GA**. The few references to Nietzsche's correspondence can be located in *Nietzsche Briefwechsel, Kritische Gesamtausgabe*, edited by Colli and Montinari, Berlin, Walter de Gruyter, 1975–1984. In most cases easily available English translations (which I have often modified without notice in quoting Nietzsche) will be co-cited with the KGW according to aphorism or section number (or heading), as well as by page number. The translations used are as follows (with abbreviations):

Beyond Good and Evil, trans. R. J. Hollingdale, Penguin, Harmondsworth, Middlesex, 1973 (**BGE**).
The Birth of Tragedy and the Case of Wagner, trans. Walter Kaufmann, Vintage, New York, 1967 (**BT** and **CW**).
Daybreak, trans. R. J. Hollingdale, Cambridge University Press, Cambridge, 1982 (**D**).

The Gay Science, trans. Walter Kaufmann, Vintage, New York, 1974 (**GS**).

Human, All Too Human, trans. R. J. Hollingdale, Cambridge University Press, Cambridge, 1986 (**HAH I – HAH III**).

On the Genealogy of Morals and Ecce Homo, trans. Walter Kaufmann and R. J. Hollingdale, Vintage, New York, 1967 (**GM** and **EH**).

Philosophy and Truth: Selections from Nietzsche's Notebooks of the Early 1870s, trans. Daniel Breazeale, Humanities Press, New Jersey, 1979 (**PT**).

Philosophy in the Tragic Age of the Greeks, trans. Marianne Cowan, Gateway, Chicago, 1962 (**PTAG**).

Thus Spoke Zarathustra, trans. R. J. Hollingdale, Penguin, Harmondsworth, Middlesex, 1973 (**Z**).

Twilight of the Idols and The Antichrist, trans. R. J. Hollingdale, Penguin, Harmondsworth. Middlesex, 1968 (**TI** and **AC**).

Untimely Meditations, trans. R. J. Hollingdale, Cambridge University Press, Cambridge, 1983 (**UM I–UM IV**).

The Will to Power, trans. Walter Kaufmann, Vintage, New York, 1968 (**WP**).

Details of other literature can be found in the bibliography.

Introduction

We, openhanded and rich in spirit, standing by the road like open wells with no intention to fend off anyone who feels like drawing from us – we unfortunately do not know how to defend ourselves where we want to: we have no way of preventing people from *darkening* us: the time in which we live throws into us what is most time-bound; its dirty birds drop their filth into us; boys their rubbish; and exhausted wanderers who come to us to rest, their little and large miseries. But we shall do what we have always done: whatever one casts into us, we take down into our depth – for we are deep, we do not forget – *and become bright again.*[1]

A philosopher: a man who constantly experiences, sees, hears, suspects, hopes, dreams extraordinary things.[2]

THE CHALLENGE OF NIETZSCHE'S THOUGHT

In a characteristic passage from *Beyond Good and Evil*, Nietzsche writes that 'It seems to me more and more that the philosopher, being *necessarily* a man of tomorrow and the day after tomorrow, has always found himself and *had* to find himself in contradiction to his today: his enemy has always been the ideal of today.'[3] Nietzsche is well known for the provocative and confrontational style of his writings. He sees his own time as a low point in human culture, as a time of decadence, mediocrity and complacency. In book after book he attacks the 'idols' of modernity, unmasking the 'songs and ditties' of contemporary ideologists, attempting to awaken his readers from the torpitude of modern self-congratulation. Very often, when it seems to Nietzsche that his readers might warm to a particular point or passage, he lashes out: I do not mean you, he objects, if you are taking comfort from this, you do not understand me. Nietzsche is the opposite of the kind of writer who seeks to ingratiate himself with his readers: he warns them off, he puts them off, he recoils from hearing his own statements uttered by others. Throughout his career, he is convinced that his 'untimeliness' will necessarily result in the miscomprehension of his thought. He revels in his isolation, as if this is a continuing confirmation of his philosophical position.

Nevertheless, Nietzsche has become one of the most popular writers of the twentieth century: the philosopher who regarded himself as the bad conscience of his age has been embraced from every part of the cultural–ideological spectrum. As an explanation for this one may naturally point to Nietzsche's literary brilliance. Successive generations have been dazzled by his prose, which lends itself almost irresistibly to quotation, exploitation, and identification. But the style of Nietzsche cannot be considered independently of the content of his thought. For the modern educated public, the name Nietzsche stands above all for his leading philosophical motifs: 'nihilism', the 'death of God', the 'Overman', and 'will to power'. It appears that, contrary to Nietzsche's expectations, his ideas have not only come to be widely understood, but have received widespread (albeit reserved on particular points) assent. It seems that Nietzsche, as the saying goes, was ahead of his time, that he was (as he maintained himself) a prophet who saw further than his own contemporaries, that the twentieth century has by now fully caught up with Nietzsche's thought, that what was formerly so controversial, so provocative and so difficult, has become commonplace. We are also in the position, so we like to think, to correct Nietzsche where necessary, to avoid the excesses and idiosyncracies of his thought, to obtain a balanced picture of Nietzsche and his limitations. From its original status as an enigma, Nietzsche's philosophy has become a resource for many intellectual disciplines and cultural-ideological tendencies. A certain appreciation of his thought has become a requirement of modern sophistication.

The emergence of Nietzsche as a timely thinker has become particularly pronounced over the last few decades. After its misuse by the Nazis, his philosophy fell under a cloud of suspicion in the immediate post-war period, but since the early 1960s it has once again risen to prominence, this time championed not by the fascist right but by the quasi-anarchistic left. Among the 'politically correct', Nietzsche now enjoys the reputation of a 'pluralist' and 'anti-dogmatic' thinker, of an exemplary practitioner of that 'critique of authority' which identifies with the marginalized and disenfranchised elements of culture. Appropriately purged of his offensively 'subjective' attitudes to politics and society, Nietzsche has been brought within the fold of modern democratic egalitarianism. The heart of his philosophy has been sought in an epistemological doctrine which sanctions 'equal rights to all perspectives', in a view of language which overcomes 'logocentrism' in favour of 'metaphorical' discourse, in an abandonment of 'closure' and 'system' for the 'free-play' of thought and writing. In this way, so it seems, Nietzsche has become relevant: he opens our eyes to the multidimensionality of experience and life, he awakens us to the 'ruses' of anonymous authority structures, through his 'genealogical' method he puts us on guard against the hidden interests of conventional thought and language.

This approach to Nietzsche, which is exemplified above all by the contemporary postmodernist commentators influenced by such writers as Gilles Deleuze, Michel Foucault and Jacques Derrida, presents itself, and is widely taken to be, radical in its implications. In politico-ideological terms, this designation may indeed be justified, but whether this is so in a philosophical context is another question. Just what philosophical radicalism consists in is seldom reflected upon, especially among those who most loudly insist upon it. More often than not, a rather unclear

but supposedly obvious meaning is transposed from a
political to a philosophical level: to be radical is to demand
change, to want a lot and need a lot, to be daring and
shocking to the establishment, to flout convention, to
parade one's 'difference', to be avant-garde. Radicalism in
this sense frequently amounts to the same thing as fash-
ionability, however much it is presented as oppositional
and antagonistic to entrenched norms. The requirement of
solidarity produces a strong tendency to conformism, a
sense of mission justifies the anathematization of traitors to
the cause along with the idolization of its heroes, an in-
group consciousness cultivates an in-group jargon. All this
amounts to a familiar phenomenon, recognized and criticized by philosophers as far back as Plato and Aristotle.
Nor is it anything new for such 'radicals' to inscribe the
names of the great philosophers on their banners.

The present study attempts to bring to light the genuine
radicalism of Nietzsche's thought as opposed to the
pseudo-radicalism of his contemporary postmodernist
commentators.[4] What I hope will emerge is the 'challenge'
of Nietzsche's thought, in contrast to the tranquillizing and
domesticating character of the 'new Nietzsche' which they
present. Of course, the postmodernists would agree that all
genuine philosophy must challenge, but, as Nietzsche
knew, what is experienced as challenging varies greatly
between individuals. Just what the really challenging
questions are, just how philosophy in fact challenges, can
be decided only within philosophy itself. Nietzsche himself never tired of stressing that philosophy can never be
challenging, i.e. can never be genuine philosophy at all, if it
proceeds from an unproblematized moral standpoint. In
the case of the postmodernist commentators, however, it is
precisely such a standpoint which is all-determinative:
modern democratic pluralism is the constant and unex-
amined basis of the kind of 'radicalism' which 'challenges'
through a 'critique of authority'.[5] As we shall see in
Chapter One, the celebration of Nietzsche's 'perspectivism' is only one instance of this: his 'rejection of truth' is

comprehended as part and parcel of an 'anti-dogmatic' outlook.

From the moral-political standpoint of the postmodernist commentators, it seems challenging and radical to say 'there is no truth'. By contrast, it will be shown in the following chapters that Nietzsche thinks of truth precisely as the fundamental radical demand and challenge of all genuine philosophy. Nietzsche continually comes back to the problem of truth, not because he wants to expel this concept from philosophy, not because he wants to 'liberate' thought from the 'dogma' of truth, but because he seeks to validate the idea of philosophical truth. In his view, traditional metaphysics has taken the problem of truth too lightly, it has been over ready to take perspectives as truths, it has been unwilling to enter into the radical kind of existence which philosophical truthfulness demands. One can acknowledge, along with the postmodernists, that Nietzsche does not simply wish to present an alternative set of truths: as we shall see, the assertions contained in his own writings are not meant as such. Instead, he wants to exhibit the attitude of truthfulness, the particular stance towards reality which is definitive of truth. It is this attitude, and not any new historical reality, which is behind Nietzsche's confrontation with nihilism. The common view that Nietzsche reacts to nihilism by saying 'there is no truth' is superficial, for it is only Nietzsche's truthfulness which allows the full force of nihilism to become visible for him. Previous philosophers, in his opinion, had failed to come to terms with nihilism. They had overlooked this phenomenon, however, not because it is so new, but because of their deficient philosophical resolve.[6] To enter into this phenomenon, to pose the problem of truth in this context, is the challenge which Nietzsche's philosophy attempts to meet. Only thus, in his view, can philosophy be what it essentially is: a process of radical questioning.[7]

TRUTH AND REDEMPTION

One of the foremost concerns of the present study will be to show that, contrary to popular current opinion, Nietzsche holds to an absolutistic conception of philosophy and of philosophical truth. In this connection, the Nietzschean motif of redemption is singled out for special treatment in Chapter Three. In its normal usage, the term has religious connotations, which is probably why, despite the frequency of its appearance in Nietzsche's texts, it has been all but ignored by the postmodernist commentators. Whether and to what extent Nietzsche is himself religious are questions which will arise at the appropriate stage, and it is advisable to resist any premature conclusions at the outset. For Nietzsche, the interrogation of philosophy and religion go hand in hand, and it may be expected that his ambivalence on the former will be paralleled in the latter case. In any event, the concept redemption runs through his writings (with some interruption in the middle works) as an indication of the existential value of philosophical truth. Nietzsche's major objection to the metaphysical conception of truth is that it lacks this existential dimension: it makes little difference to life, failing to connect with the ultimate reality of individual existence. Redemption is a concept which signifies the radicality of the demands which philosophy makes on the individual who enters into it, the radical (absolute) difference between the philosophical life and the normal life.

With the concept of redemption, Nietzsche makes the problem of truth into a subjective problem. In its familiar Christian context, the subjective need for redemption consists in a condition of sinfulness, of having 'turned away from God'. This is a condition which, from the point of view of the individual, has both positive and negative aspects. On the one hand it allows him to enjoy the things of this world, but on the other hand the impoverishment of his spiritual life is experienced as a burden and as consciousness of guilt: alienation from God is also self-alienation, for it prevents human beings from attaining their own godly nature. Despite Nietzsche's critical attitude to Christian doctrine, an analogous idea governs his understanding of the relation between human beings and truth. In his view, the natural or everyday condition of human existence is one of untruth, such that the vast majority live out their entire lives in this state. Human beings cling to untruth and make this the foundation of their existence. Just as atheists, who feel at home in ungodliness, tell themselves that 'there is no God', so do those who feel at home in untruth continually reassure themselves that 'there is no truth'. The idea of truth appears useless, a diversion from practical problems, anti-social, threatening, even wicked. For Nietzsche, the fundamental perversity and corruption of human beings is that they give their heart to untruth, that their lives are therefore a constant slander of truth, of something which is in fact the only proper object of honour and reverence. Redemption is release from this condition: it is 'a passing over into truth', understood, however, not as a matter of beliefs, but as a comprehensive existential reorienation.

In an analogous way to Christianity, Nietzsche sees the path to redemption as a path of suffering. Truthfulness goes against the grain, very much must be given up along the way, particularly the 'good opinion of men' and the cherished self-image of the ego. To go along this path requires more than an ordinary degree of courage. There are always many (Nietzsche calls them 'the herd') who are anxious to pull one back, to pour scorn and ridicule on the truth-seeker, to contrast the 'fantasies' of the philosopher with the tangible benefits of the common life. More than any other philosopher, Nietzsche stresses the psychological difficulties of truthfulness. The philosophical life, as distinct from the pseudo-philosophical intellectual life, is 'questionable': throwing away the props of existential mendaciousness implies risks which are unknown to the non-philosopher. However, in another parallel with the

Christian idea, Nietzsche sees redemption into truth as a kind of bliss or joy. In the case of Zarathustra, this is experienced in the 'tremendous moment of affirmation' which comes through willing the 'eternal return of the same'. Truth would not be truth unless it can be so experienced: this is the ultimate 'subjective' motivation of the philosopher, the answer to that enigmatic question with which Nietzsche opens *Beyond Good and Evil*: 'why do we want truth?'

SCHOPENHAUER AND HEIDEGGER

Nietzsche is well known for his view that philosophers have hitherto lacked historical sense.[8] From this it should not be concluded that he is an historicist or in any sense an historical relativist. He sees his own problems not as peculiarly modern but as perennial problems, as the same problems which have occupied philosophers since before the time of Plato, as problems which assume a particular historical guise but which are always at bottom the same inevitable problems of human existence as such. Historical situatedness gives a particular form to these problems, setting limits to the possibilities of their expression, but it does not create them.[9] Nor, as Nietzsche found in the case of many of his philological colleagues, does any amount of historical erudition and intellectuality guarantee a genuine comprehension of these problems. Since they relate to the phenomenon of existence itself, these problems must be recognizable prior to and independently of any particular (historically determinate) symbolical expression. They are the prior problems of existence, which make themselves felt at all times and places, but there are also strong forces which mitigate against their recognition. It is common to confuse them with the lesser, more timely problems of the vast majority, problems which seem more capable of resolution and whose relevancy is easily attested to. Nor does Nietzsche think, as we shall see, that philosophical problems are created by texts: rather, he considers that the philosophy (and the philosopher) behind the text can under certain circumstances become visible or audible. The major factor determining this is the intuition of the reader. Philosophy presupposes an intuitive sensitivity to its problems, and this is what Nietzsche looks for first of all in those he reads himself. Nietzsche reads and studies other philosophers not in order to become influenced by them, but because they further open up the problems with which he himself is occupied, because they allow these problems to be further entered into and more genuinely appropriated.

Such considerations are behind the particular contextualization of Nietzsche attempted in the present study. I have restricted my focus to the primary philosophical meaning of Nietzsche's writings. Although not ignoring the historical context of Nietzsche, I take it for granted that the latter alone can never provide the kind of comprehension Nietzsche demands of us. We must study carefully what Nietzsche says about his problems, we must beware of reading the problems of today back into Nietzsche, and of reading back the problems of other philosophers. In the case of Schopenhauer, however, we have a philosophical context the relevance of which Nietzsche stressed himself. There are more references to Schopenhauer in Nietzsche's writings than to any other philosopher (and more than to any other individual except Wagner). As is evident from the third 'Untimely Meditation', Nietzsche found in Schopenhauer his own problems, tackled in an appropriately radical way and expressed through an appropriate 'pathos'. Nietzsche's early readers, prior to the First World War, also found the same problems in both thinkers, and were often (e.g. Thomas Mann) equally influenced by both. By the early twenties, however, Schopenhauer's direct influence, which had been strong through the years 1860–1900, was on the wane, partly because Nietzsche dealt with his problems in a more modern context, and partly because of what Nietzsche called the 'motley leopard skin' of Schopenhauer's metaphysical system. Schopenhauer, although himself a supremely lucid writer, presents his readers with more technical difficulties than does Nietzsche. In order to come to the heart of his philosophy, which is contained in Book Three and especially Book Four of *The World as Will and Representation*, one has to wade through the quasi-Kantian epistemology of Book One, and then the disturbingly speculative metaphysic of will in Book Two. Nietzsche seemed to have distilled whatever was of genuine value in Schopenhauer, but without himself falling into the snares of a metaphysical system. This perception was reinforced from the mid-thirties by the influence of Heidegger, whose lectures on Nietzsche are uniformly dismissive of and hostile to Schopenhauer. After the Second World War, Schopenhauer became more and more forgotten, his writings seldom read by those interested in Nietzsche.

The attention given to Schopenhauer in the present study is not because I wish to emphasize the influence of Schopenhauer on Nietzsche, but because the relation between the two philosophers is a context which allows Nietzsche's problems to come into view. The early Nietzsche felt such a profound affinity with Schopenhauer that he rapidly fell into Schopenhauerian philosophical terminology and schemata. The lasting significance this had for the formulae of Nietzsche's thought is in no way diminished by the fact that in his later period Nietzsche took a more distant and critical attitude to Schopenhauer. One example (to be examined in detail in Chapter Three) is the Schopenhauerian polemical opposition between 'life affirmation' and 'life denial'. This opposition has a defining role in both Schopenhauer's pessimistic philosophy of life denial and Nietzsche's 'Dionysian' (in a certain sense optimistic) philosophy of life affirmation. The fundamental opposition itself comes from Schopenhauer and is not seriously questioned by Nietzsche at any time of his career. All the major oppositions in Nietzsche's philosophy ('this-

world' versus 'other world', 'Dionysus' versus 'the Cru-
cified' etc.) are indebted to this original Schopenhauerian
dichotomy. We shall see in Chapter Three that in some
ways Nietzsche's Schopenhauerianism inhibits him in his
basic aims, but this is not to chastise Nietzsche for being
'too Schopenhauerian'. What Schopenhauer provided for
Nietzsche is a way of formulating his own problems, thus
a way of working through them and making progress in his
own philosophical pilgrimage. Nietzsche never fettered
himself with Schopenhauerian doctrines, indeed he was
often too hasty in dismissing them, often too anxious to
refute Schopenhauer within the latter's own framework.
The present study, while not attempting any comprehensive review of Nietzsche's relation to Schopenhauer, brings
in the Schopenhauerian context of Nietzsche's ideas where
this is most important for his basic problems. In this way
the difference between Nietzsche's problems and those of
his postmodernist commentators will also come to light.

Just as Nietzsche is bordered on the far side by
Schopenhauer, so is he bordered on the near side by
Heidegger. Of course, Heidegger is only one of many
twentieth-century thinkers to have been influenced by
Nietzsche. The question in each case, however, is whether a
thinker is first of all in a position to be genuinely influenced,
something which depends on whether Nietzsche's problems (including the way in which he works them through)
are genuinely in view. There are many who are interested in
Nietzsche, who interpret him, who write about his philosophy, who utilize Nietzsche in various ways. All this, as
Nietzsche stressed himself, does not necessarily indicate a
profound comprehension of his thought. Heidegger once
said that 'there is much noise around Nietzsche', implying
(according to his well-known metaphor) that the
'audibility' of Being, as the true region of Nietzsche's
problems and philosophical questioning, is drowned out by
incessant 'chatter' about the 'death of God', 'nihilism', the
'Overman', the 'will to power' and of course (especially

these days) 'perspectivism'. Although I have devoted a separate chapter to Heidegger's relation to Nietzsche, many readers will recognize the pervasive influence of Heidegger in the present study. This does not mean, however, that I attempt a Heideggerian interpretation of Nietzsche, no more than my attention to Schopenhauer signifies a Schopenhauerian interpretation. My presupposition is that Schopenhauer, Nietzsche and Heidegger represent three successive stages in the progressive working through of the same fundamental problems, and that, when seen in their interrelation, each can be better understood on his own account. This, as stated, is a presupposition, the plausibility of which can only emerge in the course of the study. Since my focus is on Nietzsche himself, no more than a preliminary indication can be given of his relation to these other thinkers.

METHOD AND PLAN OF THE PRESENT STUDY

A new conception of philosophical truth implies a new conception of the unity of truth. Everyone knows that many of Nietzsche's statements contradict one another, that Nietzsche disavows the philosophical system and repudiates the idea of a final interpretation. Amongst the postmodernist commentators, this means that Nietzsche's philosophy does not possess a 'centre', that his works display a kind of undogmatic 'fragmentary writing' which does not need to justify itself before the 'authoritarian' tribunal of truth. In practice, this latter attitude provides a licence to exploit Nietzsche for any convenient purpose, while remaining immune from the (authoritarian) charge of distortion. My own view, as already indicated, is that behind Nietzsche's writings there is a unitary conception of the problems of philosophy, as of philosophical truth itself. To show that this is so requires examining Nietzsche's works in their totality, including the *Nachlaß*, taking full account of their chronological order and of Nietzsche's self-interpretations. It is necessary, in order to avoid the dangers of generalization and abstraction, to let Nietzsche speak for himself, but also to provide the contexts which make his statements intelligible. I have not regarded it as permissible to marginalize certain aspects of his thought as subjective, or as belonging to a youthful stage, but have tried to see his development as he saw it himself, as an organic process of philosophical growth. Nor am I attracted by the tendency to resolve Nietzsche's philosophical problems by referring to his style, rhetoric, parody or to the idea of philosophy as literature. Nietzsche did not spend his whole life worrying about philosophical problems because he thought that philosophy is literature. He lived and wrote in the way he did because he thought that philosophical problems were, in a sense we shall have to determine, 'obligatory'. The meaning of the obligatory character of philosophy is the basic question asked by Nietzsche: he does not for a moment doubt this obligatoriness, he does not (as many do today) breathe a sigh of relief and say 'there is nothing obligatory after all'. As we shall see, Nietzsche tests, and finds wanting, the obligatoriness of philosophy as hitherto conceived (within metaphysics) only to affirm what he sees as a more radical and rigorous obligatoriness.

In Chapter One I deal with some common misconceptions of Nietzsche's 'perspectivism', particularly those which associate it with pluralism and relativism, thus with a rejection of 'absolute truth'. We shall see that, as Nietzsche understands it, perspectivism does not rule out, but rather presupposes, an absolutistic conception of truth. Only when this is understood can the authentically philosophical radicalism of Nietzsche's thought emerge, as opposed to the mere epistemological radicalism of postmodernist pluralism and other forms of relativism. In this first chapter some attempt is also made to locate Nietzsche with respect to his contemporary philosophical situation, especially to the critiques of metaphysics of Kant and Schopenhauer. It will be shown that Nietzsche retains a faith in philosophy to the extent that, with the aid of Schopenhauer, he frees himself from the conceptualism (intellectualism) of Kantian scepticism. Nietzsche's reply to Kant is to posit a form of truth which is neither knowledge nor morality, but something prior to both, an original 'orientation to reality' which can be expressed but never represented (made present) in language or other symbolism. Chapter Two explains this existential conception of truth in more detail, through Nietzsche's idea of the 'hierarchy of the spirit'. For Nietzsche, truthfulness does not pertain in the first instance to discourse, statements, or theories but to certain kinds of existence: it is the measure of the 'rank-order' of human beings. By looking at the way Nietzsche ranks various 'types' of human beings we can discover what he regards as relevant to truthfulness and indicative of it. Nietzsche's basic criterion, an affirmative stance towards life, is further examined in Chapter Three, and brought into relation with the redemptive character of truthfulness. The question is raised as to whether 'redemption as life-affirmation' may not be rather more occluded than clarified by some of Nietzsche's other ontological formulae, particularly the opposition this-world/other world, and the well-known doctrine of 'eternal return'. Finally, Chapter Four sets Nietzsche's problems in the context of Heidegger's idea of the *Sache* (subject matter, substance, the 'what-ness') of philosophy. We shall see that, for both thinkers, philosophy is less a matter of producing philosophical theories (or of writing various texts) than of awakening to certain phenomena, of staying awake, of an appropriation of this wakefulness as the essence of one's being.

1
Perspectivism and its Limits

Truth will have no other gods beside it. – Belief in truth begins with doubt as to all 'truths' believed in hitherto.[1]

Nitimur in vetitum: in this sign my philosophy will triumph one day, for what one has forbidden so far as a matter of principle has always been – truth alone.[2]

For this alone is fitting for a philosopher. We have no right to *isolated* acts of any kind: we may not make isolated errors or hit upon isolated truths. Rather do our yeas and nays, our ifs and buts, grow out of us with the necessity with which a tree bears fruit – related and each with an affinity to each, and evidence of *one* will, *one* health, *one* soil, *one* sun.[3]

PERSPECTIVISM AND TRUTH

The postmodernist commentators present perspectivism as the basic idea behind Nietzsche's critique of metaphysics. Against the supposition of a metaphysically privileged viewpoint corresponding to a metaphysically privileged ontology, perspectivism, in the words of Jean Granier, 'defends an ontological *pluralism*: the essence of Being is to show itself according to an *infinity of viewpoints*.'[4] Whereas metaphysical philosophy seeks a final authoritative theory of reality, it is just this possibility, so the postmodernists contend, which Nietzsche rejects by drawing attention to the anthropocentricity and therefore perspectival character of all interpretation. Since there are unlimited possibilities for human subjectivity, there are also unlimited perspectives on the world, perspectives which cannot be judged in terms of an (epistemologically impossible) adequacy relation to independent reality. Thus Alan Schrift sees

Nietzschean perspectivism as 'demystifying the philosophical pretensions to truth and knowledge', and as an effective antidote to 'the philosopher's arrogant claims to
knowledge.'[5] Debra B. Bergoffen depicts Nietzsche as
'inaugurating a higher history of humanity by constructing
a philosophy of perspectivism where the concept of the
interpretative center replaces the convention of absolute
centredness.'[6] Babette Babich reports that 'Nietzsche's
multivalently heterogeneous perspectivalism anticipates
the inherent ambivalence of the postmodern challenge to
hierarchized discourse, specifically to the question of the
authorial or traditional authority and the presumption of a
final word.'[7] Alexander Nehamas equates Nietzsche's
perspectivism with 'a refusal to grade people and views
along a single scale.'[8] Gilles Deleuze, one of the founding
figures of Nietzschean postmodernism, plainly states that
'Nietzsche does not criticize false claims to truth but truth
itself and as an ideal.'[9]

   This last claim of Deleuze provides a convenient oppor-
tunity for concisely specifying the thesis of the present
chapter. I shall be arguing, *contra* Deleuze and the whole
tendency of postmodernist commentary, that Nietzsche
does criticize false claims to truth, but not truth itself as an
ideal. This means that Nietzsche's perspectivism is not, as it
is commonly taken to be, a perspectivalization of truth
itself. Of course, the view that all truth is perspectival is
faced with the paradox of self-reference. If the philosophy of perspectivism is itself perspectival, then it would
seem to have no more validity than any other philosophy,
and if it is not, then perspectivism has at least one exception
and can no longer be seen as a fundamental philosophical
position. The advocates of a perspectivist Nietzsche have
never succeeded in resolving this paradox, attempting
instead to sidestep it in various ways. As I hope to show,
however, once the place of perspectivism within
Nietzsche's total philosophy is understood, the paradox
does not arise. In particular, I shall elucidate the meaning of

'perspectival truth' in such a way that its subordinate position vis-à-vis 'absolute truth' can come to light. Only on the basis of such clarification can Nietzsche's much-publicized 'overcoming of metaphysics' be understood in its authentic tendency.

The view of Nietzsche as a perspectivist originates, despite the protestations of its advocates, in an epistemological conception of philosophy. By the latter I mean a conception of philosophy which is oriented to knowledge and which identifies truth with knowledge. Nietzsche's relativization of all knowledge to perspectives is thus taken to imply a relativization of truth itself. The perspectivist commentators are well aware of Nietzsche's stated hostility to epistemology, but they misinterpret his reasons for this attitude: they think that rejecting epistemology is the same thing as rejecting the quest for a final authoritative doctrine. I shall argue that, although Nietzsche does indeed reject the possibility of such a final perspective this is not the focus of his philosophy, and by itself does not at all imply an overcoming of epistemology. As long as the implicit identification of truth with knowledge remains unquestioned, the perspectivalization of knowledge/truth remains an epistemological proposition, albeit an unstable one due to the above-indicated problem of self-reference. It is no accident that perspectivist commentators on Nietzsche play up his critique of dogmatism and ignore, or attempt to explain away, his critique of relativism. They do this because, according to the epistemological assumption that truth is knowledge, dogmatism and relativism are the basic alternatives in philosophy. Nietzsche takes an entirely different attitude: what he seeks, and what he also assumes, is a conception of truth which is beyond the opposition of dogmatism and relativism. At times Nietzsche can seem dogmatic, at other times he can seem more relativistic. The way to resolve this difficulty is not to ignore one (or explain it away, perhaps as a matter of Nietzsche's political views) in favour of the other, but to understand the extra-epistemological conception of truth underlying it. It will then emerge that Nietzsche's apparent 'dogmatism' and 'relativism' (these terms are not really applicable outside of epistemological problematics) belong to different 'levels of truth' and are not at all in opposition.

Despite the 'radical' credentials of Nietzsche's perspectivist commentators, it is precisely Nietzsche's radicalism which they do not understand. For them, what is radical about Nietzsche's thought is the supposed implication of 'equal rights to all perspectives', a maxim which is admirably suited to the politico-ideological pluralism which they expound. This kind of radicalism, however, has its origins in the democratic egalitarianism which Nietzsche sees as the sworn enemy of philosophy. By contrast, the present study maintains that the radicalism of Nietzsche's thought consists not in its pluralistic and therefore anti-dogmatic implications, but in its transcending of the whole opposition between dogmatism and relativism through an extra-epistemological conception of existential truth. What this means will be elucidated in the course of the following chapters, but as a preliminary indication it can be said that existential truth relates to the 'stance' of the concrete human being to that 'primordial reality' which Nietzsche calls 'life'. This stance, which Nietzsche attempts to illuminate through his idea of 'Dionysian affirmation' as well as in other ways, is not 'primordially' cognitive and therefore is not 'primordially' expressed in discourse. As we shall see, it is the particular way of existence in which the problem of existence itself is taken up, and in which, just on account of this, the phenomenon of existence first of all becomes visible. For Nietzsche, this is the stance of all authentic philosophy and the original truthfulness of all authentic philosophers: truth as pertaining to statements, propositions, theories, points of view, perspectives, indeed truth as pertaining to anything linguistic at all, is derivative. The stance of existential 'truthfulness' (Nietzsche sometimes prefers this term to 'truth') opens up and holds open what we may call, following Heidegger, the *Sache* of philosophy.[10] Strictly speaking, it is not his own conception of philosophy but the *Sache* of philosophy which Nietzsche takes to be radical: one is radical, in other words, simply by being a philosopher. Once Nietzsche's conception of the existential radicalism of philosophy is understood, it will become plain that Nietzsche cannot be a perspectivist at this level. The postmodernist commentators, on the other hand, put all the emphasis on the distinction between discourses which recognize the perspectival character of all interpretation and those which do not. In this way the dogmatism/relativism couplet is maintained: metaphysical discourses which make a claim to unconditional truth are counterposed to post-metaphysical 'playful' or 'metaphorical' discourses which acknowledge their own relativity. Nietzsche's philosophy is then regarded as itself a discourse of the latter kind.

THE ESSENCE OF PERSPECTIVISM
It is well known that Nietzsche's views in the 'theory of knowledge' were much influenced by Friedrich Albert Lange's *History of Materialism* (1866), which gives a psychological interpretation of Kant and defends a version of phenomenalism. In his study of Nietzsche's relation to Lange, George Stack goes so far as to state that Lange's theory of the species-organization of consciousness 'is clearly the model for Nietzsche's theory of perspectivalism.'[11] This is an over-simplification, for what Nietzsche found in Lange was confirmation of ideas which he had already encountered, albeit in more metaphysical garb, in Schopenhauer. In both cases, Lange and Schopenhauer, it is essentially Kantian ideas which are determinative. However, the genealogy of perspectivism will be considered in later sections of this chapter. In this section, I shall attempt an initial clarification of Nietzsche's perspectivism through a close examination of several key passages from his later writings. The first comes from aphorism 354 (Book V: 1887) of *The Gay Science*:

This is the essence of phenomenalism and perspectivism as *I* understand them: owing to the nature of
animal consciousness, the world of which we can
become conscious is only a surface-and-sign-world, a
world that is made common and meaner; whatever
becomes conscious *becomes* by the same token shallow,
thin, relatively stupid, general, sign, herd signal; all
becoming conscious involves a great and thorough
corruption, falsification, reduction to superficialities,
and generalization. Ultimately, the growth of consciousness becomes a danger; and anyone who lives
among the most conscious Europeans knows that it is
a disease. You will guess that it is not the opposition of
subject and object that concerns me here: this distinction I leave to the epistemologists who have become
entangled in the snares of grammar (the metaphysics
of the people). It is even less the opposition of 'thing-
in-itself' and appearance; for we do not 'know' nearly
enough to be entitled to such a distinction. We simply
lack any organ for knowledge, for 'truth', we 'know'
(or believe or imagine) just as much as may be *useful* in
the interests of the human herd, the species.[12]

This passage is one of the most important philosophical
statements in Nietzsche's writings. The aphorism as a
whole, which runs over some three pages and is entitled
'On the "Genius of the Species"', displays a dense
argumentation concerning such matters as the origin of
consciousness, the need for communication, the 'surface-
and-sign-world', the difference between the 'herd' nature
of man and individual existence, and finally, knowledge
and truth. In the last part of the aphorism (given above),
Nietzsche recapitulates more concisely his foregoing argument, beginning over again with the words 'This is the
essence of phenomenalism and perspectivism as I understand them.'

The essence of perspectivism (the meaning of the
equation with phenomenalism will presently become clear)

is that 'the world of which we become conscious (*bewußt*) is only a surface-and-sign-world (*nur eine Oberflächen- und Zeichenwelt*)'. We must first ask what Nietzsche means by consciousness and becoming conscious. A little earlier in the same aphorism, he writes:

> Man, like every living being, thinks continually without knowing it; the thinking which rises to consciousness is only the smallest part of all this – the most superficial and worst part (*der oberflächlichste, der schlechteste Teil*) – for only this conscious thinking takes the form of words, which is to say signs of communication.

For Nietzsche then, 'consciousness' and 'thinking' are not the same: as he indicates, conscious thinking is only the 'most superficial and worst part' of thinking.[13] The reason he gives, that conscious thinking 'takes the form of words', is clarified a little further on in the aphorism where he says that 'consciousness does not really belong to man's individual existence but rather to his social or herd nature'. No opposition has more valuational import for Nietzsche than that between individual existence and the 'herd'. If pre-conscious thoughts, as Nietzsche also goes on to say, are 'translated back into the perspective of the herd', then a great deal, in his view, must be lost in translation. This translation, however, has a certain necessity: the social or communicative nature of consciousness flattens thoughts out to the level of practical utility. As determined by consciousness, perspectives are significant biologically. They are necessary for survival.

Nietzsche has taken the expression 'genius of the species', which remains in quotation marks in the title of the aphorism, from Schopenhauer's essay 'Metaphysics of Sexual Love' (Chapter 44 of the second volume of *The World as Will and Representation*). In that essay, Schopenhauer speaks of the ongoing conflict between the genius of the species and the genius of the individual, arguing that the sexual organs of humans as of other living beings are in the service of the species, more particularly that their power over the individual is the expression of the all-encompassing force of primal will. However, Nietzsche's employment of the term 'genius of the species' in connection with consciousness follows a more general Schopenhauerian line of thought, i.e. his view that the intellect, and the 'world as representation' constructed by it, have nothing more than a biological function. For Schopenhauer, the 'world as representation' as it appears to the human animal determined by practical needs, is really, when considered from the standpoint of philosophical intuition, just the 'veil of Maya'. Nietzsche's position, in the aphorism we are considering, is not very different: although it is not actually an illusion, the world of perspectives (the so-called 'surface-and-sign-world') is 'shallow', 'thin', 'corrupt', 'false' etc. In both cases, the contrast is between the world as revealed through the practical needs of the species, and the world as revealed through the 'metaphysical' needs of the individual.

Nietzsche's talk of translation implies a three-term structure: something to be translated, something which does the translation, and the translation itself, the end product. Let us take these in reverse order. The translation is the surface-and-sign-world. Nietzsche is allowing a multiplicity of perspectives and is generalizing over them. He is saying something about all perspectives as located within an overarching surface-and-sign-world: that all perspectives are falsifications and corruptions. The second, intermediate term, which does the translation, is the 'genius of the species' itself. Following Schopenhauer's biological Kantianism, Nietzsche is saying that consciousness is structured according to the exigencies of survival. Schopenhauer thinks that this structuration is determined by a small number of invariant principles (the *a priori* of consciousness), but Nietzsche's attitude on this matter is not clear from the given aphorism. From other contexts it may be concluded that, in Nietzsche's view, there is considerably more flexibility in perspective creation than Schopenhauer allows. However, it should be noted that, neither in the passages quoted above nor in aphorism 354 as a whole, is the diversity of perspectives emphasized, or even mentioned. Instead, Nietzsche concentrates on the distinction between pre-conscious and conscious thought, together with the point that the latter is 'shallow', 'false' etc.

The crucial question concerns the first term in the structure, i.e. that which is translated, that which 'becomes conscious'. What is this? One tempting misinterpretation should be warded off straight away, namely that Nietzsche is speaking of unconscious psychological processes. Such a view is untenable because in this aphorism Nietzsche is talking about the value of conscious versus unconscious thought: his references to corruption and falsification indicate that he is alluding to thoughts which are prior to consciousness not at the level of mental events but at the level of worth. The reason that 'the growth of consciousness becomes a danger' and a 'disease' in modern European culture is that the herd value of utility has become the universal standard through which thoughts are assessed and understood. This applies to philosophers as much as to anyone else: by remaining at the level of conscious (i.e. verbal) thought, philosophy (as epistemology) becomes 'entangled in the snares of grammar'. The laws of conscious thought are taken as the laws of truth itself, what serves herd utility is taken as knowledge. At first sight it may appear that, at the end of the passage initially quoted, Nietzsche rejects the concepts of truth and knowledge outright, as symptomatic of the overestimation of epistemology. However, in view of the fact that, in other contexts to be examined later in this study, Nietzsche employs just these concepts with respect to his own thought, this would be an unwarranted assumption.

Although Nietzsche rejects epistemological conceptions of truth and knowledge, the whole thrust of the given aphorism, when seen in this broader context, is that these must be redefined at the level of pre-conscious or pre-verbal thought. If Nietzsche sometimes (by no means always) hesitates to call the latter truth or knowledge, this is because of the weight of epistemological prejudice in interpreting these terms. The distinction between the kind of thinking which relates to individual existence and the kind which relates to herd utility is decisive in this regard: throughout Nietzsche's writings, this is a philosophical and by no means a mere psychological distinction.

The greatest obstacle to understanding what Nietzsche means by pre-conscious or pre-verbal thought, as well as the kind of 'truth' and 'knowledge' which is defined at this level, is the implicit imposition of an epistemological standard of reference: the question will constantly insinuate itself as to how such thought could be 'correct' in a sense which is philosophically relevant. In the ensuing chapters, we shall see how Nietzsche transposes this correctness onto an existential level where it means something prior to the 'adequacy' of discursive thought. The present section concludes with some further preparatory indications, taken from another aphorism in Book V of *The Gay Science*. Again, these relate to the limits of perspectivism.

This aphorism (no. 373), entitled '"Science" as a Prejudice', is a critique of the materialist doctrine of 'a "world of truth" that can be mastered completely and forever with the aid of our square little reason'. Nietzsche counters the materialists by saying that 'one should not wish to divest existence of its rich ambiguity: that is a dictate of good taste, gentlemen, the taste of reverence for everything which goes over your horizon.'[14] In the present context, the relevant question is what 'over your horizon' (*über euren Horizont*) means. In particular, does it mean, as the perspectivist commentators would have to say, 'beyond your perspective'? Is it that, for Nietzsche, the materialists lack 'the taste of reverence' (*der Geschmack der Ehrfurcht*) for the variety of other possible perspectives? But Nietzsche does not use the word perspective or its cognates at this juncture, although earlier in the aphorism he had used these (in attacking 'Spencerian perspectives'). At this later stage of the aphorism, to make quite a different point, Nietzsche uses the word 'horizon' instead of 'perspective'. He does this because he wishes to contrast the perspectival world of consciousness, otherwise the surface-and-sign-world, with something else, something which, on coming to consciousness, becomes corrupt and false. It is this something else which is over the horizon of the materialists. Nietzsche does not mean that the materialists regrettably lack reverence for the whole range of other perspectives or for perspectivity as such. He is making the quite different claim that they lack reverence for what is over the surface-and-sign-world as such, for what is prior to all 'coming to consciousness' as such. Nietzsche speaks, not of what is 'beyond' (*jenseits*), but of what is 'over' (*über*) the horizon of the materialists: the word 'over' has valuational connotations, it concerns distinctions of worth (e.g. 'Overman').[15] This same aphorism opens with the statement that 'it follows from the laws of the order of rank that scholars, in so far as they belong to the spiritual middle class, can never catch sight of the really *great* problems and question marks'. The materialist scholars can never catch sight of the great problems because these lie 'over the horizon' of the intersubjective and linguistically determined surface-and-sign-world.

There is another point to be noted about this aphorism. In the title, the word 'science' appears in quotation marks. The reason for this is that Nietzsche does not want to criticize science as such, but certain pretentions to philosophy among the 'materialist natural scientists'. He means that when science ceases to be what it rightfully is and claims some kind of absolute validity for itself, then it becomes a prejudice. Towards the end of the aphorism, when

Nietzsche says that 'a "scientific" interpretation of the world ... might be one of the most stupid of all possible interpretations', the word science is again in quotation marks. It is necessary to distinguish Nietzsche's views on science from his views on 'science'. Scientists in the true sense (who Nietzsche otherwise calls 'scholars') are simply not concerned, *qua* scientists, with the 'great problems and question marks', but when they make a pretence at this concern, when they attempt to philosophize within the 'horizon' of scientific theory, they become 'scientists' and therefore 'stupid'. Scientists in the proper sense are exponents of the 'thinking which becomes conscious' and their results have validity at this level. The 'square little reason' of the scientists has its legitimate role in the service of man's herd- or species-needs, but these latter are not what move the philosopher in his 'taste of reverence'.

In conclusion, when we put together what we have discovered from the two aphorisms examined, Nietzsche's position can be summarized as follows. 1. A distinction is to be made between verbal thoughts located within the surface-and-sign-world of consciousness and pre-verbal thoughts which in some sense are 'prior to consciousness'. 2. The former are governed by 'herd-utility', whereas the latter pertain to 'individual existence'. 3. The former kind of thinking is 'false', 'superficial' and 'corrupt' in comparison with the latter kind. 4. 'Perspectival' thinking is located within the surface-and-sign-world and therefore is 'false' etc. in this sense. 5. What is 'over the horizon' of the surface-and-sign-world (thus of perspectives) pertains to 'great problems and question marks'. 6. Access to this extra-perspectival realm depends on a 'taste of reverence'. Of course, these interim findings are still in need of interpretation. In particular, we need to understand them in the wider context of Nietzsche's relation to traditional philosophical problematics.

KANT, SCHOPENHAUER, AND THE PROBLEM OF THE ABSOLUTE

During his Basel years, when Nietzsche thinks about his relation to philosophy and the philosophical tradition, it is primarily in terms of Kant and Kantianism that he attempts to situate himself. Like many thinkers of this period who were breaking away from theology to embrace enlightenment, Nietzsche sees Kant as the decisive philosopher for modern times. The *Nachlaß* of 1872–1874, including such well-known pieces as 'Truth and Lies in the Extra-Moral Sense', shows Nietzsche's attempt at philosophical self-orientation in the sceptical, post-Kantian epoch.[16] Kant had discredited metaphysics and speculative theology. He had shown that the Thing-in-itself is unknowable. More controversially, however, Nietzsche takes the essential Kantian lesson to be that, although scientific knowledge is legitimated in relation to the world of physical phenomena, it is devalued because it cannot attain the 'in-itself' of reality: metaphysical knowledge turns out to be impossible, while scientific knowledge emerges as strictly subjective. In this way the philosophical ideal of knowledge which has determined the whole Western tradition since Plato is undermined. The project of philosophical knowledge founders on the alternatives of speculative pseudo-science on the one hand, and subjectivism on the other.

Reacting to this new philosophical situation, Nietzsche calls himself a 'philosopher of tragic knowledge' who 'finds the removed ground of metaphysics tragic but can never satisfy himself with the colourful hurly-burly of the sciences.'[17] The common solution, which Nietzsche repeatedly criticizes in the *Nachlaß*, is to throw oneself into the special sciences, either without worrying about the impossibility of absolute knowledge, or taking scientific knowledge as an acceptable substitute. As Nietzsche puts it, the positive sciences 'judge more and more according to the degree of certainty and seek smaller and smaller objects.'[18] They are not choosy about what they study, for the main criterion is just that something be knowable. Nietzsche's new kind of 'tragic philosopher', by contrast, has the task of mastering the uncontrolled drive to knowledge which has gained ascendancy in modern culture. Since this cannot occur through old-style metaphysics, Nietzsche proposes a new philosophical dignity for art.

Nietzsche's attitude to the Kantian critique of metaphysics is frequently misunderstood in contemporary commentary, particularly by those writers who see perspectivism as a radicalization of Kantian phenomenalism. This puts Nietzsche, very misleadingly, on the trajectory of that post-Kantian relativism which culminates in Derrida and other postmodernists. In fact, if Nietzsche is to be judged by what the postmodernists would regard as properly post-Kantian epistemological criteria (the perspectival character of truth), he would appear as pre-Kantian or anti-Kantian. From his early period onwards, and notwithstanding the influence of Lange, Nietzsche sees Kant above all through Schopenhauerian lenses, i.e. through lenses which still perceive a 'metaphysical need'. It is already clear in *The Birth of Tragedy* that he has inherited Schopenhauer's ambiguous attitude on the Thing-in-itself. For Schopenhauer, the impossibility of representing the Thing-in-itself implies on the one hand rejection of *a priori* metaphysics, on the other hand rejection of positive science as a vehicle of philosophical knowledge. On this latter point, Schopenhauer does not so much differ from Kant as effect a shift of emphasis, picking up on an ambiguity inherent in the Kantian philosophy itself. Because they yield only representational knowledge, Schopenhauer denies that the positive sciences can ever be a substitute for metaphysics. For Kant himself, the only possible substitute is his own transcendental philosophy which, rather than providing knowledge of the Thing-in-itself, remains reflection on the conditions of phenomenal knowledge. There has been a tendency, beginning already before Schopenhauer and lasting through to the present day, to reduce Kant's philosophy to a theory of science, implicitly assuming the cognitive supremacy of the exact sciences. Schopenhauer sees the implications of Kant very differently. If representational knowledge cannot gain access to the Thing-in-itself, Schopenhauer contends, then there must be some kind of non-representational knowledge which can. The latter is what he calls intuition, i.e. inner experience, as distinct from the outer experience of empirical (Kantian) perception.[19]

Schopenhauer believes in the possibility of an empirical metaphysics, as long as 'experience' is not understood too restrictively. This, he considers, was Kant's error. Kant had assumed that because there could not be any objective knowledge of the Thing-in-itself, it could not be known at all. He had implicitly equated objective knowledge with knowledge as such, he had made the standards of 'outer' (scientific) experience govern all experience whatsoever. It turns out, however, that even Schopenhauer's subjective way to the Thing-in-itself cannot reveal the latter in all its pristine nakedness. Whereas inner experience is free of the spatial and causal determinations of outer experience, it is still temporally structured, so that to this extent the Thing-in-itself will always be veiled. Schopenhauer is actually vacillating on this point. In the first volume of *The World as Will and Representation*, we learn that the Thing-in-itself, revealed through inner experience, is primal will, and Schopenhauer has quite a lot to say about it. In the second volume, however, we are told that will is only the way in which the Thing-in-itself appears to our inner experience, i.e. to beings whose subjectivity is constituted in such and such a manner.[20] If this is the case, no kind of metaphysic can attain the Absolute, but inner experience will lead us as close as humanly possible. Schopenhauer stresses, however, that all the scientific (representational) knowledge in the world will not bring us one step closer to satisfying the innate 'metaphysical need' of human beings.

Nietzsche views the post-Kantian philosophical situation against this Schopenhauerian background. This means that,

for Nietzsche as for Schopenhauer, the Kantian critique of
metaphysics does not abolish the Absolute as such, but only
precludes this from becoming an 'object of knowledge' in
the sense of 'representation'. From the roles of the primal
One and the Dionysian in *The Birth of Tragedy*, it is clear
that the Absolute remains philosophically accessible. Like
Schopenhauer, Nietzsche derives relativistic consequences
from Kant only in respect of knowledge and not at all in
respect of truth. To be sure, Nietzsche describes himself as
a 'philosopher of tragic knowledge'. The difficulty he has
in dispensing with the word knowledge (*Erkenntnis*) shows
that some kind of insight is assumed, but this is an insight
of a different order to that provided by knowledge in the
usual sense. Kant had wanted to restrict knowledge in order
to make room for 'faith'. Nietzsche wants to do the same in
order to make room for tragic wisdom and 'the Dionysian'.
In both cases a realm of absolute value is intended: for Kant
the moral law, for Nietzsche the 'primal One' or 'life'
itself. Nietzsche repudiates the Kantian moral law not on
account of its absolute status but because of its moral
status, because he sees it as implying that the essence of
reality is 'good' and in some sense 'rational'. Kant will
always remain for Nietzsche an idealist, a rationalizer of
Christian moral prejudices, someone who projects his own
needs and wishes onto reality. By contrast, Schopenhauer's
'de-theologized' Kantianism, in which the world becomes
merely a blind, meaningless upsurge, appealed to Nietzsche
from the beginning. Notwithstanding his rejection of
Schopenhauer's attempt at a theory of will in Book Two of
The World as Will and Representation, it is at bottom this same
will which appears as the primal One of *The Birth of
Tragedy*.

For Nietzsche, tragic art serves a philosophical purpose,
and thus, in an essential sense, serves 'truth'. It is easy to fall
into confusions here because of Nietzsche's vacillating
terminology. Such concepts as knowledge, truth and the
Absolute are so laden with the weight of the Platonist–

intellectualist tradition that it is initially difficult to give them new meanings, or to extricate a core meaning which one wants to retain. Schopenhauer, who like Nietzsche also seeks to break from intellectualism, refuses to use such terms as 'Being' and 'the Absolute', because he sees them as contaminated with Hegelianism. But in the end these are not altogether inappropriate ways of referring to the Schopenhauerian will. Once the systematic intentions of Schopenhauer are understood, these terminological issues become less important. One can see that will is not the same as Being or the Absolute if these latter imply (as with Hegel) something accessible to the rational intellect. But if these terms are revised to mean a base level of reality, 'primordial' reality so to speak, one can admit them. Nietzsche often finds himself in terminological embarrassment. It is a cliché that one can quote Nietzsche in selective fashion to almost any effect. This does not mean that one should ignore his terminology and avoid quotations. What is needed is close attention to the systematic interconnections of his ideas.

Nietzsche sees art not as an alternative to truth, but as an alternative way of expressing truth. However, what does Nietzsche mean by art? It may seem that the dichotomy between art and science is adequate to explain what Nietzsche intends. A difficulty emerges when we remember that, for Nietzsche, science too is 'artistic' in the sense that all concept formation is metaphorical. It will not do to say that science deals with reality, while art is concerned with appearance: this would imply the pre-Kantian idea that scientific (or metaphysical) concepts can correspond to Being-in-itself. The difference which Nietzsche has in mind is that art strives for beauty, whereas the 'artistic' activity of science serves utility. In *The Birth of Tragedy*, Nietzsche says that 'only as an aesthetic phenomenon is existence and the world eternally justified.'[21] This is sometimes taken as the purest kind of aestheticism: realizing that reality is unknowable, that the very idea of

correspondence between concept and object is non-sensi-
cal, the 'pathos of truth' is aestheticized, one saves oneself
from epistemological despair by giving oneself over to
beauty, or better, one becomes beautiful (a work of art)
oneself. But where does this leave the original insight that
reality is unknowable? Is it really aestheticism when a
certain kind of aesthetic experience (the Dionysian) is
asserted to possess the power of justification? I shall not
linger over terminological questions. What is important to
realize is that, for Nietzsche, 'beautiful appearance' is
beautiful only on account of its relation to the primordial
ground of reality. Different forms of art are adequate in
varying degrees as expressions of this primal One.[22] As
such they are in varying degrees truthful or untruthful.

Nietzsche's writings as a whole attempt to forge a closer
link between philosophy and art than has been customary
within the philosophical tradition. To understand this
correctly, however, the notion of aestheticism is less
helpful than the distinction between verbal and pre-verbal
thought observed in the previous section. We must also
distinguish between the verbalization of pre-verbal
thought, and thought which is verbal in an originary sense.
The former still counts as 'intuitive' thought for
Nietzsche, while the latter is considered 'abstract', 'conceptual', and 'metaphysical'. In the first case the thought
always exceeds what is available in the verbal expression,
while in the second case it is identical with this. Because
verbal thought is actually constituted within intersubjective
relations, there is in principle no difficulty of comprehension at this level. Intuitive thought, however, is capable not
only of verbalization in the strict sense (words), but may be
symbolically expressed in a variety of ways, as both verbal
and non-verbal art. The essence of Nietzsche's aestheticism
is that the symbolic rendition of pre-verbal thought
requires artistry. Whereas science requires analytical ability
and can be learned, philosophy involves an irreducibly
irrational dimension which he calls, following
Schopenhauer, the quality of 'genius'.

In recent literature on Nietzsche, much attention has been paid to the posthumously published essay 'On Truth and Lies in an Extra-Moral Sense' (1873). This has proved a favoured source for the perspectivist commentators, for whom even the early Nietzsche is an incipient postmodernist who abolishes truth with a capital T, sees metaphysics as serving authoritarian structures of power, and equates the denial of the Absolute with liberation. However, if the essay is read against the background provided thus far, a very different interpretation will result.[23] There is no denying that in 'Truth and Lies', as well as in many other writings from the same period, Nietzsche takes a critical attitude to 'truth'. Our difficulty is to determine which concept of truth he rejects, and which, if any, he accepts. A clue comes early in the essay where Nietzsche asserts that 'the intellect, as the means for the preservation of the individual, unfolds its principle powers through dissimulation.'[24] This is a straightforward borrowing of Schopenhauer's doctrine that the intellect knows only the world as representation. Whether representation is determined by invariant structures of subjectivity (as with Schopenhauer) or by the conventions and metaphors of which Nietzsche speaks throughout the essay, makes no essential difference. The point, for Nietzsche as for Schopenhauer, is that the intellect has no access to the Absolute, and does not need such access, because it serves practical functions and nothing more. If no attention is paid to what 'intellect' means within this specifically Schopenhauerian framework, if the distinction between intellect and intuition is simply overlooked, then the ground is laid for a total miscomprehension of Nietzsche's essay. This is what happens in the case of the postmodernist authors: Nietzsche's critique of intellectual truth, a critique which is also present in the writings on the Presocratics and in *The Birth of Tragedy*, is mistaken for a critique of truth as such. What Nietzsche wants to criticize in this essay is not the kind of 'dogmatism' which would deny 'perspective', but, quite explicitly, the assumption that 'language is the adequate expression of all realities.'[25] Only by forgetting the conventionality of language, Nietzsche wants to show, can one imagine oneself to 'possess' the truth in the sense of 'adequate expression' or 'correspondence'.

The critique of abstract, conceptual and linguistic truth which one finds in 'Truth and Lies' cannot be taken as a critique of truth *per se* because it is inapplicable to precisely that kind of intuition which Nietzsche (implicitly in this essay and explicitly elsewhere, particularly in the lectures on the Presocratics) connects with philosophical truthfulness. Only if the evidence for this connection is ignored can the conflict between abstract thought and intuition be taken as a conflict between different styles in the sense maintained by the postmodernists.[26] Nietzsche does say, in 'Truth and Lies', that the abstract thinker and the intuitive thinker 'both desire to rule over life: the former, by knowing how to meet his principle needs by means of foresight, prudence, and regularity; the latter by disregarding these needs and, as an "overjoyed hero", counting as real only that life which has been disguised as illusion and beauty.'[27] If these are two styles, however, the choice between them cannot avoid implicit reference to truth. As Nietzsche explains, 'the man who is guided by concepts and abstractions only succeeds by such means in warding off misfortune, without ever gaining any happiness for himself from these abstractions', whereas the intuitive man 'reaps from his intuition a harvest of continually inflowing illumination, cheer, and redemption (*Erhellung, Aufheiterung, Erlösung*)'. This is the kind of language which Nietzsche uses of the philosopher. One *Nachlaß* fragment from this period states that the philosopher wants 'his own transfiguration and redemption (*Verklärung und Erlösung*). The will strives after purity and enoblement (*Reinheit und Veredelung*): from one level to another'.[28] Another fragment asserts that 'the will to existence (*der Wille zum Dasein*) uses philosophy for the purpose of a higher form of existence (*höheren Daseinsform*)'.[29] To say that the difference between the intuitive and the abstract man is one of diverging styles (or perspectives) does not do justice to Nietzsche's ranking of these two kinds of men, to his view that the existential stance of the intuitive man is higher than that of the abstract man. This stance is precisely what Nietzsche understands by the 'truthfulness' of the philosopher.

The particular stance of the philosopher continues to occupy Nietzsche in the 1875 *Nachlaß*. Above all, it is a certain kind of 'individualism' which concerns him: 'man remains an individual only within three forms of existence: as philosopher, as saint and as artist'.[30] Even Christianity, Nietzsche points out, demands that each individual seek his own 'blessedness' (*Seligkeit*), but the vast majority of people have so little sense of themselves that they live, in what is euphemistically called a 'modest' attitude, for anonymous 'others', for 'society' and 'public opinion'. In contrast to this general situation, 'it is characteristic of the free man to live for himself and not for others'.[31] The difference between the philosopher and the scientist is explicable in these terms: 'the individual who wants to stand *for himself* needs *ultimate knowledge* (*letzte Erkenntnis*), philosophy. The others need slowly accumulating scientific knowledge'.[32] Nietzsche distinguishes existence *for the sake of existence itself* from existence which possesses merely instrumental value for something else: it is this self-oriented existence which Nietzsche understands as philosophical existence. On the other hand, such postmodernist motifs as pluralism and multiplicity are not to be found in any of Nietzsche's works (or *Nachlaß*) from any period. Nietzsche does not criticize dogmatism to establish pluralism, but to make way for intuition, for the kind of 'ultimate knowledge' through which the individual exists for his own sake. When he criticizes the Absolute of abstract thought, this is because it is a pseudo-Absolute. One must exercise care in reading Nietzsche, for his conception of the Absolute is peculiarly difficult to grasp: as we shall see in due course, its elusiveness belongs to its essence. Nietzsche's conception of truth can seem like relativism, just as, in his later writings, the death of God can seem like nihilism. This appearance, however, depends on traditional ways of thinking about truth and value. Having effected a radical shift of ground, Nietzsche's artist-philosopher and *Übermensch* emerge on the other side of both relativism and nihilism.[33]

The perspectivist commentators call for interpretations of Nietzsche which avoid the totalization or closure of his thought. On this score they have been especially severe on Heidegger's conception of Nietzsche as the 'last metaphysician' who thinks the Being of beings as will to power. Such a view, they consider, is dogmatic, depriving Nietzsche's thought of its multi-'facetedness'. Prescinding at this stage from the specific question of Heidegger's Nietzsche, one must ask whether all attempts to establish the unity of Nietzsche's thought, to discover a centre from which all his thinking flows, are necessarily dogmatic, or whether, on the contrary, this latter charge evinces a basic mis-comprehension of philosophy, perhaps even an hostility to philosophy, an abandonment of thought and truth in favour of the modern ideological value of pluralism. Philosophy, as Nietzsche recognizes, is precisely totalizing thinking, not in the sense of theoretical systems, but, as he says in the Preface to *On the Genealogy of Morals*, as thinking which proceeds from 'one will, one health, one soil, one sun'. The idea that 'centering' Nietzsche's thought somehow impugns the richness, complexity and ambiguity of his writings, demonstrates only an inadequate understanding of the One–many relation. If, as has been maintained in this section, Nietzsche believes in a 'primal One' as the essence of reality, this does not mean that his attention is diverted from the many expressions of this One, nor that these expressions are dispensable. For Heraclitus, for Plato, for Hegel, the One and the many form an indissoluble unity, and so it is also for Nietzsche. Of course, the specific relation between the One and the many is different in each of these thinkers. Nietzsche thinks of the One–many relation in terms of the primal Dionysian upsurge objectifying itself in the world of appearance. In this sense his framework is essentially Schopenhauerian: for all his reservations about philosophical pessimism, will remains the most appealing metaphor, even into the late period. Like Schopenhauer, Nietzsche believes that, notwithstanding Kant, the Absolute is in a sense accessible for philosophy, and in this sense is the sole 'object' (the *Sache*) of philosophical thought.

BEING AND BECOMING
In the Preface to *Beyond Good and Evil*, Nietzsche writes:

> It seems that, in order to inscribe themselves in the hearts of humanity with eternal demands, all great things have first to wander the earth as monstrous and fear-inspiring grotesques (*Fratzen*): dogmatic philosophy, the doctrine of the Vedanta in Asia and Platonism in Europe, was a grotesque of this kind. Let us not be ungrateful to it.[34]

This typical Nietzschean statement, full of ambiguity as it is, may help to clarify my findings in the previous section. There would be no difficulty in pulling out of Nietzsche's texts quotations to show that, in his view, the Absolute and the Thing-in-itself are metaphysical 'grotesques'. The interesting question is whether they nevertheless express 'eternal demands'. Enough evidence has already been presented to indicate that this is indeed the case. Although Nietzsche writes against the metaphysical tradition, although he is convinced that this tradition harbours much that is poisonous and destructive for the human spirit, he is unwilling to pronounce upon it a final condemnation. This is not only because he realizes the difficulty of breaking free from a tradition which has determined the structure of Western thought for over two millennia. Nor has it anything to do with romantic 'nostalgia', a convenient psychological explanation which can be used to justify minimizing whatever one does not like in Nietzsche. Fundamentally, Nietzsche's ambivalence about the metaphysical tradition stems from his love for eternity, a love perhaps most poignantly expressed in the 'Song of Yes and Amen' at the end of *Zarathustra* III, but evident throughout his writings. As a lover of eternity, Nietzsche will himself always feel bound by eternal demands and will feel related to whomsoever he takes to share this feeling. Such eternal demands have their seat in conscience, as the voice of an unfathomable but unavoidable 'thou shalt':

> But there is no doubt that a 'thou shalt' still speaks to us too, that we too still obey a stern law set over us – and this is the last moral law which can make itself audible even to us, which even we know how to live, in this if in anything we too are still men of conscience...it is only as men of this conscience that we still feel ourselves related to the German integrity and piety of millennia, even if as its most questionable descendants, we immoralists, we godless men of today, indeed in a certain sense as its heirs, as the executors of its innermost will.[35]

As a man 'of this conscience' Nietzsche does not simply turn away from the 'grotesques' of metaphysics, but attempts to understand the eternal demands behind them. This is Nietzsche's philosophical 'piety', something which his postmodernist commentators cannot share insofar as they reject the very notion of eternal demands as totalizing and therefore dogmatic. No concept has been more central in the metaphysical quest for eternity than that of Being. Nietzsche's repudiation of this concept is well known, and among the postmodernists is taken as one more indication of his anti-dogmatic and perspectival approach to truth. In the present section we shall see that the situation is somewhat more complex. Although Nietzsche takes the concept of Being as paradigmatic for what he wants to overcome in philosophy, he also has difficulty in ridding himself of it. The reason for this is that Being is not necessarily a metaphysical concept (in Nietzsche's sense) at all, but a way of indicating the ultimate 'object' of all eternal demands.

Nietzsche's early lectures on the Presocratic philosophers reveal him as a 'Heraclitean' who opposes the living flux of Becoming (*Werden*) to the frozen pseudo-reality of Parmenidean Being (*Sein*). It should be noted, however, that while identifying very closely with Heraclitus' 'complete repudiation of Being',[36] Nietzsche has no reservations in embracing the Heraclitean *logos* as 'the inner, unifying lawfulness' of Becoming.[37] Nietzsche equates a Heraclitean denial of Being with a denial of 'things', but he reconciles this with the *logos* as the law behind the flux, as 'the One' (*das Eine*) of which all coming-into-being and passing-away provide a 'continuous revelation' (*fortwährende Existenzoffenbarung*).[38] The One of Parmenides and the One of Heraclitus are altogether different, because 'the multiplicity which according to Parmenides is a deception of the senses is for Heraclitus the proper garb, the form of appearance of the One, on no account a deception: the One cannot appear in any other way.'[39]

Nietzsche criticizes Parmenides for the primacy he accords to abstract thought and conceptualization: 'according to Parmenides the content of our thinking is not at all given in perception but comes from somewhere else, from a supra-sensible world to which we have direct access through thought.'[40] The basic elements of Nietzsche's critique of a Platonic-metaphysical 'higher-world' are already visible in this statement. 'Thought' (*das Denken*), as Nietzsche uses the word here, means the operations of abstraction. Against the Parmenidean doctrine of Being,

Nietzsche appeals to the Kantian critique of knowledge, to the point that thought is only capable of grasping reality according to pre-determined forms: 'Through words and concepts we can never penetrate behind the wall of relations, for example into some fantastic primal ground of things and even in the pure forms of sensibility and of understanding, in space, time, and causality, we cannot attain anything resembling a *veritas aeterna*'.[41] Nietzsche sees Parmenides as the first philosopher to declare the sovereignty of the concept in the realm of truth, thereby pronouncing the senses to be deceptive and setting up 'that quite erroneous division between "spirit" and "body" which, especially since Plato, has lain upon philosophy like a curse.'[42] Parmenides accuses the senses of the false impression that 'non-existent things also exist (*auch das Nichtseiende sei*), that Becoming also has a Being (*auch das Werden habe ein Sein*)'.[43] Anticipating Plato, Parmenides retreats into a realm of 'the palest and most remote generalizations' where he himself becomes 'bloodless like an abstraction and enmeshed everywhere in formulae'.[44] This belief in the authority of abstraction, in the identity of Being and the concept, is for Nietzsche the fundamental faith of the whole metaphysical tradition. But now, Nietzsche believes, this faith of two thousand years has been undermined by Kant and Schopenhauer, so that with fresh vision it is possible to get back behind Parmenides and Plato, to the pre-conceptual or 'intuitive' thought of Heraclitus.[45]

Nietzsche does not deny the possibility of a *veritas aeterna* as such. What he denies is that this is attainable 'through words and concepts'. To 'know' the Heraclitean *logos* is the same thing as to participate in the *veritas aeterna*. Such knowing is also called 'intuition' by Nietzsche, but he does not intend this in a subjective or psychological sense. What is intuited is intuition itself, just 'that all-observing intuition (*jener alles überschauenden Intuition*)...which reigns over all contradictions and overlooks the universal *polemos*'.[46]

Philosophical wisdom does not come through an external intellectual relation to an independently given reality, but consists in 'becoming One (*Eins zu werden*) with this observing Intelligence (*anschauenden Intelligenz*)'.[47] Nietzsche finds much more in Heraclitus than a Kantian critique of speculative metaphysics: he finds a sublime image of the philosopher, and of the philosopher's relation to the world. Heraclitean truth is participation in that which is common to all existing things. Although the *logos* rules over them, human beings typically believe only in their own private opinions: they are, as Heraclitus says, 'asleep' or 'drunk'. Unphilosophical human beings, unalert to the *logos,* failing to understand it 'either before they have heard it or after they have heard it', live in the untruth.[48] Nietzsche is thoroughly in sympathy with the Ephesian philosopher's low opinion of the 'the many', praising Heraclitus for his 'highest form of pride' and his 'involuntary identification of himself and the truth'.[49] This pride is not personal arrogance, because Heraclitus' statement 'I searched out myself', and his conviction that wisdom does not come from listening to many opinions or from learning many things, presuppose the *logos* as an all-encompassing Intelligence in which any human being, if he only be 'awake', can participate.[50]

This contraposition of Parmenidean Being and Heraclitean Becoming is not a contrast between absolute and relative truth, but between different kinds of absoluteness. Parmenides, as Nietzsche understands him, equates truth with absolute knowledge in the sense of conceptualization and abstraction. This kind of knowledge is governed by the criterion of certainty: the concept is supposed to grasp (*begreifen* = *griefen*) and fix the object of knowledge. The intellect serves the species as well as the individual by forming concepts, by allowing experience to be articulated in words: 'Every word becomes immediately a concept in so far as it stands precisely not for the unique and absolutely individualized primordial experience (*ganz und gar individualisierte Urerlebnis*) to which it owes its origin, as a kind of remembering, but simultaneously for countless more or less similar but strictly speaking never identical cases.'[51] What counts as truth in the realm of the intellect is the assimilation of different cases under a single word. This is dissimulation, however, because it is unfaithful to what is given in the flux of Becoming. Words and concepts are 'metaphors' because they do not stand for anything 'in-itself' but reflect conventions of social life. All conceptualizations are abstractions which remove Becoming from the power of human comprehension. The greatest abstraction of all is the concept of Being, to which Parmenides is driven by his desire for absolute (non-conventional, non-metaphorical, but still conceptual) certainty.

For Nietzsche, conceptualization can achieve nothing more than the schematization of reality: it is not capable of philosophical insight. The conceptual truth sought by Parmenides presupposes an adequacy relation between intellect and object which cannot obtain: 'the adequate expression of the object in the subject appears to me a contradictory un-thing: for between two absolutely different spheres there can exist…at best an aesthetic relation, a gesturing rendering (*andeutende Übertragung*), a stammering translation (*nachstammelnde Übersetzung*) into a quite foreign tongue'.[52] Rather than attempting, after the manner of Parmenides, to intellectualize truth, the Heraclitean philosopher is lead by intuitions 'before which man is struck dumb, or speaks solely in metaphors and unheard of concept-combinations (*unerhörten Begriffsfugungen*).'[53] The philosopher speaks in this way because he realizes the general inadequacy of all language, even his own 'unheard of' language, for expressing the *logos*. By so speaking, by indicating that the nature of the instrument and the purpose for which it is now employed are fundamentally at variance, the philosopher hopes to gesture at a truth which exceeds all linguistic comprehensibility. It is important to realize that Nietzsche does not favour speaking in 'metaphors and unheard of concept-combinations' just for its own sake. He does not mean that, because no form of language can achieve an adequate expression of the *logos*, every form of language is in general permissible, and that the more daring, the more experimental this is, the better. In Heraclitean terms, only those 'metaphors and concept-combinations' which are founded on a genuine intuition of the *logos* are of any value in philosophy. At the same time, there can be no intersubjective procedure for distinguishing between what is genuinely founded in the *logos* and what is not: such procedures exist only within conceptual knowledge, where conventions and definitions provide a fixed point of reference. For Nietzsche, the value of any piece of philosophical discourse, in whatever kind of language, is assessed by intuition and in no other way.

Eugen Fink writes that 'Nietzsche's encounter with Greek philosophy is peculiar. The fundamental ontological problematic of the Greeks appears not to touch him at all.'[54] Similarly, Heidegger remarks in several places that Nietzsche uncritically takes over the hackneyed and ontologically fallacious opposition between Being and Becoming.[55] A reading of the lectures *Philosophy in the Tragic Age of the Greeks* will confirm that, by and large, Nietzsche interprets the difference between Parmenides and Heraclitus in terms of the Schopenhauerian distinction between abstract thought and intuition. Heraclitean Becoming is explained by reference to Schopenhauer's idea of intuitively apprehended will,[56] while Parmenidean Being is rejected on Kantian grounds, as evincing the 'untutored naivety of the critique of the intellect' of Presocratic times.[57] In the present context, we are concerned not with the historical-philological accuracy of Nietzsche's interpretations but with what they show about his own thought. On this score, it is noteworthy that, unless Nietzsche has changed his mind in the one year between *The Birth of Tragedy* and *Philosophy in the Tragic Age of the Greeks*, his rejection of Being is not meant as inconsistent with (Dionysian) affirmation of the primal

One. It is easy to fall into error on this point, because in the former work, the Primal One seems to be the Thing-in-itself, whereas in his lectures on the Greeks it seems that the latter is associated with Parmenides and is no longer admissible. But as we have already seen, Nietzsche equates the primal One with the Thing-in-itself only in a loose sense, i.e. only in the sense that it is the primal 'reality'. In his view, the Thing-in-itself is strictly speaking a conceptual posit, the grounding posit of the abstract thinker. If *The Birth of Tragedy* had assumed the Thing-in-itself in this strict sense, its language would have been theoretical-discursive, which it is not: it is 'aesthetic' in the ambiguous sense earlier discussed. When considering *The Birth of Tragedy*, one must not look for a nicely smoothed out philosophical terminology but must attend to the all-pervasive theme of primordiality. Despite vacillating terminology, Nietzsche continually reinforces the point that Dionysian truth acquaints us with something absolute. Nietzsche does not want to be taken as a Parmenidean metaphysician when he says that the Dionysian brings us into contact with 'the truly existent primal One' (*das Wahrhaft/Seiende und Ur-Eine*),[58] or that the voice of the Dionysian lyrist 'sounds from the depth of Being' (*tönt aus dem Abgründe des Seins*),[59] or that the Dionysian experience provides 'true knowledge' (*wahre Erkenntnis*) of 'the horror or absurdity of Being' (*das Entsetzliche oder Absurde des Seins*).[60] Nietzsche does not want to be a metaphysician of the intellect, but he calls himself an 'artist-metaphysician' because what he seeks to express is 'primordial reality' and by no means an optional 'perspective' on the world.

Nietzsche's 'repudiation of Being' is further clarified by the aphorisms collected under the heading 'Thing-in-itself and Appearance' in Book Three of *The Will to Power*. Since all these post-date *Zarathustra*, they cannot be intended as inconsistent with the resurrected idea of the Dionysian and other quasi-mystical motifs such as 'eternal return'. Nietzsche objects to Kant's distinction between appearance and Thing-in-itself because Kant himself 'rejected as impermissible making inferences from phenomena to a cause of phenomena – in accordance with his conception of causality and its purely intra-phenomenal validity.'[61] This criticism is not original to Nietzsche: it had been widely made in Kant's own lifetime and was commonly regarded as one of the principle difficulties with the *Critique of Pure Reason*. Nietzsche was no doubt aware of it at the time he was using the expression 'primal One' in *The Birth of Tragedy*. It is essentially the same criticism that he had made of Schopenhauer in an early (1867) fragment, to which John Sallis has recently drawn attention, where Nietzsche complains that Schopenhauer gives the will/Thing-in-itself 'determinations' which would be legitimate only at the level of phenomena.[62] We can conclude that Nietzsche's own 'primal One' (or 'life'), although intended in some sense as 'primordial reality', is not to be confused with any kind of causal ground. This is reinforced by Nietzsche's comment that 'One would like to know how things-in-themselves are constituted (*wie die Dinge an sich beschaffen sind*); but behold, there are no things-in-themselves.'[63] The question of how something is constituted is a question which asks for knowledge, for determinations, for qualities, properties or predicates. However, all these have meaning only at the level of phenomena. If the 'primal One' is a philosophically acceptable idea, it cannot be legitimate to ask 'what' it is (as Schopenhauer asks, and gives a highly differentiated answer, in respect of will as Thing-in-itself) nor, which comes to the same thing, to ask for (conceptual) knowledge of it. As Nietzsche says: 'The question "what is that?" is an imposition of meaning from some other viewpoint. "Essence", the "essential nature" is something perspectival and already presupposes a multiplicity. At the bottom of it there always lies a "what is that for me?"'[64] The great error is the assumption that 'things possess a constitution in themselves (*eine Beschaffenheit an sich*)' for this presupposes that 'interpretation and subjectivity are not essential, that a thing freed from all relationships would still be a thing.'[65]

If metaphysics aims at a theory of reality which is somehow non-perspectival, then Nietzsche is from the very beginning a declared opponent of metaphysics. But if we take metaphysics as seeking a more fundamental truth than theoretical truth, i.e. a truth quite different to that of things and their properties, then Nietzsche is indeed a metaphysician. What Nietzsche seeks as an 'artist-metaphysician' is the supra-theoretical truth of Becoming rather than the theoretical truth of Being. Conceptual knowledge falsifies the truth of Becoming into doctrines about stable, unchanging things. This occurs under the rule of logic, and functions in the service of man's biological needs. Nietzsche does not believe that human beings can get along without the concept of thing. He believes that the world of thing-ification, a world conditioned by language and needs, is the natural medium of human existence. This world is false, however, in a different sense to the falsity of the metaphysical Thing-in-itself or metaphysical Being. These latter notions are false because they rest on the philosophical error of absolutizing what is merely an exigency of survival. Human beings live within the falsity of the thing-world to the extent that they are oriented to survival and pragmatic ends, but the metaphysics of Being is a philosophical error which attempts to absolutize that which can only be relative (to survival). For Nietzsche's project to make sense, the truth of Becoming must in some manner be accessible. If the animal nature of man cannot be altogether cancelled, it must still be possible to go beyond this: 'We must be raised up – and who are they, who raise us up? They are those true *human beings, those who are no longer animal, the philosophers, artists and saints.*'[66]

The tendency of postmodernist commentary is to reduce Nietzschean Becoming to an anti-dogmatic (perspectivist) motif. From my considerations thus far, it is clear that this is an erroneous view. To be sure, it is not wrong to emphasize that for Nietzsche all interpretations are perspectives. What is wrong is to take this as implying that all truth is perspectival. Nietzsche intends exactly the opposite. The fact that interpretation is perspectival means that truth in the philosophical sense cannot be the truth of interpretation, i.e. that it cannot be theoretical or discursive truth of any kind. If, as Nietzsche insists, 'linguistic means of expression are useless for expressing Becoming',[67] this does not mean that Becoming is altogether inaccessible and inexpressible. It does not mean that philosophical truth is a mistaken idea which must henceforth be recognized as 'arrogant' and 'dogmatic'. For how does Nietzsche see the falsity of metaphysical-theoretical definitions of truth? How does he 'know' that Becoming is not theoretically knowable? These questions, if posed within perspectivism, are unanswerable: Nietzsche's 'seeing' and 'knowing' can be nothing more than a conflicting point of view. The way out of this difficulty is the way out of perspectivism itself, i.e. by reference to that supra-perspectival intuition which Nietzsche presupposes from the very beginning, and out of which all his writings flow, not as 'theoretical knowledge' but as philosophy.[68] Nietzsche is convinced that 'each word of Heraclitus expresses the pride and majesty of truth, but of truth grasped in intuitions rather than through the rope ladder of logic.'[69] While this intuitively apprehended truth is absolute in the sense of primordiality, because it is non-conceptual it remains inexpressible as doctrine.

It might seem that Nietzschean Becoming, in the indicated sense as the primordial object of philosophical intuition, begins to resemble Being, in function if not in content. This suspicion is supported by signs that Nietzsche's metaphysical definition of Being is not the only one he is prepared to entertain. In the third *Untimely Meditation*, published only a year or so after his lectures on the Presocratics, he writes:

This eternal Becoming (*ewige Werden*) is a deceitful puppet-show....That heroism of truthfulness (*Wahrhaftigkeit*) consists in one day ceasing to be its plaything. In Becoming everything is hollow, deceptive, flat and worthy of our contempt: the puzzle which man has to solve can be solved only out of Being (*nur aus dem Sein*), in So-being and not Other-being, in the everlasting (*im Unvergänglichen*). Now he begins to examine how deeply he has grown into Becoming and how deeply into Being – a tremendous task looms up before his soul: to destroy everything which becomes and to bring to light everything which is false.[70]

This passage, which appears to flatly contradict his more well-known evaluation of Being and Becoming, should warn us against any too hasty stereotyping of Nietzsche's ontological views. Although Nietzsche here associates Being with the 'heroism of truthfulness', whereas elsewhere he accords this status to Becoming, this is not a contradiction, but only indicates his basic hesitancy and indecision in respect of ontological terminology. Whether he calls it 'Being' on the one hand, or 'Becoming' on the other, Nietzsche understands philosophical truthfulness as oriented to a 'primordial reality' which in some sense is 'eternal' and capable of generating 'eternal demands'. A much later passage from Book V (1887) of *The Gay Science*, where Nietzsche is discussing aesthetic creativity, points to the same conclusion. Nietzsche wants to distinguish creation which is prompted by 'desire for Being' from creation prompted by 'desire for Becoming'. But he notices the following difficulty:

But both of these kinds of desire are seen to be ambiguous when one considers them more closely...The desire for *destruction*, change and Becoming can be an expression of an overflowing energy that is pregnant with future (my term for this, as is known, is 'Dionysian'); but it can also be the hatred of the ill-constituted, disinherited, and under-privileged, who destroy, *must* destroy, because what exists, indeed all existence, all Being, outrages and provokes them. To understand this feeling, consider our anarchists closely.[71]

The major failing of postmodernist commentary on Nietzsche – that it is content to rest in perspectivism as a standing refutation of all philosophical 'arrogance' – may indicate that, in these circles, Being is indeed viewed as an outrageous and provocative concept. On the other hand, one may ask whether Nietzsche could grant those who are not so outraged and provoked their own 'desire for Being', and whether this would really be incompatible with his rejection of the metaphysical Being which he associates with Plato and Parmenides. Finally, the opposition of Being and Becoming seems thoroughly questionable when in *The Will to Power*, referring to two central themes of his later writings, Nietzsche says that 'to impose upon Becoming the character of Being (*dem Werden den Character des Seins aufzuprägen*) – that is the supreme will-to-power', and also 'that everything recurs is the closest approximation of Becoming to a world of Being (*extremste Annäherung einer Welt des Werdens an die des Seins*): – high point of the meditation.'[72] These statements, which are important for Heidegger's interpretation of Nietzsche, will receive further discussion in Chapter Four below. It is already evident, however, that Nietzsche's 'repudiation of Being' is more questionable than appears at first sight.

TRUTH AND THE LIMITS OF LANGUAGE
In the *Metaphysics* (1010a12), Aristotle refers to a radical Heraclitean philosopher Cratylus 'who finally did not think it right to say anything but only moved his finger'. Nietzsche does not follow Cratylus' example, but despite

his large literary output, there is no thinker who is more
conscious than Nietzsche of the difficulty, if not the
outright impossibility, of philosophical communication.
As he puts it in *Twilight of the Idols*:

> We no longer have a sufficiently high estimate of
> ourselves when we communicate. Our true experi-
> ences are not garrulous. They could not communicate
> themselves if they wanted to: they lack words. We
> have already grown beyond what we have words for.
> In all talking there lies a grain of contempt. Speech, it
> seems, was devised only for the average, medium,
> communicable. The speaker has already *vulgarized*
> himself by speaking.[73]

For Nietzsche, language and concept formation serve the
needs of the herd (or herd self) rather than the individual,
and hence cannot be the medium of philosophical truth.
Becoming, the peculiar 'object' of philosophical thought,
ceases to be what it is when it takes on determinate
conceptual form: strictly speaking one cannot even say 'it'
or 'is' of Becoming, hence Cratylus' quandary. Nietzsche
does not remain silent, but his writings (especially in the
later period) abound in warnings to distrust all words,
including his own. He refuses to be held to account for
what he has written, and becomes progressively more
convinced of its necessary miscomprehension:

> He who has sat alone with his soul day and night, year
> in and year out, in confidential discord and dis-
> course...finds that his concepts themselves at last
> acquire a characteristic twilight colour, a smell of the
> depths and of must, something incommunicable and
> reluctant which blows cold on every passer-by. The
> hermit does not believe that a philosopher – supposing
> that a philosopher has always been first of all a hermit
> – has ever expressed his real and final opinions in

books: does not one write books precisely to conceal what lies within us? – indeed, he will doubt whether a philosopher *could* have 'final and real' opinions at all.[74]

The postmodernist commentators give much emphasis to Nietzsche's disavowal of final opinions, but they misconstrue this as equivalent to their own pluralistic antidogmatism. If Nietzsche's texts do not contain final opinions, this means, on their account, that different texts with different opinions are always permissible. Schrift calls this 'interpretative pluralism'.[75] Derrida thinks of it as the necessary plurality of styles.[76] Nehamas takes it to imply that 'there is no view of the world that is binding on everyone'.[77] These commentators see the impossibility of any final perspective as following from the open space of perspectivity, taking Nietzsche's statement that 'facts are precisely what there is not, only interpretations'[78] as an invitation to the infinite task of 'writing'.[79] All this misses the essential point. Although Nietzsche rejects facts in the sense of things or states of affairs which correspond to concepts, he does not mean that the philosopher has no access to that primordial reality which he calls 'Becoming'. Such access, in Nietzsche's view, is not to be had through interpretations if by this is meant the kind of conscious thought which is linguistically determined, but rather through pre-conscious or intuitive thought. His point is not simply that purported facts must henceforth be recognized as interpretations, but, more radically, that the truth of philosophy cannot be linguistically expressed and therefore cannot consist in interpretations at all. He refuses final opinions not on the grounds that there are (or should be) equal rights to all perspectives, but because any perspective whatsoever is limited to the 'surface-and-sign-world'. Far from supporting a pluralistic flowering of writing and styles, Nietzsche disavows all writing and every style which is not oriented to the *Sache* of philosophy and to truth in the philosophical sense. Because 'true experiences are not garrulous', he calls for *less* writing in general and for more intuition.[80]

The inability of writing to convey his philosophical meaning often leads Nietzsche to consider whether he should not have used another medium to express himself, the medium of music. Nietzsche's youthful aspirations to a musical career are well known, as is his association with Wagner from the late 1860s till the mid-1870s. As late as 1882 he can still remark, in a letter to the conductor Hermann Levi, that 'perhaps there has never been a philosopher who is in such a degree a musician as I am', adding that he is fundamentally a 'frustrated musician'.[81] In his early period, Nietzsche shares with Wagner an admiration for the philosophical justification of music presented by Schopenhauer in *The World as Will and Representation*: the idea that music is the 'unmediated objectivation of will' plays a central role (albeit under certain modifications) in *The Birth of Tragedy*. Nietzsche then wonders, in the 'Attempt at Self-Criticism' attached to the new (1886) edition of this book, whether he 'should have sung and not spoken'.[82] He attaches to *The Gay Science* a 'Prelude in Rhymes' and an 'Appendix of Songs'. The climax of *Thus Spoke Zarathustra* is 'The Song of Yes and Amen'. In the last aphorism of *The Gay science*, we read:

> I hear all around me the most malicious, cheerful and koboldish laughter: the spirits of my book are attacking me, pull my ears, and call me back to order. 'We can no longer stand it', they shout at me; 'away, away with this raven black music! Are we not surrounded by bright morning? And by soft green grass and grounds, the kingdom of the dance? Has there ever been a better hour for gaiety? Who will sing a song for us, a morning song...?[83]

In *The Case of Wagner*, he writes:

> Has it been noticed that music liberates the spirit? gives wings to thought? that one becomes more of a

philosopher the more one becomes a musician? – The grey sky of abstraction rent as if by lightning; the light strong enough for the filigree of things; the great problems near enough to grasp; the world surveyed as from a mountain. – I have just described the pathos of philosophy.[84]

It is this 'pathos of philosophy' which is incommunicable in words. On the other hand, if this pathos is indeed communicated in Nietzsche's writings, the latter must themselves be understood extra-discursively, in a sense as 'music'. Nietzsche indicates as much. In *Ecce Homo* he calls his *Zarathustra* 'eloquence become music' and a 'dithyramb on solitude'.[85] His 'style', so he tells us, tries to communicate an 'inward tension of pathos', but whether this actually occurs depends on whether there are 'ears capable and worthy of the same pathos'.[86] One does not understand *Zarathustra* unless one sees (or 'hears') beyond the words that are contained in it, one does not comprehend its 'truth' if one searches for it in these words themselves independently of their 'rhythmical' effect.

The 'Yes-saying pathos' of Nietzsche's philosophy is a kind of 'attunement' (*Stimmung*) in the sense that Heidegger gives this term (sometimes translated as 'mood') in *Being and Time*: not as a psychological accompaniment to philosophical thought, not as an external and ethereal 'atmosphere' which surrounds it, but as originally *disclosive*, as opening up (and holding open) the *Sache* with which the philosopher is concerned.[87] In Nietzsche's case, what language and theory cannot reveal becomes accessible in Dionysian 'intoxication' or 'gay' science. Since the essence of reality is the terrible Dionysian abyss, the intellectual optimism of Socratic rationalism is philosophically false. It is false because it is a non-attunement to Dionysian reality, because within the particular kind of existential stance which it is, this reality cannot emerge. For Nietzsche in *The Birth of Tragedy*, it is through the 'Dionysian dithyramb' alone that the primal One can achieve expression: although the lyric poet uses 'Apollinian' metaphors, the specifically tragic effect depends on the ability of Dionysian melodies to set the hearer 'into motion'. The Dionysian reveller does not intellectualize tragic wisdom but 'dances' it. This symbol of the dance, ubiquitous in Nietzsche's writings, indicates not only that philosophical truthfulness is a kind of activity (or 'stance', as I have been saying) but conveys something of the celebratory nature of this activity. The 'object' of Dionysian celebration, whatever we may call it, cannot be independently described or made available for theory, for this would mean entering into a quite different (non-celebratory) kind of stance. There can be no greater barrier to communication than the different attunements to reality which belong to different stances. This is a familiar experience in everyday life, but so entrenched is the theoretical conception of truth that its philosophical import is overlooked.

It may be objected that, in the end, Nietzsche remains a 'writer', that his philosophy is passed on to us in the form of written texts and should not be sought elsewhere. However sensible and sound this observation may appear to be, it begs the essential question, falling back into the epistemological-theoretical framework which Nietzsche is trying to overcome. Of course, Nietzsche's texts (together with other written reports of his life and thought) are the only testimony which we possess of his philosophical activity, but when we reify these texts, when we think of his philosophy as 'in' these texts themselves, their testimonial character, which Nietzsche himself never tires of stressing, is lost sight of.[88] Such reification appears a perfectly natural and justifiable procedure because within the mainstream metaphysical tradition, and particularly in the modern scientific age, philosophy is considered as a 'theory' of the world, whose 'validity' is to be assessed according to the intersubjective protocols of conceptual-theoretical discourse. It is thus assumed that the 'meaning' of Nietzsche's philosophy will emerge from a thorough examination of the internal relations of all his central concepts. But although meticulous and patient attention to detail is necessary in reading his texts, Nietzsche is very much aware that this alone will not lead to comprehension. The kind of reading which Nietzsche wants is not just 'philological': it must also be 'philosophical'.[89] As the postmodernists emphasize, Nietzsche can be read in many different ways and to many different purposes, but this (ultimately rather boring point) is not the issue. Nietzsche can only be read in the way he himself intended if he is read as a philosopher, i.e. only if the reader has the *Sache* of philosophy all the while in view. It is precisely this *Sache* (the 'primal One' or 'life', to use Nietzschean expressions) to which all words and concepts are inadequate: unlike the situation in theoretical discourse, the 'object' of philosophy is not 'constructed' but must be given from the outset, 'given', moreover, in a mode of self-evidence prior to all cognition as normally understood. The limitation of language is that it cannot bring the *Sache* originally or primordially into view, it cannot be the medium or vehicle through which one in the first place 'becomes a philosopher'. Since the *Sache* of philosophy is, to recall our earlier findings, 'over the horizon' of the 'surface-and-sign-world', a reading of Nietzsche texts which remains at this latter level will not recognize it, and Nietzsche himself, as he always feared, will be mistaken for what he is not. On the other hand, if this *Sache* is indeed in view (in the case of the 'right reader', as Nietzsche says) then his writings can be understood in their proper testimonial character. This has nothing to do with romantic sentimentalism, or with any kind of psychological reductionism. Nietzsche gives testimony to himself only as philosopher, and thus to the *Sache* of philosophy itself. His writings do not theorize but exhibit the situation of the philosopher in multifarious aspects, particularly in a world which is 'unphilosophical'. Nietzsche's writings pose problems, but problems which are (provided that the *Sache* is in view) recognizable rather than originally opened up in the texts themselves. Ultimately, and despite his sometimes excessive literary pride, Nietzsche considers his own writings to be of secondary value:

> For what things do we write and paint, we mandarins with Chinese brushes, we immortalizers of things which *let* themselves be written, what alone are we capable of painting? Alas, only that which is about to wither and lose its fragrance!...And it is only your *afternoon*, my written and painted thoughts, for which alone I have the colours, many colours perhaps, many many-coloured tendernesses and fifty yellows and greens and reds: – but no one will divine from these how you looked in your morning, you sudden sparks and wonders of my solitude, you my old beloved – *wicked* thoughts![90]

TRUTH AND INTEREST

One of the things upon which the postmodernist commentators most uncompromisingly insist is the 'interested' character of Nietzschean truth: in rejecting the age-old metaphysical shibboleth of 'disinterested truth', so it is claimed, Nietzsche exposes the 'dogmatism' which would disguise specific interests as universal. Jean-Luc Nancy writes that 'in order to be able to begin to recognize Nietzschean truth, one must begin by acknowledging, without dissimulation or deception, the hidden evaluation and the secret interestedness of truth, of all our truths.'[91] Derrida evinces the same attitude with his thesis of 'the *a priori* link between philosophy and politics.'[92] The 'secret interestedness of truth' plays a fundamental role in the project known as deconstructionism, where authoritative definitions in all areas of life are 'unmasked' in their relation to specific structures of power/interest. Within this politicization of perspectivism, 'equal rights to all perspectives' translates into 'equal rights to all interest-constellations', i.e. into politico-ideological pluralism. Just as there is no metaphysically guaranteed theory of the world, so there is no metaphysical or supra-perspectival source of political authority. The struggle between perspectives is at bottom a struggle between different political forces, between the opposed interests of different categories of social actors.[93] If Nietzsche himself does not seem to be a political pluralist, a distinction can be made between his reactionary 'political ideology' on the one hand, and 'the internal integrity of his critical, postmodern insights' on the other.[94]

This politicization of Nietzsche stems from the same miscomprehension of perspectivism already revealed. Nietzsche does indeed see perspectival truth as inherently interested: this is a matter of definition for him. When he 'unmasks' a particular perspective, he finds a utility-value behind its claim to authority, he finds a specific 'herd-interest' at work. But because the postmodernist commentators do not appreciate the difference between perspectival truth and philosophical truth in Nietzsche, they do not grasp the critical meaning of Nietzschean unmasking. On their view, the absence of any supra-perspectival vantage point means that unmasking takes place as a 'strategical' act between perspectival interests. In reality, however, Nietzsche sets out to unmask the interested and therefore unphilosophical nature of sundry perspectival authority claims, including claims made by 'so-called' philosophers who declare their service to truth. Nietzsche does not criticize authority in order to promote pluralism within the 'surface-and-sign-world', but insofar as the authority of philosophy is usurped by interests which are extra-philosophical. Acceptance of ('obedience to' would not be putting it too strongly) the authority of philosophy is what Nietzsche understands as 'decency': 'It is my fate that I have to be the first *decent* (*anständige*) human being; that I know myself to stand in opposition to the mendaciousness (*Verlogenheit*) of millennia – I was the first to discover truth (*Ich erst habe die Wahrheit entdeckt*) by being the first to experience lies as lies.'[95] This is a different kind of decency to that commonly recognized: 'when mendaciousness at any price monopolizes the word "truth" for its perspective, the really truthful man is bound to be called the worst names.'[96] Whoever ('the really truthful man') does not show solidarity to commonly accepted interests will be branded as 'immoral', or alternatively, as happens to Nietzsche in postmodernist commentary, will be domesticated, castrated and sent out to pasture with the herd.

We have seen that, for Nietzsche, the philosopher looks 'over the horizon' of all perspectives to the 'great problems and question marks' attaching to human existence as such. In this realm, what the postmodernists call 'interest' (and Nietzsche calls 'herd utility') no longer operates. Nietzsche's position is again rather similar to that of Schopenhauer, who distinguishes between the 'representational' thought governed by utility-values (survival of individual and species), and the philosophical intuition of the 'pure, will-less subject'. Although Nietzsche criticizes the Schopenhauerian will-less subject, his intentions in this regard can be easily misunderstood. What Nietzsche objects to in Schopenhauer is the philosophical pessimism, the idea of will-denial as world-denial. But the will which is affirmed in the tragic (and ostensibly anti-Schopenhauerian) wisdom of Dionysus is by no means 'interested' will in the sense which Schopenhauer wants to 'deny', it is by no means the will of a herd-self as expressed through a herd perspective. Similarly, although Nietzsche insists, against the 'Schopenhauerian' ideal of selflessness, that philosophy concerns the self and serves the self, this is anything but an egoistic self which seeks its personal or herd advantage. Schopenhauer's philosophy is built on a granite foundation of anti-egoism and anti-utilitarianism, and on these issues Nietzsche does not differ from him in the least. Philosophers, as Nietzsche understands them, are governed by what he calls the 'pathos of distance':

> It was out of this *pathos of distance* that they first seized the right to create values and to coin names for values: what had that to do with utility! The viewpoint of utility is as remote and inappropriate as it possibly could be in face of such a burning eruption of the highest rank-ordering, rank-defining value judge-ments: for here feeling has attained the antithesis of that low degree of warmth which any calculating prudence, any calculus of utility, presupposes – and not for once only, not for an exceptional hour, but for good.[97]

As for the pursuit of egoistic or herd advantage, Nietzsche has this to say:

> Common natures consider all noble, magnamimous feelings inexpedient and therefore first of all incred-ible. They blink when they hear of such things and feel like saying 'Surely, there must be some advantage involved; one cannot see through everything'. They are suspicious of the noble person, as if he surrep-titiously sought his advantage....What distinguishes the common type is that it never loses sight of its advantage, and that this thought of purpose and advantage is even stronger than the strongest instincts; not to allow these instincts to lead one astray to perform inexpedient acts – that is their wisdom and pride.[98]

Nietzschean unmasking is directed not against the idea of philosophical truth as such, but against its all too frequent abuse. The real philosopher, he considers, is an exception, while those whom the public take as philosophers are just 'advocates who do not want to be regarded as such, and for

the most part cunning pleaders for their prejudices.'[99] It is
quite comprehensible that Nietzsche, for whom philosophy is the highest value, should be so preoccupied with
exposing false claims to wisdom; the same attitude is taken
by all defenders of philosophy, e.g. by Plato in *The
Republic* and other dialogues, when exposing the 'interested' character of sophistry. Like Plato, Nietzsche believes
that while the authentic philosopher is often 'misunderstood, misjudged, misindentified, slandered, misheard
and not heard',[100] there are always many who are anxious
to lay claim to this title. It is necessary to expose the interests
of these false pretenders. When Nietzsche says that the
philosopher 'has today the duty to be mistrustful, to squint
wickedly up out of every abyss of suspicion', he is
speaking not of the common mistrust which is anxious on
behalf of its own herd advantage, but of philosophical
mistrust, of the mistrust of the philosopher who is aware
that interest is adept at disguising itself as truth.[101] The
postmodernist commentators, on the other hand, in connection with their campaigns of deconstruction, do not
observe a distinction between philosophical suspicion and
suspicion governed by interest; indeed, there is no room for
such a distinction if it is always one perspective which
unmasks another.

   In defense of the postmodernists, it may be suggested
that the 'interestedness' of Nietzschean unmasking consists
in something other than perspectival herd or ego advantage. Might it be possible, after the manner of Mark
Warren, to see Nietzsche's guiding 'interest' as 'free
agency', or 'power as subjectivity'?[102] In this case the
individualism of Nietzsche's philosophy would indicate his
concern with 'autonomy' and the politico-ideological
forces which inhibit its realization. Nietzsche would provide, as Warren puts it, an 'implicit critique of domination',
with his method of unmasking telling 'a political story
about the relation between oppression, culture, and the
constitution of subjects.'[103] While Warren in this way

draws parallels between Nietzsche and the Marxist critique of ideology, other postmodernist authors incline towards quasi-anarchistic politics. For Gilles Deleuze, Nietzsche 'announces the advent of a new kind of politics', the politics of the 'nomad' who wants to 'evade the codes of settled people', particularly the codes of 'the despotic and bureaucratic organization of the party or state apparatus.'[104] Derrida, in a move which has been particularly influential, has attempted to make Nietzsche relevant for the feminist critique of 'phallocentric' discourses: on his view, Nietzsche shows that woman, 'precisely because she does not believe in truth itself, because she does not believe in what she is, in what she is believed to be' occupies a privileged position within the politics of truth: she is the site of the 'untruth of truth'.[105] In this way woman is credited with a 'universal' mission somewhat reminiscent of that of the proletariat within Marxism.

But the difficulties of equating the 'interest' of Nietzsche's philosophy with a particular perspectival interest are not overcome by resorting to mythologies of privileged subjectivity, whether Marxist, feminist or anarchist (the mythology of the disenfranchised and marginalized elements). If autonomy is posited as the universal interest behind Nietzsche's thought, we must ask precisely what kind of autonomy is intended. The postmodernist commentators founder at this point, for their fear of dogmatism prevents them from giving any positive meaning to autonomy: to specify a 'freedom-to' would be dogmatic, so in the last resort they must be content with the negative (quasi-anarchistic) ideal of 'freedom-from'. This is the kind of freedom Nietzsche is referring to when he says that:

> the longing for freedom, the instinct for the happiness and the refinements of the feeling of freedom, belong just as necessarily to slave morality and morals as the art of reverence and devotion and the enthusiasm for them are the regular symptoms of an

aristocratic mode of thinking and valuating. [106]

For Nietzsche, the negative ideal of freedom expresses nothing more than 'their [the anarchist's] total and instinctive hostility towards every form of society other than that of the *autonomous* herd'. [107] Such negative freedom is reactive, proceeding from experienced repression, exclusion or wounded dignity, and turning on the sources of these, wanting 'liberation'. [108] It is accompanied by the characteristic mistrust of the slave, the mistrust which always suspects ulterior motives where values are spoken of or commands issued. If it wants anything in particular (which it often does not) this will be something thoroughly perspectival, variable, changing from one moment to the next. On Nietzsche's reckoning, liberation into herd autonomy does not amount to any kind of liberation worth mentioning. This does not make him into a political reactionary, as Warren concludes. It indicates that his 'seriousness lies elsewhere':

> For a few must first of all be allowed, now more than ever, to refrain from politics and step aside a little: they too are prompted to this by pleasure in self-determination; and there may also be a degree of pride attached to staying silent when too many, or even just many, are speaking. Then these few must be forgiven if they fail to take the happiness of the many, whether by the many one understands nations or social classes, so very seriously and are now and then guilty of an ironic posture; for their seriousness lies elsewhere, their happiness is something quite different. [109]

In what kind of self-determination, then, does the Nietzschean philosopher take pleasure? The answer is given in one of the most well-known mottos of Nietzsche's writings, the imperative to 'become who you are'. [110] Yet this answer is itself an enigma, open to many interpretations, including the pluralist injunction to 'do your own thing'. A detailed discussion of the problem of the self in Nietzsche will be postponed until Chapter Three, but in the present context it may be noted that the postmodernist commentators, by insisting on the comprehensive social determination (perspectival constitution) of the self, i.e. by refusing the distinction between the herd self and the philosophical self, pass over one of the most profound and intriguing questions of Nietzsche's philosophy (and not only Nietzsche's), namely the question of how the universal is attainable through a process of individualization. Within the framework of perspectivism, the individual has simply no right to the universal, because this would imply a point of view which is a 'view from nowhere'. As already indicated, the solution of this difficulty is that supra-perspectival truth (the 'universal' which is sought by the philosophical self) is not any kind of 'view'. By the same token, the supra-perspectival self is not 'interested' in the same sense as the perspectival self, and indeed may not even seem like a self at all, as normally understood.

If the Nietzschean philosopher can be said to have an 'interest', it is in human existence as such. This is to be distinguished from the local, limited, perspectivally constituted interests which occupy the herd. The former is the concern of the 'intellectual' conscience, the latter are the concern of the 'moral' or 'herd' conscience.[111] In an aphorism from *The Gay Science* entitled 'The Intellectual Conscience', Nietzsche says the following:

> The great majority of people does not consider it contemptible to believe this or that and to live accordingly, without first having given themselves an account of the final and most certain reasons pro and con, and without even troubling themselves about such reasons afterward: the most gifted men and the noblest women still belong to this 'great majority'. But what is goodheartedness, refinement, or genius to me, when the person who has these virtues tolerates

slack feelings in his faith and judgements and when he does not account the *desire for certainty* as his inmost craving and deepest distress – as that which separates the higher human beings from the lower.[112]

This passage is difficult to reconcile with Nehamas' contention that Nietzsche refuses 'to grade people and views along a single scale'.[113] The opposite is true: Nietzsche takes the uncompromising attitude that the only thing which counts is the degree to which an individual is governed by the intellectual conscience. Of course, the 'desire for certainty' of which Nietzsche here speaks is not the theoretical certainty of Cartesianism, it is not indicative of foundationalism in the sense of an epistemologically guaranteed view of reality. Nietzsche's desire for certainty is the desire for something very epistemologically uncertain indeed, for something which cannot be encountered within the 'grasping' and 'securing' (i.e. utilitarian) structures of theoretical cognition. This means that the interest of the philosopher is 'incomprehensible and impractical' by the standards of herd interest.[114] To the question of why one must enter into philosophical regions, Nietzsche is content to reply, without reservation or embarrassment: 'That one wants to go precisely out there, up there, may be a minor madness, a peculiar and unreasonable "you must"'.[115]

It is Nietzsche's claim of a higher interest for the philosopher which is behind his ill-deserved reputation for personal arrogance. In fact, Nietzsche loathes nothing more than intellectual and spiritual complacency. Nothing strikes him as more ridiculous than the delusion of already 'possessing' the truth, but by the same token nothing strikes him as more worthy of contempt than the resentful revolt against philosophy and truth so characteristic of his own time. Nietzsche is aware that there are many who applaud the failure of dogmatic metaphysics out of a feeling of revenge, out of that 'revenge against the spirit' which finds nothing so outrageous than the claim to higher insight.[116] These are people who 'honourably, wrathfully, revengefully represent by word and deed the *unbelief* in the lordly task and lordliness of philosophy', who themselves preach 'a timid epochism and abstinence doctrine: a philosophy that does not even get over the threshold and painfully *denies* itself the right of entry.'[117] Having unburdened themselves of any relation to truth, such people retreat into their own sphere of 'interests' secure in the thought that they are no longer required to account for themselves. Somewhat surprisingly, however, they still want to be listened to as 'philosophers', and, in what amounts to a kind of 'higher dogmatism', they attempt to make their own pluralism morally prescriptive. The passion of a moral purpose stands in place of true philosophical resolve:

> O you good natured and even noble enthusiasts, I know you! You want to win your argument against us, but also against yourself, and above all against yourself! and a subtle and tender bad conscience so often incites you against your enthusiasm! How ingenious you then become in the outwitting and deadening of this conscience!...You drive yourself to the point of hating criticism, science, reason! You have to falsify history so that it may bear witness to you, you have to deny virtues so that they shall not cast into the shade those of your idols and ideals!...How you thirst for those moments when your passion bestows on you perfect self-justification and as it were innocence; when in struggle, intoxication, courage, hope, you are beside yourself and beyond all doubting; when you decree: 'he who is not beside himself as we are can in no way know what and where truth is!' How you thirst to discover people of your belief in this condition – it is that of intellectual vice – and ignite your flame at their torch! Oh your

deplorable martyrdom! Oh your deplorable victory
of the sanctified lie! [118]

The great currency of the perspectivist Nietzsche has much
to do with the sacrosanctity of democratic pluralism in the
countries of his contemporary interpreters. But its roots go
deeper than this. For, as Nietzsche recognizes, the modern
culture of egalitarianism provides a perfect outlet, a
perfect moral justification, for the anti-philosophical senti-
ment of the majority, for the inevitable suspicion of
philosophy and truth among those for whom 'reality' is
defined by their own shifting 'interests'. Perspectivism
effects a domestication of Nietzsche's thought by subvert-
ing the authoritative character of philosophical truth.
Where there is no authority, there is no challenge, and in the
end, no seriousness either, no perserverence and no resol-
uteness. It has never been difficult to do what Derrida's
translator Gayatri Spivak recommends, i.e. to 'reverse
perspectives as often as possible.'[119] This has always been
the way of the non-philosophical majority who are moved
by many things, including a taste for 'variety', which are
other than truth. What is difficult is not to move laterally
within the shallows, but vertically into the depths. While
those who feel comfortable in the shallows may reassure
themselves on 'epistemological' grounds that 'there are no
depths', this will not convince a philosopher like Nietzsche:
he has experience, he has been down there.

2
Hierarchy of the Spirit

It is the *problem of the order of rank* of which we may say it is *our* problem, we free spirits.[1]

The *order of castes*, the supreme, the dominating law, is only the sanctioning of a *natural order*, a natural law of the first rank over which no arbitrary caprice, no 'modern idea' has any power. In every healthy society, there can be distinguished three types of man of divergent physiological tendency which mutually condition one another and each of which possesses its own hygiene, its own realm of work, its own sort of mastery and feeling of perfection. Nature, *not* Manu, separates from one another the predominantly spiritual type, the predominantly muscular and temperamental type, and the third type distinguished neither in the one nor the other, the mediocre type – the last as the great majority, the first as the elite.[2]

RANK ORDER AND VALUE

We have seen that, for Nietzsche, the philosopher attains to a 'higher' form of existence than that of other human beings. The 'pathos of distance' not only limits the possibilities of communication open to the philosopher, it not only detaches him from mundane herd involvements, but it elevates him, it distinguishes him, it honours him as a more 'worthy' human being. Nietzsche takes 'nobility' and its counterpole 'plebianism' as philosophical categories. Unlike the postmodernist commentators, who distribute truths along a horizontal axis of perspectives, Nietzsche distributes human beings, in their concrete forms of existence, along a vertical axis of philosophical truthfulness, and thus along a vertical axis of 'worth'. It is common to speak of Nietzsche's 'aristocratic temperament', but this kind of talk all too often amounts to a psychological reductionism which is anxious to delete 'subjective' elements from his thought. As we shall see, Nietzsche does not believe in 'hierarchy of the spirit' because he is an aristocrat, but more the other way around: because of the 'hierarchical' nature of truth, he is forced to become an aristocrat, to continually renew and reacquire his aristocratic values.

Let us begin with a statement from the *Genealogy of Morals*: '*All* the sciences have from now on to prepare the way for the future task of the philosophers: this task understood as the solution of the *problem of value*, the determination of the *order of rank among values*.'[3] Two questions arise. First, what are values? Second, in respect of what are values to be ranked? Values do not exist just as abstract ideals but as concrete practices, as specific modes of living and acting. Throughout his works, Nietzsche ranks in the sense that he 'evaluates' values, e.g. the values of the religious life, political activity, money making, family life, honour seeking, the pursuit of sensual pleasure, scholarship and science. On the measure of rank, Nietzsche gives various criteria. In one late fragment he says simply 'First question concerning order of rank: how solitary or herd-bound (*herdenhaft*) one is.'[4] A passage from *Beyond Good and Evil* invokes another theme familiar from my previous discussions:

> There is an *instinct for rank* which is more than anything else already the sign of a high rank; there is a *delight* in the nuances of reverence, which reveals a noble origin and noble habits....He whose task and practice is to explore the soul will avail himself of precisely this art in many forms in order to determine the ultimate value of a soul, the unalterable innate order of rank to which it belongs: he will test it for its *instinct of reverence*.[5]

It was noticed earlier how Nietzsche connects lack of

reverence with blindness for the 'great problems and question marks'. In another passage from *Beyond Good and Evil*, we find that it is precisely one's fitness for the 'supreme problems' which determines one's spiritual rank:

> In the last resort there exists an order of rank of states of soul with which the order of rank of problems accords; and the supreme problems repel without mercy everyone who ventures near them without being, through the elevation and power of his spirituality, predestined to their solution. Of what avail is it if nimble commonplace minds or worthy clumsy mechanicals and empiricists crowd up to them, as they so often do today, and with their plebian ambition approach as it were this 'court of courts'. But coarse feet may never tread such carpets: that has been seen to in the primal law of things.[6]

Further, because the 'supreme problems' are accessible only through a certain kind of suffering, rank order can 'almost' be determined through the capacity for suffering:

> The spiritual haughtiness and disgust of every human being who has suffered deeply – *how* deeply human beings can suffer almost determines their order of rank – the harrowing certainty, with which he is wholly permeated and coloured, that by virtue of his suffering he *knows more* than even the cleverest and wisest can know, that he is familiar with, and was once 'at home' in many distant, terrible worlds of which '*you* know nothing!' ... this spiritual, silent haughtiness of the sufferer, the pride of the elect of knowledge, of the 'initiated', of the almost sacrificed, finds all forms of disguise necessary to protect itself against contact with importunate and pitying hands and in general against everything which is not its equal in suffering.[7]

What do solitariness, reverence, fitness for the supreme problems and capacity for suffering signify? The answer has already been indicated: Nietzsche's measure of rank is truth. To avoid falling into epistemological ways of thinking, the term truthfulness may be preferable. Zarathustra, who is surely a figure of the highest rank, is said to be 'more truthful (*wahrhaftiger*) than any other thinker', indeed 'his doctrine, and his alone, has truthfulness (*Wahrhaftigkeit*) as the highest virtue.'[8] On the other hand, Nietzsche is by no means averse to speaking simply of 'truth' (*Wahrheit*): 'How much truth does a spirit *endure*, how much truth does it *dare*? More and more that became for me the measure of value.'[9] It is not so much the terminology which matters as whether truth is understood in an existential sense, as a stance towards and within existence. What 'stance' means here still needs elucidation, but we may anticipate by saying that, for Nietzsche, the stance of truth(fulness) is that of 'justice' (*Gerechtigkeit*). It is the will to justice, so Nietzsche maintains in his early essay on history, which distinguishes the genuine from the mendacious truth-seeker.[10] The genuine philosopher ranks (i.e. values, judges) according to justice, giving everything what is in truth due to it, while the apparent philosopher is driven by one or more of a variety of motives: e.g. 'curiosity, escape from boredom, enviousness, vanity, play instinct, drives which have nothing whatsoever to do with truth.'[11] It is this sense of justice which allows the philosopher to distinguish the supreme problems from regional or trivial problems, and in the final event to accord supreme value to philosophy itself.

The postmodernist commentators are not unaware that rank order is a prominent motif in Nietzsche's writings. But because it does not sit well with their prime desideratum of pluralism, they adopt one or other of two strategies (or a combination thereof) to deal with it. Either, like Mark Warren, they consign it to Nietzsche's regrettable 'political views' and deny any organic connection with his basic philosophical standpoint. Or, like Alexander Nehamas, they try to subordinate the principle of rank order to perspectivism itself, thus arriving at the absurd notion of 'noble' and 'plebian' perspectives. Nietzsche obviously does not speak in a very pluralist spirit when comparing his own philosophy to other outlooks, but this, according to Nehamas, only reflects his right to a forthright and creative defense of his own perspective. [12] The strategies of Warren and Nehamas only indicate the embarrassment of the postmodernists when faced with Nietzsche's actual texts. Their extravagent attempts to explain away the texts make Nietzsche into an advocate or rhetorician rather than a philosopher: he must always be taken as saying something which, according to his own principles, is highly exaggerated and unreasonable. Besides such explicit references to rank order as those just quoted, it can hardly escape the notice of even the most casual reader that metaphors of height and depth frequently occur in Nietzsche's writings, specifically in connection with philosophical insight. If Nietzsche were really a perspectivist in the sense maintained by the postmodernist commentators, then his rhetoric far exceeds what he is entitled to philosophically, and it must be concluded that he is a very arrogant and impertinent man.

It may also be noted that, once rank order is written out of Nietzsche's philosophy in the manner of the postmodernists, his critique of morality likewise disappears from view. What we find under this rubric in Nietzsche's actual texts is a critique of that morality of equality and levelling which he associates with Christianity. On the other hand, because the perspectivist standpoint of the postmodernist commentators precludes substantive criticism, because perspectivism can recognize only the formal *metacritique* which deconstructs dogmatic definitions of truth, the content of Nietzsche's critique remains occluded. All deconstructive criticisms come to the same predictable conclusion that a closure has been effected, that some specific and contextual definition has been totalized. Since at this level of abstraction any closure whatsoever is equally objectionable, Nietzsche's substantive critique of morality can be ignored, or can be referred to his suspect 'political views'.

Although the idea of rank order appears politically suspect to the postmodernist commentators, in Nietzsche's writings it has, at bottom, nothing to do with political or socio-economic categories: it is a rank order of the spirit. To be sure, on quite frequent occasions, Nietzsche makes a correlation between 'master morality' and those who are political masters, as between 'slave morality' and those who are political slaves. But this is a contingent and entirely defeasible correlation. His examples are almost always taken from ancient society (Greece and Rome) and are used to illustrate virtues and vices which are independent of politics as normally understood. Political metaphors are used to clarify spiritual attitudes. Nietzsche does not believe that free spirits will ever be political overlords or are likely to occupy positions of socio-economic influence. He is simply not concerned with such matters: as a philosopher his 'seriousness lies elsewhere'. Rank order pertains to individuals as psychological types: the relevant opposition, to simplify in a manner which Nietzsche does himself, is between the 'ill-constituted' (and therefore resentful) types on the one hand, and 'the well-constituted' (and therefore philosophical) types on the other.[13] While membership of a lowly socio-economic category may accentuate the resentment of the ill-constituted type, or bring it further out into the open, resentment itself does not have political or socio-economic roots. The same principle applies to those 'nobles' possessed of 'the great health'.[14] Nietzsche is aware that his own egalitarian age sees evil as fundamentally the responsibility of 'society', but he is at pains to distinguish himself from those who would distort the meaning of 'free spirit' along socio-political lines:

In all the countries of Europe and likewise in America there exists at present something that misuses this name, a very narrow, enclosed, chained up species of spirits who desire practically the opposite of that which informs our aims and instincts....They belong, in short and regrettably, among the *levellers*, those falsely named 'free spirits' – eloquent and tirelessly scribbling slaves of the democratic taste and its 'modern ideas', men without solitude one and all, without their own solitude, good clumsy fellows who, while they cannot be denied moral respectability, are unfree and ludicrously superficial, above all in their fundamental inclination to see in the forms of existing society the cause of practically *all* human failure and misery: which is to stand the truth happily on its head....their two most oft-recited doctrines and ditties are 'equality of rights' and 'sympathy with all that suffers'.[15]

So far I have spoken rather loosely of rank order as it pertains to values and individuals. An individual's position in the order of spiritual rank will be determined by the rank of those values with which he most closely identifies. However, the valuational activity of human beings is complex. As Nietzsche recognizes, many different values will struggle against each other for supremacy, so that the overall valuational orientation of the individual may be quite unstable.[16] Values of different rank may be co-present, and their claim upon the individual may vary at different points of time. It may be possible to rank individuals in terms of those values which are most enduring and stable for them, but even if this, as Nietzsche suggests, constitutes their 'innate, unalterable order of rank', it is an outcome which must be continually reaffirmed and reacquired. In this sense, and in this sense alone, rank order is indeed a matter of 'politics' but, as Leslie Thiele has put it, of 'the politics of the soul'. The spiritual aristocrat is what he is not through resting on his laurels, but through fighting those 'gravitational' forces which would bring him down to the rank of spiritual pleb.[17] In Thiele's words, 'the language that best facilitates the description and analysis of the soul is political. The world of politics serves as a conceptual and terminological resource for the "reader of souls".'[18] The 'political' struggle takes place primarily within one's own self, and only secondarily between oneself and others.

Because Nietzschean rank order defines 'levels' or 'degrees' of truthfulness, it is a pluralism of sorts, but it has no resemblance to the relativistic pluralism of the postmodernist commentators. Nietzsche could hardly be more explicit on this:

> Are they new friends of 'truth', these coming philosophers? In all probability: for all philosophers have hitherto loved their truths. But certainly they will not be dogmatists. It must offend their pride, and also their taste, if their truth is supposed to be a truth for everyman, which has hitherto been the secret desire and hidden sense of all dogmatic endeavours....In the end it must be as it is and has always been: great things for the great, abysses for the profound, shudders and delicacies for the refined, and, in sum, all rare things for the rare.[19]

Nietzsche considers that philosophical truth is 'undogmatic' because it is not a 'truth for everyman'. All this means, however, is that not everyone is capable of philosophical truthfulness. This is about as undogmatic and pluralist as saying that, since only a few are capable of power, the powerlessness of the many should be recognized as right for them. Truth, like power, is a normative, valuational, concept: it signifies a greater good. There may be an equal right to truths at all levels of the spiritual hierarchy, but, for Nietzsche, some of these truths are more equal than others.

In the following three sections I shall analyse Nietzsche's hierarchy of the spirit in terms of the three categories spiritual lower class, spiritual middle class, and spiritual aristocracy. These are categories which Nietzsche employs himself, but it should now be clear that no individual belongs purely to one category or another. My method of treatment is merely a convenient way of referring to forces which are operative within every individual. Nietzsche is not the first to have looked at human spiritual life in this way. In *The Republic*, for example, Plato distinguishes three parts of the soul (reason, spirit, and desire) corresponding to three classes of the state (guardians, auxiliaries and workers), while Aristotle, in the *Nichomachean Ethics*, talks of the conflict between the higher (rational) and lower (desiring) parts of the soul.[20] Thiele maintains that Nietzsche returns to such ancient models of the 'soul as plurality' in opposition to the Christian doctrine of 'soul atomism', but this suggests an oversimplified conception of Christian thinking on the soul, perhaps a confusion between the soul as a whole (i.e. the whole of spiritual life) and that part of the soul which is immortal (for Plato as well as Christianity). Nietzsche is himself given to oversimplified judgements on Christianity, perhaps more so than on any other subject. Although he undoubtedly views his own idea of spiritual rank order as anti-Christian, there are many parallels within the Christian tradition. Notwithstanding its 'levelling' morality, hierarchy of the spirit is one of Christianity's most characteristic conceptions, reflected in both its theology and ecclesiastical structure. The idea of spiritual progress which one finds in such Christian authors as Pseudo-Dionysius and John Climacus is not dissimilar to Nietzsche's, especially in so far as, at the summit of the 'ladder of divine ascent', truth (God) is encountered as something unsayable and unknowable.[21] Whether Nietzsche can be rightfully associated with such religious thought, however, is a matter reserved for later discussion.

The final three sections of the chapter look at Nietzsche's ranking of the historical epochs of the spirit: the Greek spirit, the spirit of Christianity and the spirit of modernity. In opposition to modern notions of progress, Nietzsche sees the history of the spirit since the Greeks as a decline into decadence, but I shall not attempt to assess this sweeping claim as an historical hypothesis. My main concern will be to draw out the implications of Nietzsche's historical evaluations for the economy of the spirit. In different epochs of history, different aspects of the spirit come to the fore which do not show themselves with comparable clarity at other times.[22] Nietzsche sees the philosophical significance of historical knowledge as the uncovering of spiritual possibilities which in our own times have been lost from view or have withered away to pale shadows of their former selves. Once Nietzsche's historical reflections are understood in this way, the essential meaning of his critique of modernity will more clearly come to light: not, as the postmodernists would have it, as a critique of dogmatism, but as a critique of that very pluralism and '*largeur* of heart' which the postmodernists celebrate as their own highest virtue.

THE SPIRITUAL LOWER CLASS
The spiritual lower class is made up of those who, by the nature of their spiritual economy, are farthest removed from truth and truthfulness. Such removedness is expressed in various character traits and their associated values. Again, Nietzsche's interest in the character of the spiritual pleb has clear antecedents in Greek philosophy, particularly Plato and Aristotle. The philosopher, as a lover of wisdom, must always wonder at the motivations of those who are either indifferent to wisdom or positively disdainful of it.[23] Only through understanding the non-philosopher can the philosopher also be comprehended: these are just different sides of the single problem of truth.[24] In many of his dialogues, Plato exposes the base

motives which fetter the vast majority of human beings to pre-philosophical or even anti-philosophical forms of existence. Aristotle does the same thing in the *Nichomachean Ethics*. Contrary to what might be expected from such a vigorous anti-Platonist, Nietzsche's view of the spiritual lower class evinces a good deal of common ground with these founders of the metaphysical tradition. There is a similar emphasis on petty pride and ambition, on the general inclination to take things easily, and on the corrupting power of the lower 'brown pleasures'.[25] However, I shall attempt to understand such familiar themes in terms of a number of characteristic Nietzschean motifs, discernible in his works from an early date.

The weakness of the spiritual pleb is an obvious starting point. But it is all-important that weakness and strength be understood in the frame of reference intended by Nietzsche, and not, as so often happens, in terms of vague appeals to the 'will to power'. This phrase explains nothing unless we know what type of 'power' is relevant. I shall come back to 'will to power' at a later stage, when discussing Heidegger's view of Nietzsche. From the general thesis adumbrated above, i.e. that rank order is for Nietzsche an order of truthfulness, it can be said at this point that it is the power to truthfulness which is intended. The spiritual pleb possesses this power in a very limited degree. This is not because he lacks what could be broadly called 'intellectual accomplishments'. Nor does it necessarily mean absence of cleverness, mental agility and alertness. The characteristic weakness of the spiritual pleb is quite consistent with a well-rounded education and an acute intelligence. Nor is the power to truthfulness, in the philosophical sense intended, identical with the power of 'theoretical' understanding. Nietzsche is consistently scathing of modernity on all these points, claiming that superficial and ornamental accomplishments of learning are mistaken for genuine spirit.[26] What really matters, as far as Nietzsche is concerned, is one thing only: the power to face, and actually enter into, the 'great problems and question marks' of human existence. It is this power which is lacking in the spiritual pleb. This is his defining 'weakness'.

What Nietzsche means by 'weakness' is inseparable from his understanding of the 'great problems' (the *Sache*) of philosophy itself. This is already evident in *The Birth of Tragedy*, where he laments the weakness of the Socratic intellectual in recoiling from the 'terrible' Dionysian truth: Socratism is the expression of the 'senile, unproductive love of existence' of those who fear the sight of Dionysian abysses.[27] Nietzsche looks forward to a rebirth of tragedy from those who 'turn their back on all the weaklings' doctrines of optimism in order to "live resolutely" in wholeness and fullness'.[28] The connection between intellectualism and weakness is also maintained in Nietzsche's early writings on the Presocratics, where Heracliteanism, as the courageous embracing of the eternal 'strife' of existence, is contrasted with Parmenideanism, as the anxious yearning for security.[29] Weakness is cowardice, the desire for a prop in a sea of uncertainty, the need for a panacea against the ambiguity of existence, the nervous anxiety over one's own fragile self. Fundamentally, weakness of the spirit is a flight from truth:

> This ultimate, most joyous, most wantonly extravagent Yes to life represents not only the highest insight but also the *deepest*, that which is most strictly confirmed and born out by truth and science....To comprehend this requires courage and, as a condition of that, an excess of strength: for precisely as far as courage may venture forward, precisely according to that measure of strength one approaches the truth. Knowledge, saying Yes to reality, is just as necessary for the strong as cowardice and the flight from reality – as the 'ideal' is for the weak, who are inspired by weakness.[30]

Nietzsche presupposes that, at some level and however obscurely, all human beings are acquainted with the phenomenon of the Dionysian. But the cowardice inscribed in the psychology of the average human being means that, more often than not, this awareness occurs in a 'turning away'. In his later writings, Nietzsche tends to assimilate this kind of cowardly avoidance of truth with the psychology of *ressentiment*. Especially in the third essay of *The Genealogy of Morals*, it seems that *ressentiment* encompasses almost the whole range of human values and activities. Conventional existence emerges as a tissue of escape mechanisms for those who wish to revenge themselves on their underlying philosophical weakness. The degree to which one turns away from life seems to depend primarily on one's psychological-physiological constitution. Nietzsche reserves his special scorn for the 'worm-eaten' types who insist on elevating their own weakness to the status of a religion. The inability to stand up to life is then promulgated as the highest virtue, while strength is denigrated as wickedness and injustice:

> They walk among us as embodied reproaches, as warnings to us – as if health, well-constitutedness, strength, pride, and the sense of power were in themselves necessarily vicious things for which one must pay some day, and pay bitterly: how ready they themselves are at bottom to *make* one pay: how they crave to be *hangmen*. There is among them an abundance of the vengeful disguised as judges, who constantly bear the word 'justice' in their mouths like poisonous spittle, always with pursed lips, always ready to spit upon all those who are not discontented but go their way in good spirits.[31]

The true spiritual plebs are those who seek a revenge against the spirit, a revenge for their own weakness in spirit. Moreover, and this is what particularly aggravates

Nietzsche, they have, in modern culture, largely succeeded in their campaigns of vengefulness. Paradoxically, the weak have triumphed over the strong, at least at the level of cultural institutions and public opinion. Especially since the movements of democratic egalitarianism came to the fore in the nineteenth century, *ressentiment* has enjoyed a good public conscience. This has had the effect of poisoning the general stock of human beings, of stunting the strong in their growth, of hampering and perhaps altogether crippling those who might otherwise have taken their place among the spiritual aristocracy. Again, Nietzsche's critique of doctrines of equality is not directed at socio-economic power structures, but at the levelling of the spirit which has, as a matter of historical fact, accompanied the development of social egalitarianism. It is the levelling out of values which occupies Nietzsche, the levelling down to values which are uniformly pre-philosophical, which are uniformly constituted in the flight from life (in the Dionysian sense) rather than in its radical affirmation.

If weakness of the spirit is cowardice before the primordial phenomenon of life, it is also and equally cowardice before one's own self. The spiritual pleb flees from life into the herd. This is a place of familiarity, reassurance and security. Precisely because the 'terrors' of the Dionysian phenomenon are incommunicable, precisely because they are only 'knowable' to a radically individualized self, the herd pronounces them unreal. The spiritual pleb does not believe in 'himself', more accurately, he believes only in a 'self' which is conferred upon him by the herd:

> Whatever they may think and say about their 'egoism', the great majority nonetheless do nothing for their ego their whole life long: what they do is done for the phantom of their ego which has formed itself in the heads of those around them and has been communicated to them; as a consequence they all of

them dwell in a fog of impersonal, semi-personal opinions, and arbitrary, as it were poetical evaluations, the one for ever in the head of someone else, and the head of this someone else again in the heads of others: a strange world of phantasms – which at the same time knows how to put on so sober an appearance![32]

Since the spiritual pleb believes only in a herd self, he is fearful of solitude, which for him can be nothing more than a great and painful emptiness, a separation from his own kind. He is at home only in the 'market-place', and is constantly in need of its busyness and garrallousness. This garrallousness often finds expression in reading and writing, as conduits for the constant flow of opinion. A critique of the 'scribbling rabble', as they are called in *Thus Spake Zarathustra*, runs through all Nietzsche's works. These are people who are possessed by language and constantly entangled in language. In the end they come to believe that language is the only reality. Since they are unable to see beyond language and are therefore disconnected from that which is truly worthy of thought, their discourse takes on, especially when they 'philosophize', a tortuous self-referential character.

The postmodernist commentators, by insisting that Nietzsche does not believe in anything but a socially constituted (and therefore perspectival) self, overlook the difference between the herd self and the supra-perspectival philosophical self which, as Nietzsche says, wants to 'become what it is'.[33] The spiritual pleb loses touch with his genuine self and becomes an actor, waiting on the evaluations of others, tossed this way and that way by their good and bad opinions. By contrast, although the spiritual aristocrat will also have his 'masks', although he will be forced to act out comprehensible social roles when he enters the 'marketplace' and interacts with others, he will never confuse himself with his public face.[34] The masks of the spiritual aristocrat do not indicate, as the postmodernists imagine, a new kind of 'undogmatic' subjectivity, but are a means of self-protection from the spiritual plebs, a way of avoiding their irritating misunderstandings. It is indeed remarkable that anyone could believe that Nietzsche's books were written for the 'socially constituted self'.[35] But the de-personalization of Nietzsche's thought which occurs at the hands of the postmodernists is indicative of what always happens with the *politicization* of philosophy: the individual reduces to the thinnest of abstractions, a mere bearer of social determinations. Nietzsche, on the other hand, understands his books as written for the self of the 'subterranean man', for the self which tunnels and burrows beneath perspectival reality.[36] The postmodernists are blind to this latter self, which explains why they are also blind to the very prominent motif of solitude in Nietzsche.

The spiritual pleb is concerned with problems which have reality for the herd. These will reflect the pettiness of herd ambitions, limited as they are to self-preservation, to power, money, and rivalry within the herd.[37] It is not only possible, but is actually the rule, that human beings pass through life with no other problems than these. In this sense the life of the spiritual pleb sinks to the level of the animal, although in another sense it is even lower than the animal, which at least has no higher possibilities to be forfeited. It can seem at times that Nietzsche is himself resentfully obsessed with the spiritual plebs, as if he cannot quite reconcile himself to their existence. They are, in the varying descriptions given to them ('men of the marketplace', the 'last men', the 'rabble'), a recurring object not only of his contempt, but of an almost physiological disgust or nausea. As *Zarathustra* III approaches its climax in the section 'The Convalescent', the necessity of the 'little man' emerges as the final obstacle to Zarathustra's affirmation of eternal recurrence: 'And eternal recurrence even for the smallest! that was my disgust at all existence.'[38] The same problem disturbs Nietzsche in *The Gay Science*, where he looks forward to a time when he will no longer need to 'accuse', when 'looking away shall be my only negation.'[39] This ambition is not fulfilled, for in the works of his last productive year, particularly the *Antichrist*, Nietzsche's vituperation of the spiritual plebs reaches the highest level of intensity: 'It is a painful, a dreadful spectacle which has opened up before me: I have drawn back the curtain on the *depravity* of man.'[40]

In essence, Nietzsche's critique of spiritual plebianism is identical with his critique of the 'herd instinct' in man. It is noticeable how little a role this plays in postmodernist discussions of Nietzsche's 'critique of morality'. Instead, the postmodernists focus on Nietzsche's alleged (but in truth almost non-existent) exposure of the 'repressive' power of custom and acculturation in 'normalizing' the individual: once again, it is society which is at fault, not the individual himself. What is in force here is the liberal assumption that the individual wants autonomy in the first place, and that only through the imposition of authority does normalization take place. Nietzsche takes a more realistic if less politically correct attitude: he posits the herd instinct as a fundamental and in most cases overriding instinct of human beings:

> The reproaches of conscience are weak even in the most conscientious people compared to the feeling: 'This or that is against the morals of *your* society.' A cold look or a sneer on the face of those amongst whom and for whom one has been educated is feared even by the strongest. What is it that they are really afraid of? Growing solitude! This is the argument that rebuts even the best arguments for a person or cause. – Thus the herd instinct speaks up in us.[41]

What the postmodernists overlook is the degree to which individuals normalize themselves, i.e. positively want to be normal, to be accepted and recognized, to belong, to be part of the herd. Of course, Nietzsche is not unaware of those anonymous ideological forces which channel the herd instinct along particular paths, often to the benefit of the ruling stratum of society. Unlike the postmodernists, however, he gives due consideration to the fact that ideological normalization presupposes not only an inherent susceptibility in those who are subjected to it, but an actual need which makes them complicit in the entire process. This is a rather unflattering portrayal of human beings, but for Nietzsche it is not the business of philosophy to flatter:

> We know well enough how offensive it sounds when someone says plainly and without metaphor that man is an animal; but it will be reckoned almost a *crime* in us that precisely in regard to men of 'modern ideas' we constantly employ the terms 'herd', 'herd instinct', and the like. But what of that! we can do no other: for it is precisely here that our new insight lies....Now it is bound to make a harsh sound and one not easy for ears to hear when we insist again and again: that which here believes it knows, that which here glorifies itself with its praising and blaming and calls itself good, is the instinct of the herd animal man: the instinct which has broken through and come to prevail over the other instincts. [42]

It is not surprising that postmodernism, which seeks to establish itself as the intellectual orthodoxy of our time, is rather hard of hearing when it comes to such passages as these. For the conformism which is so characteristic of this movement is loathe to admit a herd instinct at all: instead, what Nietzsche understands under this heading is obscured through self-laudatory phraseology about 'solidarity', 'communication' and 'co-operation'. It is not that Nietzsche accords no value to genuine human fellow-feeling. On the contrary, he values it too highly to confuse it with its semblance. All his life Nietzsche yearned for nothing more than true philosophical companionship. The reason he never found it is that, in the end, what he always encountered in others was the herd self. This is not an experience original and peculiar to Nietzsche. It was the experience of Schopenhauer before him, and, at the very beginning of philosophy, it was the experience of Plato: 'So only a very small remnant survives, Adeimantus, of all those worthy to have dealings with philosophy.'[43]

Is the condition of the spiritual plebs their own responsibility? Is their turning away from life and truth a matter of free choice, or is it something like a physiological necessity? If free choice were involved, there would be some grounds to compare the spiritual plebs with the 'sinners' of Christianity; if there were no choice they could be pitied or despised only in an amoral sense. Nietzsche does not come to an unambiguous conclusion on this matter. Immediately following the above-quoted statement on the 'depravity' of man, he insists that 'in my mouth this word is protected against at any rate one suspicion: that it contains a moral accusation of man. It is – I should like to underline the fact again – free of any *moralic acid*.' This characteristic disclaimer is not altogether convincing. The fact that Nietzsche finds depravity 'precisely where hitherto one most consciously aspired to "virtue", to "divinity"', does not show that some *other* (i.e. non-Christian, as he understands it) kind of morality is excluded.[44] Nietzsche often asserts that the concept of guilt belongs inseparably to the morality of *ressentiment*, but in practice he comes close to simply reversing the application of the concept: the guilty are no longer the strong and powerful, but the weak and powerless. It is difficult to understand the intensity of Nietzsche's invective if the weak and resentful are only 'sick' in a physiologically determined manner. The spiritual pleb has forsaken his existential responsibilities, and this makes him 'guilty' in some sense. These responsibilities are taken up fully only

by the philosopher, i.e. by 'the man of the most comprehensive responsibility who has the conscience for the
collective evolution of mankind.'[45] It seems at times that,
in Nietzsche's view, the vast majority of human beings are
altogether lacking in conscience. But he acknowledges an
inner resistance to this conclusion, remarking that, like all
noble types, he 'unjustly' persists in ascribing a conscience
to everyone.[46] There are problems here which Nietzsche
never satisfactorily resolves. Are there responsibilities
which are imposed on man *qua* man? If there are not, from
where do the responsibilities of the philosopher derive? I
shall come back to these problems in Chapter Three below.

THE SPIRITUAL MIDDLE CLASS

When Nietzsche speaks of the spiritual middle class, it is
invariably 'scholars' (*die Gelehrten*) and 'scientists' (*die
Wissenschaftler*) that he has in mind. He sees the difference
between the spiritual middle class and the spiritual plebs as
of much less importance than the difference between both
these groups and the spiritual aristocracy. The middle class
possess a certain discipline and refinement of spirit which is
absent among the plebs. There is a flicker of reverence
among the middle-class spirits, the conscience insinuates
itself in their case somewhat more forcefully, but they still
do not possess the strength of will for the 'really great
problems and question marks' which occupy the spiritual
aristocrat. Nietzsche often expresses respect for the craftsmanship of the genuine scholar, presupposing as it does a
certain control over the coarser emotions of *ressentiment*. He
approves of the 'probity' (*Probität*) which is presupposed in
every genuine *discipline*, in contrast with the 'half-genuine'
and 'histrionic' essence of spiritual plebianism.[47] By the
same token, Nietzsche experienced his greatest personal
disappointments with members of the spiritual middle
class. As professor of classical philology at Basel, he was
dismayed to discover that his university colleagues were
'only' scholars. *The Birth of Tragedy* already expresses a

distinct contempt for the proprieties of his academic profession, a contempt which was repaid with hostility and ostracism.[48] More generally, Nietzsche suffered recurring disappointments when childhood friends and youthful associates gradually abandoned their former thirst for the 'great problems' and accommodated themselves to the staid and comfortable life-style of the scholar. He felt that these people had the requisite intellectual equipment, but inadequate spiritual strength, to accompany him into more challenging waters. This feeling intensified with the advancing years, as he became progressively more isolated and convinced of his destiny as a solitary.[49] In his later works, a somewhat grudging acknowledgement of scholarly virtues is mixed with a more basic contempt:

> Today there are plenty of modest and worthy laborers among scholars, too, who are happy in their little nooks...the last thing I want is to destroy the pleasure these honest workers take in their craft: for I approve of their work. But that one works rigorously in the sciences and that there are contented workers certainly does *not* prove that science as a whole possesses a goal, a will, an ideal, or the passion of a great faith. The opposite is the case...science today is a *hiding place* for every kind of discontent, disbelief, gnawing worm, *despectio sui*, bad conscience – it is the unrest of the *lack* of ideals, the suffering from the *lack* of any great love, the discontent in the face of involuntary contentment.[50]

Nietzsche sees scholarship as a false solution to the problem posed by the death of God: fundamentally it is resignation and reconciliation to nihilism. The 'great faith' of metaphysics and theology has been given up, but nothing has been put in its place. If the middle-class spirits convince themselves that nothing needs to be put in its place, this is because they are in any case inadequate to the demands of a great faith:

It follows from the laws of the order of rank that scholars, insofar as they belong to the spiritual middle class, can never catch sight of the really great problems and question marks; their courage and their eyes simply do not reach that far – and above all, their needs which led them to become scholars in the first place, their inmost assumptions and desires that things might be such and such, their fears and hopes all come to rest and are satisfied too soon.[51]

The relative order of rank of scholars and philosophers is discussed at length in Part Six ('We Scholars') of *Beyond Good and Evil*. Nietzsche is particularly concerned to criticize the 'self-glorification and presumption of the scholar' who has declared his independence from philosophy, or even worse, equates philosophy with scholarship.[52] Such confusion, he explains, testifies to the spirit of *ressentiment* which is endemic in modern times. The scholars are 'industrious labourers' who are useful to society and feel honoured in this role. They are proud of their expertise and craftsmanship. In many cases they have encountered only charlatan philosophers and form premature judgements about philosophy as a whole. Compared with the tangible benefits, both private and public, of their scholarly occupations, philosophy seems a queer thing, leading nowhere. Since the 'great problems' have no relation to utility values, the scholar does not believe in their reality. The 'impersonal' stance of the scholar, actually a euphemism for his allegiance to herd values, cuts him off from his own self and thus from all philosophy:

Whatever remains to him of his 'own person' seems to him accidental, often capricious, more often disturbing: so completely has he become a passage and reflection of forms and events not his own. He finds it an effort to think about 'himself', and not infrequently he thinks about himself mistakenly: he can easily confuse himself with another, he fails to understand his own needs and is in this respect alone unsubtle and negligent....He no longer knows how to take himself seriously.[53]

Among scholars, the discipline of the herd is expressed through conceptual thought and intersubjective rationality. The *de facto* reduction of philosophy to scholarship is an expression of Socratic intellectualism and its suspicion of 'intuition'. Already at the time of Socrates, Nietzsche considers, it was the instinct of levelling, the resistance of any claim to superior insight, which was at the basis of the new 'theoretical' stance in philosophy. Socrates, he points out in his early lectures on the Greeks, and repeats as late as *Twilight of the Idols*, was a pleb.[54] Dialectics and theoretical knowledge were invented by a pleb in a democratic *polis*, so that everyone could have the truth equally. When truth becomes theoretical, all claims must be proven through intersubjective criteria of validity: truth is levelled out to that which is publically available and within the reach of the natural intelligence of all human beings. The ascendency of scholarship is a triumph of the democratic spirit which will not tolerate anything 'higher' and which wants truth as something calculable and checkable. The faith of the scholar is that truth must be there for everyone, attainable through clear and distinct ideas, or it cannot be there at all.

Nietzsche expects little more from the spiritual middle class than from the spiritual plebs. At best they have an instrumental value for the spiritual aristocrat, who can profit from their labours to widen his knowledge in one area or another. But even here it seems that their value is limited. One does not gain the impression that Nietzsche himself learned much from scholarly sources, apart from information in the narrowest sense. The world of classical antiquity did not open up for him in the works of his scholarly colleagues, but only in the original texts themselves, which he read with a freedom shocking to the philological establishment. Perhaps the discipline of linguistic knowledge was his greatest debt to scholarship. But this knowledge intrudes only very marginally in his writings, and it does not seem that much depends upon it. Nietzsche certainly recognizes that a training in methodical thinking and 'rationality' are indispensable for the philosopher, for these do possess their own domain of validity. Above all, however, what he took away from his experience with scholars, and as a scholar himself, was a demystified outlook. In his later period, he often regretted his 'wasted years' at Basel.[55] But that he came to see his philological studies as 'wasted' is itself of positive significance. Nietzsche attained proficiency in the intellectualism of the spirit, and came away convinced that this was not the same as philosophical truthfulness.[56] This was a lesson he had to learn for himself. He could not have made this judgement from a position of inexperience and ignorance, he could not accept a 'romantic' critique of intellectualism of the type all too common among the spiritual plebs. Nietzsche's sojourn amongst the spiritual middle class was a necessary stage in his development. It acquainted him with that level of spirituality which enjoyed official status within the Western tradition as the pathway to truth. The fact that he had experienced, during his ten years at Basel, the limits of intellectualism from the inside, goes a long way to explaining the confident tone of his later polemics.[57]

THE SPIRITUAL ARISTOCRACY

The problem of the spiritual aristocrat can be seen as the focal issue of Nietzsche's entire thought, in essence identical with the problem of truth. It may seem that, if the spiritual aristocrat is the philosopher, this reduces to the problem of the nature of philosophy, but the latter formulation already obscures what is distinctive in Nietzsche's approach. Although Nietzsche does indeed identify the spiritual aristocrat with the philosopher, he refuses to perform that abstractive operation which diverts attention from the concrete human being who philosophizes in favour of 'philosophy' as a disembodied structure of theory. The latter is the approach of the intellectualist tradition with its depersonalization of thought. By contrast, Nietzsche insists that philosophy exists for the sake of the philosopher, and that the value of philosophy can only be estimated by the human specimens which partake of it. It is this aspect of Nietzsche's thinking which justifies the label 'existential', understanding by this term an emphasis on the *facticity of existence*. For Nietzsche, existence has reality only in the concrete. This means that, in the human realm, the only thing which can have value, the only thing which can be genuinely admired, is the individual person.[58] When modern morality preaches the opposite, when it declares that it is 'society' or 'mankind' or 'philosophy' which should be the supreme objects of veneration, it turns away from realities to embrace abstractions. This is yet another confirmation of the hegemony of the herd: what is individual is passed over for what is common.

Nietzsche is interested first and foremost in the 'personalities' of the great philosophers. In the Foreword to his early *Philosophy in the Tragic Age of the Greeks*, he tells us:

I will relate the history of these philosophers in a simplified manner: I want to highlight only that point from every system which is a slice of *personality* (*Persönlichkeit*) and which belongs to that irrefutable, undiscussable, which history has preserved....The task is to bring to light that which we *must always love and honour* and which no subsequent knowledge can rob us of: the great human being.[59]

Nietzsche goes on in this study to identify Heraclitus as the paradigmatic philosophical type. While giving due consideration to the doctrine of the Ephesian philosopher,

Nietzsche emphasizes that this is inseparable from the man himself. Heraclitus' doctrine of Becoming is an expression of those character traits which Nietzsche will always associate with the spiritual aristocrat: solitude and independence, reticence, strength and courage, the large vision which sees a harmony and 'justice' behind the universal strife of existence. Heraclitus 'has the truth', but not because he 'has' the doctrine of Becoming.[60] Rather, Heraclitus' status as a philosopher, his philosophical truthfulness, depends on what he himself is. There is no other way of understanding truth than by studying the truthful type.

It goes without saying that, for Nietzsche, the spiritual aristocrat is not the philosopher as traditionally conceived. By the same token, it is no accident that the term 'philosopher' is his favoured designation for those who occupy the highest spiritual rank. If we look at the names of those to whom Nietzsche accords the status of aristocrat, we find (among others, and with some variation at different periods of his writing) Heraclitus, Empedocles, Goethe, Heine, Schopenhauer, Wagner, Montaigne, Emerson, Dostoyevsky and Stendhal. Missing from this list are the classical rationalists of the Western tradition such as Aristotle, Aquinas, Descartes, Leibniz, Kant and Hegel. Nietzsche cannot relate to 'abstract' thinkers: he has neither the patience nor the inclination to become immersed in the conceptual edifices of the metaphysicians. He will not consent to the appropriation of the term 'philosopher' for thinkers of just this type. Rather, the spiritual aristocrats listed are for Nietzsche all 'philosophers' in the literal and honoured sense of 'lovers of wisdom'. Nietzsche also uses other expressions to mean the same thing. The most important of these is 'free spirits', a term he first adopts at the time of *Human, All Too Human*. At other times he speaks as if spiritual aristocrats, as creators and lawgivers, can be regarded simply as 'artists'. Nietzsche has no fixed idea of the spiritual aristocrat. He takes for granted that, like truth itself, it is an elusive concept, indeed an elusive 'reality' which will defy all attempts at definition. But if clear-cut conceptual elucidation is ruled out, this does not imply the impossibility of intuitive understanding, based, as always, on concrete cases. On the other hand, in looking at particular cases it is necessary to focus on universal characteristics. As earlier observed, Nietzsche does not believe that anyone is purely of one spiritual rank or another. He acknowledges that he himself bears traces of the lower ranks. Heraclitus seems to be the only figure to whom he consistently gives unqualified approval and this, no doubt, is due to the scantiness of information about him. Among modern philosophers he respects no one more than Schopenhauer, among modern artists no one more than Wagner, but in both cases an early wholehearted reverence gives way in the later works to profound ambivalence. The type of the spiritual aristocrat must be unearthed from beneath the complexities and impurities of the empirical individual.

The universal characteristics of the spiritual aristocrat do not translate out into predelineated forms of life. Zarathustra tells his followers 'I now go away alone, my disciples! You too now go away and be alone! So I will have it.'[61] This does not mean, as the postmodernist commentators would have it, that Nietzsche is preaching a pluralism of lifestyles. The exhortation 'go away and be alone' is not an exhortation to 'difference'. Solitude is the medium in which the universal values of philosophy, above all the value of truth, become visible and meaningful. Although there is indeed a plurality of lifestyles available to the spiritual aristocrat, this plurality is not itself the point. Solitude, in the sense intended by Nietzsche, is not a determinate lifestyle, but a spiritual condition which governs each and every spiritual aristocrat in whatever lifestyle. Precisely because it cannot be identified with empirical aloneness, much less with loneliness, precisely because it is something concealed and masked from the coarse misunderstandings of the spiritual plebs, solitude in the Nietzschean sense is consistent with a variety of 'surface' lifestyles, including 'surface' gregariousness.

The solitude of the spiritual aristocrat is the holding at a distance of his socially constituted pseudo-self (the herd-self) in favour of his own true self. Reverence for truth and reverence for self amount to the same thing:

> What is noble? What does the word 'noble' mean for us today? What, beneath this heavy, overcast sky of the beginning rule of the rabble which makes everything leaden and opaque, betrays and makes evident the noble human being?...It is the *faith* (*Glaube*) which is decisive here, which determines the order of rank here, to employ an old religious formula in a new and deeper sense: some fundamental certainty which a noble soul possesses in regard to itself, something which may not be sought or found and perhaps may not be lost either. – *The noble soul has reverence for itself.*[62]

The aristocrat of the spirit knows the value of the self as the unique locus of truth: this is his 'faith'.[63] It is a faith which deplores nothing more than the squandering and forfeiting of the self which occurs among the lower orders of the spirit, all for the sake of spurious benefits held out by the herd. Moreover, it is a faith which (to extend the 'old religious formula') demands steadfastness in the face of the resentful howls of the rabble. The latter senses how flimsy a thing the herd self at bottom is, and takes it as an unpardonable conceit that anyone should take his own self so very seriously. In reality, the self-reverence of the spiritual aristocrat has nothing whatever to do with arrogance or conceit as these are commonly understood. Because it is unconcerned with petty gratifications, it would even seem surprisingly 'impersonal' to the spiritual pleb who could catch a glimpse of it.

This aristocratic reverence of self may even seem like a kind of asceticism, so different is it from common self-preoccupation and vanity. Despite the fact that, under the rubric 'world renunciation', Nietzsche sees asceticism as his main enemy, he is forced to concede that, in another sense, it is the natural ideal of all genuine philosophers:

> What, then, is the meaning of the ascetic ideal in the case of a philosopher? My answer is – you will have guessed it long ago: the philosopher sees in it an optimum condition for the highest and boldest spirituality and smiles – he does *not* deny 'existence', he rather affirms *his* existence and only his existence....They think of *themselves* – what is the saint to them! They think of what *they* can least do without: freedom from compulsion, disturbance, noise, from tasks, duties, worries; clear heads; the dance, leap and flight of ideas; good air, thin, clear, open, dry, like the air of the heights through which all animal being becomes more spiritual and acquires wings.[64]

It is this detachment which decisively separates the Nietzschean spiritual aristocrat from the 'great man of action', a type with whom he is often confused. Although Nietzsche frequently uses the vocabulary of politics to illustrate what he means by the 'mastery' of the aristocrat, at bottom he is always thinking of spiritual self-mastery. This type of person will be unimpressed by those 'great events' which attract so much attention in the public realm: wars and revolutions, the rise and fall of generals and statesmen, the mass movements of the people. While these can obviously be matters of life and death, the aristocrat of the spirit treats them as of secondary importance. In this respect he resembles the 'holy man', the ascetic type who has 'turned away from the world'. But as Zarathustra says, 'many a one who turned away from life, turned away only from the rabble: he did not wish to share the well and the flame and the fruit with the rabble.'[65] The Nietzschean aristocrat turns away from 'world' and 'life' as these are commonly understood, his 'will to power' is directed towards realities of which the spiritual pleb has no experience: 'the "higher nature" of the great man lies in being different, in incommunicability, in distance of rank, not in an effect of any kind – even if he made the whole globe tremble.'[66]

The reverence of self which Nietzsche ascribes to the spiritual aristocrat does not imply that this self is already a secure possession. On the contrary, as Nietzsche indicates with the dictum 'become who you are' (the supreme command of conscience), the true self always remains something to be attained. This is no easy task, for the herd self constantly attempts to take charge of the individual. From the point of view of the herd, the true self is a fiction, perhaps a romantic delusion or piece of sentimentality. To progressively break free of the herd self (this can only happen gradually, it is the 'path' of the philosopher, his philosophical 'ascent') is a dangerous and questionable undertaking, because it becomes more and more difficult to live with the herd in the world. The true self is an enigma.[67] Because it does not testify to itself with the obviousness of the herd self, the spiritual aristocrat can be plagued by self-doubt and anxiety. This is what Nietzsche means by the philosopher 'living dangerously': philosophical existence is a dangerous 'psychological' experiment.[68] It may even turn out that the path of philosophy is a path to destruction.[69] If this is so, the philosopher can be seen as one who sacrifices himself to truth, and to life in the Dionysian sense. This idea appeals to Nietzsche more and more in his later period, as his illness intensifies and his final mental collapse draws near: the philosopher must sacrifice his own health (both physical and mental) to the demands of his task, but by way of compensation rises to the 'great health' of Dionysian affirmation.

Although the Nietzschean spiritual aristocrat bears some resemblances to the Greek sage and the Christian holy man, his existence in a 'sea of uncertainty' is a difference which Nietzsche insists upon again and again. This uncertainty relates to the peculiar object of reverence of the aristocratic type, i.e. the transient realm of Becoming. But it sometimes seems that Nietzsche merely replaces one kind of certainty by another, that he rejects metaphysical certainty only to embrace a kind of intuitive certainty. While the latter supposedly has nothing of the consoling and comforting qualities of metaphysical certainty, while it cannot perform the function of a prop for those of weak spirit, it still governs the 'faith' of the philosophical type, it still commands the intellectual conscience. In a sense, it is a 'certainty of uncertainty'. Similarly, the 'incomprehensibility' of Becoming sometimes appears transfigured in a peculiar 'comprehensibility of the incomprehensible'. Nietzsche resists any attempt to resolve these kinds of paradoxes:

> But you do not understand this? Indeed, people will have trouble understanding us. We are looking for words; perhaps we are also looking for ears. Who are we anyway? If we simply called ourselves, using an old expression, godless, or unbelievers, or perhaps immoralists, we do not believe that this would even come close to designating us: We are all three in such an advanced stage that one – that *you*, my curious friends – could never comprehend how we feel at this point.[70]

Nietzsche suffers as much as he revels in this situation of philosophical-existential isolation: it is both a torment for him and a kind of liberating joy. Many critics of Nietzsche would say that he illegitimately elevates his own subjective condition to the status of a philosophical thesis, attempting thereby to justify his emotional immaturity. This criticism cannot be refuted, but it begs the question. Nietzsche's view of the emotions of the spiritual aristocrat depends on his understanding of primordial reality: the question is whether reality is such that the emotional stance of those whom Nietzsche admits to the spiritual upper class is fitting and proper. For Nietzsche, Socratic intellectualism is responsible for the prejudice that the sober emotional state of the theoretician, conceived in fact as the exclusion of all emotions other than scientific objectivity, is the natural and obvious state of all those who seek truth. Overcoming this prejudice is part of Nietzsche's redefinition of truth: he needs to redefine the 'stance' of the truthful man.

THE GREEK SPIRIT

In Nietzsche's view, the Greeks of the tragic age represent one of history's rare 'lucky hits', one of those 'chance occurrences of great success' at a collective level.[71] It is an age which ends with the figure of Socrates; thereafter, genuine Hellenism gives way to non-Greek or even anti-Greek forces, to intimations of Christianity of which Plato is the classic exemplar. Nietzsche credits himself with rediscovering the tragic culture of Presocratic Greece, more particularly the Dionysianism at the heart of Greek tragic wisdom. He begins his career, in *The Birth of Tragedy*, with a study of this phenomenon, and after ten years during which it is no longer mentioned by name, he returns to it with heightened enthusiasm in his final works:

> I was the first to take seriously that wonderful phenomenon which bears the name Dionysus as a means to understanding the older Hellenic instinct, an instinct still exuberant and even overflowing: it is explicable only as an *excess* of energy....For it is only in the Dionysian mysteries, in the psychology of the Dionysian condition, that the *fundamental fact* of the Hellenic instinct expresses itself – its 'will to life'. *What* did the Hellene guarantee to himself with these mysteries? *Eternal* life, the eternal recurrence of life; the future promised and consecrated in the past; the triumphant Yes to life beyond death and change.[72]

With Socratism, a weakening of the instincts sets in. The Greeks are already beginning to distrust life and are therefore searching for its justification in a higher world. This tendency is reinforced by Plato and comes to a head with Christianity. Nietzsche gives no credence to the distinction between Platonic philosophy and Christian religion: in his view they are one unitary phenomenon. Neither Plato nor Christianity are properly Greek, but are both of Eastern origin.[73] Together with Buddhism, they are reflections of the underlying weakness of Eastern culture, with its desperation to flee from life into a world of tranquility and repose. They are expressions of that *ressentiment* stance towards reality which in succeeding centuries gained the upper hand in Western culture.

The tragic wisdom of the Presocratic Greeks is for the most part inaccessible to modern men. Only in the case of such physiological 'lucky hits' as he himself, where the forces of *ressentiment* have been kept at bay through a resilient health, is there any possibility of comprehension. The 'cheerfulness' (*Heiterkeit*) of the Greek tragic age, with which Nietzsche is much concerned in his early works, was already transformed in later Hellenistic times into 'that pink hue of cheerfulness' which is at bottom a 'womanish flight from seriousness and terror' and a 'craven satisfaction with easy enjoyment'.[74] The latter is the cheerfulness characteristic of modern men such as David Strauß, a kind of simple-minded optimism and jollity which is unacquainted with the terrible visions of Dionysianism.[75] Authentically tragic cheerfulness, on the other hand, comes with consciousness of victory, consciousness of the strength which has overcome all trepidation and hestitation in the face of life. Tragic cheerfulness is not a mere emotion, but a truthful stance towards reality: it accepts the nature of reality for what it is, and it accepts man's place within reality. It is a stance of gratitude:

> What astonishes one about the religiosity of the ancient Greeks is the tremendous amount of gratitude

(*Dankbarkeit*) that emanates from it – the kind of man who stands thus before nature and before life is a very noble one! Later, when the rabble came to predominate in Greece, fear also overran religion; and Christianity was preparing itself.[76]

Where a great gift is received, the noble temperament distinguishes itself not by judgement, not by putting it on the scales and finding it, perhaps, too light, but by unreserved gratitude. To be able to do this one must be free of the *ressentiment* mentality of those who in their fear and weakness always want something different. Lack of gratitude for life is the closest thing to 'sin' which Nietzsche acknowledges. The inability to be grateful for the world as it is, more precisely, for the 'fact' of the world as such, is what he sees as the essence of spiritual plebianism.

Along with gratitude goes reverence. When tragic wisdom becomes displaced by Socratism, reverence gives way to an importunate insistence on drawing back the veils. Whereas Dionysian truth had been accessible only through initiation and secret rituals, the democratic instinct of intellectualism demanded that truth be public and accessible to all. In *The Birth of Tragedy* Nietzsche accuses the Socratic dramatist Euripides of sacrilege for bringing the spectator onto the stage to pass judgement on the drama.[77] The dramas of Euripides already indicate a weakening of the instincts, a self-doubt and uncertainty about life, a need for the prop of intellectual confirmation. In the end, Dionysus is 'scared from the tragic stage by a demonic power speaking through Euripides.'[78] The demonic figure of Socrates is the embodiment of irreverence. Insisting on conscious reason, he attacks the instincts, the seat of all reverence.[79] Socrates asks for reasons why life should be affirmed, and finds these lacking: he thus confuses an object of reverence with an object of rational inquiry. In *Twilight of the Idols*, Nietzsche puts the matter as follows:

In every age the wisest have passed the identical judgement on life: *it is worthless*....Everywhere and always their mouths have uttered the same sound – a sound full of doubt, full of melancholy, full of weariness with life, full of opposition to life. Even Socrates said as he died: 'To live – that means to be a long time sick: I owe a cock to the saviour Asclepius'. Even Socrates had had enough of it.[80]

The deficiencies of life which so burden Socrates were not unknown to the tragic Greeks. But they took an altogether different attitude to them. As Nietzsche explains in *The Birth of Tragedy*:

We are to recognize that all that comes into being must be ready for a sorrowful end; we are forced to look into the terrors of individual existence – yet we are not to become rigid with fear: a metaphysical comfort tears us momentarily from the bustle of the changing figures. We are really for a brief moment primordial Being itself (*das Urwesen selbst*), feeling its raging desire for existence and joy in existence; the struggle, the pain, the destruction of phenomena, now appear necessary to us.[81]

A similar description is given in *Twilight of the Idols*:

Affirmation of life even in its strangest and sternest problems, the will to life rejoicing in its own inexhaustibility through the *sacrifice* of its highest types – *that* is what I called Dionysian, *that* is what I recognized as the bridge to the psychology of the *tragic* poet. *Not* so as to get rid of pity and terror, not so as to purify oneself of a dangerous emotion through its vehement discharge – it was thus Aristotle understood it – : but, beyond pity and terror, *to realize in oneself* the eternal joy of becoming.[82]

Apart from the demonic influence of Socrates, Nietzsche does not explain why the tragic age of Greece gives way to the incipient Christianity of later Hellenism. Perhaps he does not think that any special explanation is required. If the tragic age is just a 'lucky hit' in the history of humanity, the victory of Socratism might be simply a return to spiritual normality (i.e. mediocrity) on an historical scale. In general, Nietzsche gives little attention to the mechanisms of cultural change. He tends to see the development of Western civilization as the progressive domestication of the spirit. The instinct to civilization is the instinct of weakness, for its main objective is self-preservation on a higher and higher level. Culture is built on the spiritual needs of the middle and lower orders, and if, for a brief period, the tragic age of Greece was an exception to this law, Nietzsche does not expect to see its like again. Even in *The Birth of Tragedy*, where he seems most optimistic about a cultural rebirth, he does not envisage this as a reform of socio-cultural institutions. What he hopes for is that the Dionysian type will once again become possible, but he recognizes that this can occur only within the interstices of contemporary culture. Unlike David Strauß, Nietzsche never takes on the mantle of a cultural or social reformer: in his view, what needs reforming will always be, first and foremost, the individual himself.

Walter Kaufmann has rightly emphasized that Nietzsche's relation to Socrates is by no means unequivocally hostile.[83] It is true, as Kaufmann maintains, that Socrates' disdain for public opinion, his independence and uncompromising philosophical resolve, could not fail to appeal to someone like Nietzsche. On the other hand, Kaufmann understates Nietzsche's critical attitude to Socrates. In *The Birth of Tragedy*, Socrates stands for the cardinal sin of intellectual optimism, the prototype of the theoretical man who holds 'the unshakeable faith that thought, using the thread of causality, can penetrate the deepest abysses of Being.'[84] On these grounds, Socrates represents the counter-force to tragic wisdom, and, by implication, also to Heraclitean intuition. Nietzsche does acknowledge that the honesty of Socrates ensures that intellectualism itself will at some stage break down, i.e. when logic finds itself at its impassable limit and finally 'gazes into what defies illumination (*in das Unaufhellbare starrt*).'[85] To the extent that Nietzsche does not embrace a mysticism untutored in the ways of reason, but wants, like Schopenhauer, to understand the limits of reason, the project of Socratism possesses some partial legitimacy for him. But he views it in predominantly negative terms, as displacing philosophical intuition into the channels of abstract thought.

Nietzsche has a similar attitude to Plato. While the complexity of Plato's philosophy is attested by the great diversity of interpretations both within the Platonic tradition itself (including Neoplatonism) and among its opponents, Nietzsche is not interested in such subtleties so much as in the fundamental tendency of historical Platonism, which he uses as a foil for developing his own ideas. Starting with the opposition between intellect and intuition, Nietzsche reads all the Greek philosophers within this interpretative schema.[86] The result is a historically flawed and overly undifferentiated account: a model of intellectualism largely based on modern scientific thought is read back into Plato and Parmenides. Having stigmatized a particular thinker as abstract, other aspects of his thought, possibly more in line with Nietzsche's own outlook, are glossed over or totally ignored. This is especially true in the case of Plato.[87] Nietzsche is over hasty in taking the Platonic doctrine of Ideas as a retreat from the richness of life, and in denying to Plato any vestige of mystical sensitivity. As already observed, there are aspects of Nietzsche's thought which have affinities with Platonism. This is also so in respect of Neoplatonism. Schopenhauer was an open admirer of Neoplatonism, and the Schopenhauerian motifs which are most prominent in the

early Nietzsche, especially the 'Primal One' and the Dionysian overcoming of the *principium individuationis*, are highly
suggestive of Neoplatonism. Nietzsche is no more enam-
oured with the common world of everyday life than are
Platonists of every description. He too wants to attain a
'higher world', and he will constantly struggle with the
problem of distinguishing this from the 'ideal world' of
Platonism. Just as much as Plato does Nietzsche affirm a
radical discontinuity between philosophy (as he understands it) and everything which is not philosophy, just as
much as the latter-day idealist-Platonist Hegel does he
consider philosophy an 'inverted world' where values are
turned upside down.[88] In his own mind, however, this is all
'Dionysianism' and not 'Platonism'.

THE SPIRIT OF CHRISTIANITY

Nietzsche's summary verdict on Christianity is that it is a
'capital crime against life'.[89] Previously, Nietzsche considers, Christianity had been arraigned on minor and
incidental charges, relating to its concept of God, the
historical accuracy of its assumptions, and its mythological
cosmology. Passing a severe judgement on all these counts,
modernity has not only overlooked the major offence, but
has sought to sanction it, even to sanctify it: Christian
morality has been left untouched, the 'world-denying'
morality of weakness, sickness and self-abasement. Christianity has waged 'a war *to the death* against the *higher* type of
man', it has taught man to be ashamed of himself, it has
taught an attitude of resentment rather than of gratitude
towards life. Nietzsche's critique is 'psychological': he
judges Christianity by the human types which it produces
and venerates. His first reaction to any given religious
doctrine is to ask 'Who espouses this?' or 'What kind of
character can say this?' Behind the doctrines, he looks for
the basic attitudes to life and manifestations of life which
are then judged for their worth.

The psychological type of the Christian is embodied
above all by Paul of Tarsus. It is in connection with Paul

that Nietzsche first develops, in *Daybreak* (1881), the idea of a resentful attitude to life. Paul was a 'very tormented, very pitiable, very unpleasant man who also found himself unpleasant.'[90] Paul was a fanatic, consumed by the desire to distinguish himself through the highest honours of the Jewish religion, and, possessed of the self-righteousness common to all fanatics, he had a lust to condemn and to punish. But Paul also became aware of his own inability to obey the Jewish law which he championed, indeed of the essential unfulfillability of the law. Overcome with tormented pride, he sought a way out from this impasse and characteristically found it in an act of revenge. Christianity was this act. The death of Jesus on the cross made the law unnecessary. 'At one stroke', Nietzsche writes, 'he feels himself recovered, the moral despair is as if blown away, destroyed – that is to say fulfilled, there on the cross.'[91] On Nietzsche's account, Pauline Christianity is an intensification (a kind of 'squaring') of original Jewish *ressentiment*: although Judaism was already a religion of weakness, Paul found himself too weak even for this, and Christianity was his solution. Paul distilled the *ressentiment* out of Judaism and poured it into his new creation. Nietzsche fills out this picture in *The Antichrist* of 1888, where Paul is presented as a 'genius of hatred' and 'the greatest of all apostles of revenge'.[92] At all costs Paul sought to poison the sources of human joy: hence guilt, sin, the last judgement and hell became key items in his message. It is not Paul's 'beliefs' which Nietzsche primarily finds objectionable: these are an expression of the character type itself. Paul was cowardly, timid, petty, mistrustful, self-abasing, untruthful, envious etc., and therefore believed in his theology. At the same time, Paul was a 'genius' in that through him *ressentiment* became creative: he was able to mobilize the weak into a movement of world-historic proportions. Through him the weak were able to conquer.

It is only in his final period, mainly in *The Antichrist* and *The Will to Power*, that Nietzsche has much to say about

Jesus himself.[93] He treats Paul and Jesus as antithetical personalities, absolving the latter of any responsibility for the historical phenomenon of Christianity. Jesus was a 'free spirit', completely innocent of *ressentiment*.[94] He preached a this-wordly rather than an other-worldly philosophy.[95] Although the character-type of Jesus can still be unearthed by a close reading of the Gospels, it has been distorted beyond all recognition by Pauline theology and the Church. The figure of Jesus poses certain difficulties for Nietzsche's psychology. He is not a *ressentiment* type, but nor does he seem to be an affirmative type like Zarathustra. At one point Nietzsche calls him the 'most interesting decadent', at another point he finds the term 'idiot' appropriate, used in its Dostoyevskyan meaning.[96] It is not clear on what grounds Nietzsche is entitled to feel admiration for the Jesus-type. But the fact that Nietzche does find Jesus so attractive highlights certain aspects of Zarathustra's personality.[97] The more Dionysian images of Zarathustra – as dancer, reveller, buffoon – suggest a contrast with Jesus. However, Zarathustra also values silence, unobtrusiveness, stillness, detachment, all of which suggest similarities. We shall come back to this problem – Nietzsche calls it the problem of 'the psychological type of the redeemer' – in the next chapter. For the moment it suffices to note that Jesus is completely outside the 'spirit of Christianity' as Nietzsche understands it.

As with his treatment of Greek philosophy, what Nietzsche says about Christianity, especially in polemical contexts, is over-simplified and historically unacceptable. He again draws out one tendency and portrays it as the essence. On the other hand, his works are full of remarks which indicate anything but an unqualified rejection of everything Christian. There is a distinction to be made between the *ressentiment* type of Christian and the *homines religiosi* who may call himself a Christian:

The fight against the church is certainly among other things – for it means many things – also the fight of the more common, merrier, more familiar, ingenuous, and superficial type against the dominion of the graver, deeper, more meditative, that it, more evil and suspicious human beings who brood with an enduring suspicion about the value of existence and also about their own value.[98]

Nietzsche is at pains to distance himself from the critique of religiosity to be found among 'men of modern ideas':

Every age has its own divine kind of naivety for the invention of which other ages may envy it – and how much naivety, venerable, childlike and boundlessly stupid naivety there is in the scholar's belief in his superiority, in the good conscience of his tolerance, in the simple unsuspecting certainty with which his instinct treats the religious man as an inferior and lower type which he himself has grown beyond and *above* – he, the little presumptuous dwarf and pleb, the brisk and busy head – and handyman of 'ideas', of 'modern ideas'![99]

Nietzsche's religious temperament has recommended him to many thinkers sympathetic to Christianity.[100] Paul Tillich, for example, comments that an 'awareness of eternity' distinguishes Nietzsche from the common atheism which is sometimes attributed to him.[101] An overt polemical attitude often conceals what Nietzsche actually assimilates from the Christian tradition. There are strong strains of Protestantism in him, most notably his emphasis on conscience and individual responsibility, together with his repudiation of all institutions (whether university or church) and office-holders (whether professors or priests) of the spirit. Nietzsche acknowledges that Christianity can mean different things to different ranks of the spirit. For the plebian type it is the perfect prop for an exhausted life force, an enchanting and intoxicating outlet for *ressentiment*. But it has also been, for the best part of two millennia, the only vehicle, the only spiritual medium, for the genuine *homines religiosi*. While the latter kind of person is distinguished by a resolute questioning of the value of life, the spirit of Christianity, in the narrow *ressentiment* sense, is to be criticized for the answer it gives: that this life has no value whatever, or even a negative value, and that all value pertains to the 'next world'.

THE SPIRIT OF MODERNITY

One of the unresolved problems of Nietzsche's philosophy is the relation between his critique of Christianity on the one hand, and his critique of modernity on the other. At first sight it is paradoxical that Nietzsche, with his reputation as the nineteenth century's most virulent critic of Christianity, should also be so scornful of modernity, i.e. of the period when religious belief in general, and Christianity in particular, is on the wane. If the Christian God has so long been the symbol of *ressentiment* ideals, should not the 'death of God' bring in its train a liberation of the spirit? Certainly this was the way it had seemed to many of Nietzsche's anti-clerical predecessors, to such 'enlightened' and 'scientific' critics as David Strauß, Ludwig Feuerbach and Karl Marx. But far from sharing their optimism, far from seeing modernity as an epoch of spiritual emancipation, Nietzsche speaks uniformly of decline. A typical passage is the following:

> And so as to leave no room for doubt as to *what* I despise, *whom* I despise: it is the man of today, the man with whom I am fatefully contemporary. The man of today – I suffocate of his impure breath. With regard to the past I am, like all men of knowledge, of a large tolerance, that is to say of a *magnanimous* self-control: I traverse the madhouse-world of entire millennia, be

it called 'Christianity', 'Christian faith', 'Christian church', with a gloomy circumspection – I take care not to make mankind responsible for its insanities. But my feelings suddenly alter, burst forth, immediately I enter the modern age, *our* age. [102]

What is it precisely about modern man which is so deserving of contempt? Nietzsche answers a little later in the same aphorism:

All the concepts of the church are recognized for what they are: the most malicious false coinage there is for the purpose of *disvaluing* nature and natural values; the priest himself is recognized for what he is....Everyone knows this: and *everyone nonetheless remains unchanged*. Where have the last feelings of decency and self-respect gone when even our statesmen, in other ways a very unprejudiced kind of man and practical anti-Christians through and through, still call themselves Christians and go to communion?

One might wonder how deep this critique goes if the emphasis is just on the prevalence of hypocrisy and humbug. Does Nietzsche really think that this kind of thing did not happen in other historical periods? More relevant is that Nietzsche, especially in his later writings, portrays the values of modernity as secularized Christian values. Whether or not statesmen go to church, they still believe in such values as 'equal rights', i.e. in values which, for Nietzsche, are impermissible outside of Christianity. David Strauß does not attend communion, but, in Nietzsche's view, his 'new faith' in modern morality and rationality still depends on the 'old faith' of Christianity. Nietzsche assimilates Christianity and modernity as a single spiritual phenomenon: he sees modernity as without its own principles of legitimation, as a weak duplicitous continuation of Christianity, as Christianity in decline,

Christianity which no longer believes in itself but clings to the old values for want of an alternative, Christianity which cannot bring itself to confront its own lack of foundations.

However, there is another dimension to Nietzsche's critique of modernity which is rather different in emphasis. This is the critique of nihilism. To be sure, Nietzsche sees the phenomenon of nihilism – the devaluation of all values – as an outgrowth of Christianity, as in a certain sense the product of the latter's own logic.[103] But the question must be put as to whether, in the broader context of Nietzsche's thought, nihilism has characteristics which are independent of Christianity. Nietzsche depicts nihilistic man as complacent, mediocre, without any 'great faith', without ideals, possessed by petty ambition and envy, believing in his own 'happiness': in a word, as a man of *ressentiment*. If such a man chooses to beautify himself with Christian phraseology, does this make him into a secret Christian? On the other hand, if he dispenses with such phraseology, is he still in essence Christian just by virtue of his *ressentiment*? Neither suggestion seems particularly plausible. It must be remembered that, for Nietzsche, Christianity is not the cause of *ressentiment*, but merely the vehicle for its 'creative' deployment. If, for various reasons, this vehicle becomes no longer available, the man of *ressentiment* remains what he is. If he seeks expression for his *ressentiment* through quasi-Christian ideals which (by hypothesis) he knows to be without foundation, this does not make him into a covert Christian but into a false hypocritical Christian. His lack of Christian faith is, on this way of looking at the matter, a mark against him rather than for him.

The concept of nihilism as employed by Nietzsche is notoriously difficult. Sometimes he distinguishes between 'passive' and 'active' nihilism, where the former is a resigned and demoralized submission to the devaluation of values, the latter a courageous affirmation of the 'abyss' and the creation of new values.[104] It seems that active nihilism is the prerogative of a few free-spirits like Nietzsche himself, the majority of modern men being caught up in passive nihilism. Aware that the ideals of the tradition are no longer worthy of belief, the passive nihilists lower their horizons to whatever seems practically attainable. If it is no longer permissible to believe in truth or God, they can, for example, still believe in values like 'family life' or 'the nation'; they can believe (as do the 'last men' in Zarathustra's Prologue) in 'happiness'. Such people have long ago adjusted to the death of God, they have long become hardened in their bemused and contemptuous enlightenment concerning all 'higher' demands. In this sense, the culture of passive nihilism is one of mediocrity:

> What will the moral philosophers who come up in this age now have to preach? They discover, these acute observers and idlers, that the end is fast approaching, that everything around them is corrupt and corrupt-ing, that nothing can last beyond the day after tomorrow, *one* species of man excepted, the incurably *mediocre*. The mediocre alone have the prospect of continuing on and propagating themselves – they are the men of the future, the sole survivors; 'be like them! become mediocre!' is henceforth the only morality that has any meaning left, that still finds ears to hear it.[105]

Is Nietzsche here depicting the surreptitious continuation of Christian values, or simply the collapse of Christian values? Any plausibility attaching to the first alternative depends on Nietzsche's thesis of *ressentiment* as the founda-tion of Christianity. But as we have seen, Nietzsche in certain respects also harbours a grudging admiration for Christianity, an admiration which can burst forth into open praise when comparing Christian with modern culture. Is it the case that, in modern times, *ressentiment* comes into full bloom only because of so many centuries of Christian preparation? Or is it rather that other factors are responsible for the mediocrity and levelling which Nietzsche finds so painful to behold? Granted that Nietzsche himself insists on Christian morality as the ultimate villain, may it be that this obfuscates his practical critique of modernity?

These questions are of particular importance given the tendency of much contemporary commentary to domesticate Nietzsche's critique of modernity. This occurs when Christianity and modernity are assimilated with one another and subjected to a unitary critique under the rubric of 'the death of God'. Modernity is then understood in terms of secularized Christian ideals like reason and progress, and is distinguished from postmodernity as the proper age of nihilism. The themes of mediocrity and levelling fall out of sight altogether, or are hastily subsumed under Christian morality, while the major focus of Nietzsche's critique becomes the destruction of authoritarian residues of Christianity, with an affirmation (explicit or implicit) of a 'godless' postmodernity. In reality, however, Nietzsche is much more scathing of the nihilistic-relativistic side of modernity than he is of its residual Christian elements, including the dogmatism so abhored by the postmodernists. [106] Above all he is scornful of the vacuousness of modern ideals, oriented as they are to nothing more than the 'universal green pasture happiness of the herd, with security, safety, comfort, and an easier life for all.' [107] Nietzsche sees the decadence of modernity in the circumstance that it knows no great tasks. The typical modern man is a philistine because he lacks all sense of the tragic implications of the death of God. This means that he lacks an original orientation to truth: he does not need truth, does not experience the destruction of Christian truth as a loss, and therefore does not feel the necessity of a 'revaluation' of values. No distinction can be found in Nietzsche between pre-nihilistic modernity and nihilistic postmodernity: from the Strauß essay through to *The*

Antichrist, he sees modernity as nihilistic from the very beginning. Nihilism is a slowly intensifying process: the implications of the death of God become visible only gradually over an extended period of time, as does the untenability of the various substitute faiths. Although it is only in late modernity that nihilism comes to the surface as a mass psychological phenomenon, this is an outcome which is already guaranteed by the original loss of faith going back to the Enlightenment and earlier.

Nietzsche's critique of modernity is seen one-sidely by many contemporary commentators because they assume that 'perspectivism' is his fundamental philosophical position. With this assumption in place, the critique of nihilism gets subordinated to the critique of dogmatism, something which seems perfectly justified in the light of Nietzsche's thesis of modernity as secularized Christianity. Passive nihilism, in its resignation and despair, is understood as still beholden to the now discredited Christian dogmatic ideals, while active 'postmodern' nihilism, enlightened as it is about the perspectival character of truth, becomes the way of the *Übermensch*. Once Nietzsche is released from the straightjacket of perspectivism, his critique of modernity appears in a very different light. To begin with, his hostility to democratic egalitarianism no longer has to be dismissed as 'subjective' and inconsistent with his 'epistemology', but can be seen as integral to his critique of the 'smallness' of modern values. Likewise, his ambivalence with respect to Christianity no longer must be explained away as 'nostalgia', but can be recognized for what it is, i.e. as reflecting Nietzsche's respect for a 'great faith'. Here, as elsewhere in Nietzsche's thought, it is necessary to resist any hasty smoothing out of apparent contradictions. Nietzsche sees the true test of philosophical resolve in one's willingness and ability to hold oneself out within these. Modernity is for him above all a time of trial. While there is no going back to the Christian-metaphysical tradition and the consolations of its dogmatic truths, a different kind of philosophical truthfulness must be embraced if man is not to capitulate before the emptiness of 'modern ideas'.

Once one recognizes that the main focus of Nietzsche's critique of modernity is its 'mediocrity' and 'weakness', his historical-analytical thesis of modernity's roots in Christianity can be called into question. There is no denying that residues of Christianity persist into modern times, sometimes as secularized versions of Christian values. But Nietzsche gives insufficient recognition to the autonomy of modernity. For example, the importance of the socioeconomic forces of capitalism, particularly in respect of the phenomena of 'levelling' (the world as 'market-place') are almost entirely overlooked. The historical conflicts between Christian and modern values (Galileo, Darwin et al.) are also left unaccounted for. Influential as Nietzsche's descriptive-psychological depiction of nihilism has been, his thesis of modernity as exhausted Christianity has not proved useful for understanding the dynamics of modern culture. Nietzsche is over-axious to establish the responsibility of Christianity for everything he detests about modernity, but the inadequacy of his explanatory hypothesis should not lead us away from the phenomena themselves. Nietzsche wants to bring the spirit of modernity into view as the 'spirit of mediocrity'. He wants to show modernity up as an age without 'greatness':

> And if it is true to say of the lazy that they kill time, then it is greatly to be feared that an era which sees its salvation in public opinion, that is to say private laziness, is a time that really will be killed: I mean it will be struck out of the true history of the liberation of life. How reluctant later generations will be to have anything to do with the relics of an era ruled, not by living men, but by pseudo-men dominated by public opinion; for which reason our age may be to some distant posterity the darkest and least known, because least human, portion of human history.[108]

No doubt 'private laziness' can be found in every historical age, no doubt mediocrity is not unique to modernity. However, what is different about the modern period is that mediocrity now parades itself with the best of consciences, that a contemptuous dismissal of the 'great problems' is socially sanctioned through the complacent maxim 'there is no truth'. Modernity makes a virtue out of its own retreat from the demands of philosophy: this, and not its inheritance of Christian values, is what Nietzsche understands as its essential *ressentiment*. [109]

3
Redemption and Life Affirmation

But some day, in a stronger age than this decaying, self-doubting present, he must yet come to us, the *redeeming* man of great love and contempt, the creative spirit whose compelling strength will not let him rest in any aloofness or any beyond, whose isolation is misunderstood by the people as if it were flight *from* reality – while it is only his absorption, immersion, penetration into reality, so that when one day he emerges again into the light, he may bring home the *redemption* of this reality: its redemption from the curse that the hitherto reigning ideal has laid upon it.[1]

The very fact that Dionysus is a philosopher, and that gods too therefore philosophize, seems a by no means harmless novelty and one calculated to excite suspicion precisely among philosophers – among you, my friends, it will meet with a friendlier reception, unless it comes too late and not at the right time: for, as I have discovered, you no longer like to believe in God and gods now. Perhaps I shall have to go further in the frankness of my story than may always be agreeable to the strict habits of your ears?[2]

REDEMPTION AND THE ABSOLUTE
In the famous parable from *The Gay Science*, Nietzsche depicts a 'madman' announcing the death of God to a crowd of bemused bystanders.[3] The 'men of the market-place' do not regard the madman's message as a piece of astonishing news. They have heard it before, they acknowledge it, they have adjusted to it long ago. What perplexes them, and what leads them to consider the stranger as indeed a madman, is the urgency with which the message is delivered. To these bystanders, the death of God

is no reason to be shaken to the bottom of one's being, there is no need for such terrible forebodings. When the madman forces his way into local churches and pronounces these 'tombs and sepulchers of God' they become indignant. Neither does the death of God justify interference with religious observances.

The experience of the madman is the constantly repeated experience of Nietzsche's own life.[4] As his close confidante Lou Salomé notes, the problems created by the loss of his childhood faith remain the basic impetus for Nietzsche's philosophical activity.[5] Christianity had provided European man with an Absolute, with a centre for valuation and a justification for human existence. Could all this really be given up with the equanimity of modern man? Such apparent composure would be explicable if a new Absolute had been substituted for the old one. But this had not occurred. Not only was a new Absolute lacking, but modernity, to all appearances, seemed perfectly reconciled to this situation. Henceforth, so the unanimous opinion seemed to be, mankind would have to live with mere relativities. Such a fate need not be onerous. If one could not believe in an Absolute, belief in 'progress', in 'the future', in 'reason', in 'equal rights', were adequate substitutes, and of course happiness was still attainable through such traditional means as family life, money-making or the pleasures of the senses. All these may amount to something less than absolute value, but there need be no despair on that account. The Absolute seemed dispensable after all: as it turned out, human beings could live meaningful and satisfying lives without it. Such at least was the general opinion. But Nietzsche takes a different attitude.

Nietzsche is convinced that the Christian Absolute cannot be resuscitated. He thinks the same of the metaphysical Absolute (the Good of Platonic philosophy) which to all intents and purposes he assimilates to Christianity. He further rejects the elevation of the relative values of modernity to *de facto* absolute status, as occurs when 'education', 'progress', or 'equal rights' are pursued with something resembling religious fervour. Contrary to popular assumption, however, not only does Nietzsche not reject the Absolute as such, he sees it as the one eternal demand of philosophy. His whole thought is governed by a yearning for the Absolute, by the attempt, after the death of the Christian God, to rediscover the genuine Absolute. What he objects to in the Christian God is not that it is absolute but that it is not genuine:

> What sets *us* apart is not that we recognize no God, either in history or in nature or behind nature – but that we find that which has been reverenced as God not 'godlike' but pitiable, absurd, harmful, not merely an error but a *crime against life*....In a formula: *Deus, qualem Paulus creavit, dei negatio.*[6]

Nietzsche takes the same attitude to all those concepts which, like God, have traditionally been linked with the Absolute. He does not object to them as such, but to the circumstance that 'little abortions of bigots and liars began to lay claim to the concepts "God", "truth", "light", "spirit", "love", "wisdom", "life" as if these were synonyms of themselves.'[7] All these are concepts which Nietzsche uses in his own way, not in a relativistic sense, but in connection with his own kind of Absolute. When he describes himself as the last disciple of the god Dionysus, when he portrays Zarathustra as the most truthful of all men, when he speaks of the free spirit, tragic wisdom and the affirmation of life, he does not mean to imply a reconciliation with anything less than the Absolute, he does not have in mind a standpoint in any sense optional, contingent or perspectival. What he intends is a new conception of the Absolute, therefore new conceptions of God, truth, spirit, life etc. Nietzsche is not an 'untimely' thinker because he rejects the Christian God: this was in the second half of the nineteenth century already an old story, it had already attained the status of public opinion. What makes him untimely is his refusal to accommodate himself to the nihilistic relativism of modernity. In seeking a new Absolute, in insisting that existence without such an Absolute is impossible, he appeared (for example to such Basel colleagues as Burckhardt and Overbeck, who acknowledged his genius) as a romantic or sentimentalist, as a kind of 'madman'. Even in the present day, the pathos of Nietzsche's philosophical resolve is often dismissed as idiosyncratic, so that his thought can be forced into the very categories which he so vehemently rejected. The impossibility of the Absolute has in contemporary times become such an article of faith that one 'knows' that Nietzsche, as a 'modern' thinker, must have rejected it too. One 'knows' this, despite the counter-evidence of the texts.[8]

The great difficulty in talking about 'the Absolute' is that so many different meanings may be attached to this term. We have already seen the dubiousness of attributing to Nietzsche an unequivocal rejection of 'Being'. Where he condemns this notion, it means the supreme unchanging object of metaphysical knowledge, a realm of eternal truth which can be 'possessed' through intellectual reasoning. On the other hand, he sometimes considers 'Being' a suitable term for the conceptually ungraspable 'life' intuited by the Dionysian philosopher. As for 'the Absolute', Nietzsche has a distinct distaste for this particular term. He associates it, as does Schopenhauer before him, with German idealism, especially Hegelianism. But terminology should not be allowed to mislead. Just as Schopenhauer sought an ultimate sphere of truth beyond 'representational' knowledge, so does Nietzsche invest absolute value in Dionysian truth, in the truth of 'life' itself. And, although this truth does not possess epistemological significance, although it does not translate out as an authoritative 'theory' of reality, there is, for Nietzsche, no more decisive question for a human being than his relation to just this truth.

Whether we are justified in calling Dionysian truth 'absolute' depends on what is achieved through it. Similarly, whether we are justified in calling the 'object' of Dionysian affirmation 'the Absolute' depends on the role which Nietzsche attributes to it. It was remarked above that the Christian Absolute provided a centre for valuation and a justification for human existence. Does this also hold in the case of Nietzsche's Dionysian? Despite differences in the way Nietzsche conceives both valuation and justification, the answer is undoubtedly yes. For Nietzsche, all valuation must be measured on the scale of life affirmation or life denial: this is the only measure which counts. Moreover, existence can only be justified through an affirmative stance towards life. Christianity had sought a centre of valuation through the idea of 'the good', and Nietzsche rejects this. Christianity had sought the justification of human existence through the immortality of the soul and the reward of eternal life, which Nietzsche also rejects. But Nietzsche does not dismiss the problems of Christianity: he gives different answers. Although he reformulates these problems, he does not reject them as pseudo-problems. The need for a new centre for valuation ('new law tables') and for a new principle of justification stands at the very foundation of his thought.

Of these two functions of the Absolute, valuation and justification, the latter has the primary role. The centre of valuation is itself to be valued on account of its capacity to justify. In the case of Christianity, 'the good' is valued because of the promise of heavenly rewards. For Nietzsche, the Dionysian phenomenon of 'life' is worthy of affirmation because only thereby is the justification of individual existence possible. The parallel with Christianity is indicated by Nietzsche's taking over of the term 'redemption' (*Erlösung*) as a synonym for 'justification'. It is through the Dionysian that man achieves redemption: all authentic valuation, all genuine truth, all genuine wisdom, all genuine spirit, are for Nietzsche oriented to this supreme possibility. Redemption is Nietzsche's answer to the question 'why do we want truth?'[9] At the same time, truth is his answer to the question 'how is life to be redeemed?' Of course, only a specific kind of truth comes into consideration here. Scientific-theoretical truth, for example, is non-redemptive. One does not want this kind of truth for the purposes of redemption but for pragmatic reasons, ultimately for self-preservation. Scientific truth is not absolute truth, not philosophical truth, because it does not cater for the absolute need for redemption. This is why Nietzsche thinks it perverse to devote oneself to scientific truth in the manner of the spiritual middle class, to pursue science as a grand and all-consuming passion. Redemption is the sole 'criterion of adequacy' for absolute truth: in this respect Nietzsche does not think that Christianity was wrong. Where he differs from Christianity is in his conception of the nature of redemption, and the means of its attainment.[10]

This chapter attempts to clarify the role of redemption in Nietzsche's philosophy, and thus to throw some further light on the vexed question of what he means by 'truth'. The mainly negative conclusion of Chapter One, namely that Nietzsche is not a 'perspectivist' in the sense of relativistic pluralism, will be supplemented by more positive considerations: we shall see more precisely how the 'absolutism' of Nietzsche's philosophy is to be understood. Preliminary to this, some attention must be given in the following section to Schopenhauer's philosophy of redemption. An unfortunate consequence of the neglect of Schopenhauer among contemporary commentators is that the theme of redemption, so central for Nietzsche's esteemed predecessor as for Nietzsche himself, fades almost entirely from view. We shall see that Nietzsche's thought is in many ways a response to Schopenhauer's philosophy of redemption, which in Nietzsche's view partakes too much of the Christian model. This Schopenhauerian context is especially evident in *The Birth*

of Tragedy, which will be examined in the section 'Dionysian redemption': the concept of Dionysianism will emerge
as an attempt to understand redemption in a 'life-affirm-
ing' rather than in a Schopenhauerian 'life-denying' ('pessimistic') manner. However, Nietzsche's sceptical
temperament did not easily allow him to rest content with
such a 'religiously' coloured concept as redemption. In
subsequent works he is plagued by doubt, returning again
and again to the 'psychology' of redemption, concerned to
discover if a genuine meaning can be given to a concept
which seems to have its provenance in Christianity. These
psychological considerations will occupy us in the fourth
section, 'The psychological analysis of redemption'. Till
the end of his writings, Nietzsche remains conscious that
redemption is a questionable concept, very liable to be
invested with Christian assumptions. But he never abandons it, he retains it as one of the basic 'enigmas' of his
philosophy. As we shall observe in the section headed
'Redemption and the eternal return', it plays a special role in
Thus Spoke Zarathustra, where the supreme thought of the
'eternal return' signifies nothing less than redemption from
time. Having thus arrived at the core of Nietzsche's
thought, the following section 'This world and other
world', makes an interim assessment. I ask whether
Nietzsche's polemical opposition between 'this world' and
'other world' is in fact a satisfactory framework for
dealing with the problem of redemption, or whether, on
the contrary, this seductively simple opposition hinders
Nietzsche in his basic aims. The issues raised in this section
are further elaborated in Chapter Four. The next section,
'Redemption and the self', focuses on the 'self' as the
'subject' of redemption, attempting to understand the
meaning of Nietzsche's dictum 'become who you are'. In
this connection, particular emphasis is given to the apparent
antagonism between the 'individualizing' and 'universalizing' dimensions of Nietzsche's thought. The final section
of the chapter explains why Nietzsche calls the radical
solitude of redemption a 'purification' and 'cleansing'.

SCHOPENHAUER'S PHILOSOPHY OF REDEMPTION

Schopenhauer considered himself an atheist. At one point Nietzsche praises him for his 'unconditional and honest atheism' and as 'the *first* admitted and inexorable atheist among us Germans'.[11] It is true that, for Schopenhauer, because theism claims rational knowledge in an area beyond the competence of reason, it is once and for all refuted by the Kantian critique of speculation. He thus rejected all 'doctrines' of God, all 'theology' as he understood it, from the belief systems of the common people to the refined constructions of Hegelianism. On the other hand, this does not prevent Schopenhauer's philosophy from possessing a profoundly religious character. While rejecting doctrinal theology, he embraced the experiential-moral dimension of Christianity and the Eastern religions, particularly Buddhism. The three sources of his own philosophy, he used to say, were Plato, Kant and Eastern wisdom. From Plato he learnt that the empirical world is a second-order reality dependent on an eternal realm of Being, from Kant he learnt that reason is limited to the 'world as representation' and could not know the Thing-in-itself, from Buddhism (and also Christianity) he learnt that pity, understood as the fellow-feeling of sufferers, is the foundation of morality. His philosophy attempts a synthesis of all these sources, governed by his own key idea of the 'world as will'. The latter is likewise the key to his understanding of 'redemption'.

The basic character of human life as suffering can be verified, in Schopenhauer's opinion, through unprejudiced observation, but he considers it his own distinctive achievement to have shown why this is so, to have provided a metaphysical explanation of this empirical fact. This he attempts through his idea of the essence of reality – the Thing in itself – as will, i.e. as a blind, eternal, directionless, meaningless, impersonal surge. That he calls this essence 'will' does indeed pose a difficulty. We know what will is through our own experiences of willing, and in this sense it is a 'subjective' phenomenon. Schopenhauer never comes to an adequate resolution of this problem. He maintains that the inner intuition through which we are conscious of will is, on account of its lack of spatial determinations, less subjective than the external perception which, in combination with the intellect, yields the 'world as representation'. Inadequate as this may be for establishing that will is the Thing-in-itself (which must be free of all determinations, not just spatial ones) it suffices for his basic argument on redemption. Even if will is not the Thing-in-itself, the latter manifests itself in the human sphere first and foremost in the phenomena of desiring, striving, yearning etc. But (and here the resemblance with Buddhism is evident) all such willing is accompanied by suffering. Willing is always directed to a lack which is experienced as painful, and human beings, condemned as they are by the nature of things to willing, are condemned to repeated cycles of pain (the 'wheel of Ixion'). Human willing resembles a thirst whose anticipated satisfaction always turns out to be illusory. The objects of will are like mirages whose objective properties can never justify the desperation with which they are sought. Happiness is never an accomplished fact but always a promise, a hope for the future whose deceptive character is repeatedly confirmed through ever new rounds of willing directed towards ever new objects. The sorry truth of human existence is that it is no more than a phenomenal manifestation of this blind primal striving. As one lost in the desert cannot help but stagger on towards the next mirage, so all human beings are driven by the will from one deception to another until they finally expire, 'sword in hand'. In short, neediness-for-redemption is grounded in will-bound suffering. Therefore redemption consists in breaking free of will.

The moral meaning of redemption is grounded in the circumstance that human willing is the willing of an ego. This makes willing not only painful, but also unjust, for the ego seeks its own benefit alone. Considered as Thing-in-itself, will is an undifferentiated unity. But primal will 'objectifies itself' at the level of phenomena through the *principium individuationis*, which in the case of human beings means discrete egos. Each ego considers itself the supreme reality, and would more readily will the destruction of the entire external world than its own destruction. Breaking free of will (i.e. redemption) implies the overcoming of egoism: it is the breaking through of the *principium individuationis* and the re-establishment of the original unity of all human beings, indeed of all beings whatsoever. According to Schopenhauer, this is the true foundation of the morality of compassion (or pity) to be found in Christianity and Buddhism. All human beings are essentially companions in suffering. But what prevents them from acknowledging this, and from acting towards each other out of fellow-feeling, is that they are also companions in guilt. The guilt of man does not reside in any particular form of existence, nor in any particular 'wicked' acts performed, but simply in his existence as an ego.[12] Because man exists only as a suffering and guilty ego, Schopenhauer draws his well-known 'pessimistic' conclusion: 'it would be better not to be'.

This unenviable situation of man has yet another aspect. As an ego he is condemned not only to suffering and guilt, but also to error. The only reality an ego can know is the 'world as representation', i.e. the world as constructed by the intellect for the purposes of self-preservation. However much mastery the ego achieves in this realm of scientific truth, however deeply it probes the world of space, time and causality, it remains, precisely as ego, cut off from the primal ground of its being. The ego understands its individuation as absolute, it cannot see beyond the 'veil of Maya' which is constituted through this individuation. The intellect is the slave of individuated egoistic will, and only possible objects of this will have any meaning for it. Error is not morally neutral, but reflects the fundamental guilt of ego-centred existence: man is in error because he is 'sinfully' dominated by will. Redemption, as the overcoming of will, is the simultaneous overcoming of suffering, guilt and error: it is deliverance into bliss, blessedness and truth.

In *The World as Will and Representation*, Schopenhauer distinguishes two kinds of redemptive experience: aesthetic (Book Three) and ascetic (Book Four). The former is a transitory and unstable freeing from the dictates of will, while the latter is a more enduring and perfected freeing, i.e. redemption in the full and proper sense. Aesthetic redemption is explained in terms of the Platonic Ideas.[13] Through contemplation of a Platonic Idea 'a change takes place in the subject' as a result of which it is 'no longer an individual'.[14] The distinction between subject and object is overcome: what was formerly a subject separated from its object of will now becomes a 'pure, will-less subject of knowledge' and 'loses itself' in contemplation.[15] In contrast with theoretical cognition, which is always governed by interest, the experience of beauty liberates one from individual motivation: this is what makes aesthetic experience 'pure'. In being thus released from the dominion of will, suffering is abolished, leading to that feeling of well-being, sometimes of intoxication and ecstacy, which attaches to aesthetic experience. This feeling of pleasure is purely contemplative, distinterested and impersonal: it lifts the burden of the world as will. However, Schopenhauer maintains that aesthetic contemplation cannot be an enduring condition. It is episodic and transitory, providing only a foretaste of the more comprehensive redemption to be attained through asceticism. The latter is a condition of 'voluntary renunciation, resignation, true releasement and complete will-lessness'.[16] What is at work here is the ascetic's repugnance at his own manifestation as an individual. Seeing through the *principium individuationis*, the ascetic crushes his own individual will. Asceticism is the 'greatest, most important and most meaningful phenomenon which the world can exhibit.'[17] Achieving a deep tranquillity and serenity, the ascetic no longer feels egoistic greed, fear, envy, hate or anger, but 'looks back calmly and with a smile on the phantasmagoria of this world which was once able to move and agonize even his mind, but now stands before him as indifferently as chess-men at the end of a game.'[18]

Although Schopenhauer has great respect for the more severe exponents of asceticism (e.g. Francis of Assisi), he does not insist on particularly strict ascetic practices. By 'asceticism' he understands the greatest possible indifference to objects of will, whereas extreme practices such as self-flagellation, fasting and the hair-shirt are always caught up in the logic of that which they seek to combat. What is essential is the virtue of pity, itself a state of suffering. As the genuine hair-shirt, pity signifies an overcoming of the *principium individuationis* so that one 'now identifies one's own lot with that of mankind in general: but this is a hard lot of trouble, pain, and death.'[19] The ascetic suffers out of insight and empathy, the egoist out of will. With the overcoming of will, suffering is transfigured rather than abolished: a new kind of extraworldly suffering is embraced which results in 'a melancholy mood, the constant burden of one great pain and a corresponding playing-down of all smaller joys and sorrows.'[20] The ascetic has overcome his personal guilt, but now experiences the primal guilt of mankind. His 'melancholy mood' is not a negative manifestation and as such something he would like to get rid of, though it is invariably confused with this by those living within egoism. It is the destiny of those who live in the truth, an aspect of truthfulness itself.

A serious logical problem in Schopenhauer's doctrine of redemption arises from his claim that will, i.e. that which is overcome in the ascetic condition, is the Thing-in-itself. Schopenhauer's treatment of this problem is dismissive: he speaks simply of 'exceptions' to the domination of will. The overcoming of will is not susceptible to 'rational' explanation, with Schopenhauer speaking of a 'transcendental alteration' which happens 'suddenly and as if coming from outside', of 'rebirth' and an 'act of grace'.[21] But even if we accept this kind of language, the difficulty remains that, instead of achieving a unification with the primal ground of reality, the redeemed individual appears to be actually annihilated: as Schopenhauer puts it, redemption is a 'crossing over into an empty nothingness' (*Übergang in das leere Nichts*)'.[22] This paradoxical solution is made necessary by Schopenhauer's insistence that human suffering and misery are metaphysically guaranteed. If the essence of reality is pure and purposeless will, then a return to this from the second-order level of individuation does not hold out the promise of release from suffering, nor of the other sublime aspects of the redemptive experience. Schopenhauer is therefore forced to postulate 'another world', albeit a world of 'nothingness', as an escape from the desperate situation of man. This negative characterization of redemption is not only an expression of the limits of rational understanding. What shuns nothingness is our own individual will, our nature as will-to-life. As Schopenhauer puts it in the closing sentences of his main work: 'We freely acknowledge that what remains after the complete abolition of the will is, for all who are still full of will, assuredly nothing. But also conversely, to those in whom the will has turned and denied itself, this very real world of ours, with all its suns and galaxies is, – nothing.'[23]

It is Schopenhauer's idea of redemption as an 'affirmation of nothingness' which arouses the indignation of Nietzsche. As we shall see, however, there is some doubt as to whether Nietzsche shows sufficient recognition of Schopenhauer's underlying intentions with this idea. In many passages, particularly in his later writings, Nietzsche reads Schopenhauer rather too much according to the exigencies of the latter's formal metaphysical system. But notwithstanding the radical difference which redemption is supposed to make, Schopenhauer does not see it as the literal negation of the world: he realizes perfectly well that in some sense the ascetic remains 'in the world', subject to its temptations, and burdened with its guilt. In this connection it may be noted that Schopenhauer's most popular work in Germany (although almost unknown in English-speaking circles) has always been his *Aphorisms on Life-Wisdom*, a treatise which is supposed to suspend strict metaphysical pessimism in an attempt to show how life can be made 'least unbearable'.[24] Yet the basic tendency of *The World as Will and Representation* still determines this work: the philosophy of 'practical living' which it presents is governed by the same views on human value and corruption. Implicitly at least, redemption emerges as a this-worldly possibility, as a kind of ideal, attainable in degree. Not a denial of life, not a 'crossing over into nothingness', but an alteration of existential relations is the issue. It is this aspect of Schopenhauer's thought, i.e. 'life denial' as a 'way of life', which makes it first of all relevant to Nietzsche.

DIONYSIAN REDEMPTION
Although Nietzsche's first book, *The Birth of Tragedy*, has the outward appearance of an aesthetic theory, it is more fundamentally a response to the Schopenhauerian philosophy of redemption. The Dionysian aesthetic presented in this work is an answer to the problem of redemption, to the problem of how man can justify his own individual existence in the face of the 'terrifying' and 'absurd' abyss of life. The lack of any higher 'theological' purpose to life is the point of departure for *The Birth of Tragedy* as it is for Schopenhauer. It is simply asserted as the 'tragic' insight which must be once again appropriated after the long period of optimistic intellectualism beginning with Socrates. But rather than, in the manner of Schopenhauer, concluding that life must be 'denied', Nietzsche understands redemption as the affirmation of life: not resignation and renunciation, but Dionysian 'life-intoxication' becomes the solution.

In the ancient Greek world, the Dionysian cults belonged to the so-called 'mystery religions'.[25] Of probable oriental origin, they offered an alternative to the polis-centred, ritualistic and political religion of the Greeks, gaining particularly widespread influence in late Hellenistic times when the traditional gods were in decline and the spectre of nihilism ever present. The Dionysian cults were redemptive in their basic meaning for, unlike traditional religion, they focused on the individual, inducing an alteration of consciousness into a state of 'divine madness' or frenzy. Although condemned by political authorities and periodically suppressed, the cults proved remarkably resilient, surviving well into the Christian period and providing a source of recruitment into Christian communities. In choosing the god Dionysus as the symbol of life affirmation, Nietzsche is well aware of this alternative religiosity, a religiosity which worships 'life' itself, not in its most proximate manifestations, but as the groundswell of life, as the inexhaustible upsurge of life, as primal force and origin. The Dionysian experience reveals that 'life is at the bottom of things, despite all changes of appearances, indestructibly powerful and pleasurable' (*unzerstörbar mächtig und lustvoll*).[26] This pleasurable quality, however, is not inconsistent with a kind of 'primal pain' (*Ur-Schmerz*) which, like the pains of childbirth, is in the service of life. Much later, in *Twilight of the Idols*, Nietzsche puts the matter thus:

> In the teachings of the mysteries, *pain* is sanctified: the 'pains of childbirth' sanctify pain in general – all becoming and growing, all that guarantees the future, *postulates* pain....I know of no more exalted symbolism than this *Greek* symbolism, the symbolism of the Dionysian. The profoundest instinct of life, the instinct for the future of life, for the eternity of life, is in this word experienced religiously.[27]

In *The Birth of Tragedy*, Nietzsche presents the Dionysian orgies of the Greeks as 'festivals of world redemption and days of transfiguration' (*Welterlösungsfesten und Ver-klärungstagen*) which 'destroy the individual and redeem him by a mystic feeling of oneness' (*durch eine mystische Einheitsempfindung zu erlösen*).[28] In combination with the 'Apollinian' principle of 'beautiful form', the Dionysian experience finds expression in tragic art, more precisely in the tragic artist himself, understood as 'the medium through which the one truly existing subject celebrates his redemption in appearance' (*Erlösung im Scheine*).[29] Although Nietzsche asserts that 'it is only as an *aesthetic phenomenon* that existence and the world are eternally justified', his concerns in the book as a whole are not aesthetic in any narrow sense. Rather, a particular kind of art is seen as an alternative to Schopenhauerian pessimism. The Dionysian and Apollinian principles are joined to produce 'the fundamental knowledge of the oneness of everything existent, the conception of individuation as the primal cause of evil, and of art as the joyous hope that the spell of individuation may be broken in augury of restored oneness.'[30] Through the Apollinian principle, individuation is not abolished, but as Nietzsche says, 'redeemed': 'Apollo, however, again appears to us as the apotheosis of the *principium individuationis,* in which alone is consumated the perpetually attained goal of the primal One, its redemption through appearance (*Erlösung durch den Schein*).'[31] At the level of 'beautiful appearance', the contradiction between the primal One and individuation is overcome, and the whole phenomenal world redeemed through being experienced in an aesthetic mode. This does not mean that Apollo is victorious over Dionysus: the only kind of art which serves redemption is Dionysian art, though it is as art that the Dionysian principle finds expression. In *The Birth of Tragedy*, art is no alternative to religion, but a way of understanding the alternative religion symbolized by Dionysus. This is confirmed by the fact that, when Nietzsche returns to the Dionysian motif in his late period, the specifically 'aesthetic' Apollinian principle drops almost out of sight.

Nietzsche rejects the Schopenhauerian conception of neediness-for-redemption on two major counts. Firstly, human suffering is narrowed down to specifically 'tragic' suffering. Nietzsche's 'primal pain' is not the pain of human willing with all its accompanying frustrations and resistances, it is not the natural suffering of man as a vulnerable creature in a hostile world. For Nietzsche, this kind of suffering is simply part of the human lot, and is universally accepted as long as human existence is seen as meaningful. The only kind of pain which is 'metaphysically' significant is that arising from the 'tragic insight' of the meaninglessness of existence. Secondly, Nietzsche rejects Schopenhauer's moral interpretation of redemption. Whereas Schopenhauer regards human neediness-for-redemption as equivalent to egoistic guilt, and seeks a solution through the ascetic morality of pity, Nietzsche insists that Dionysian redemption involves 'nothing reminiscent of asceticism, spirituality, or duty'.[32] In the later 'Attempt at Self Criticism' attached to the new edition of *The Birth of Tragedy* in 1886, Nietzsche refers to 'the careful and hostile silence with which Christianity is treated throughout the whole book – Christianity as the most prodigal moral theme to which humanity has ever been subjected.'[33] Nietzsche's later critique of Christian morality is clearly presaged in this early work, as when he speaks of the 'active sin' and 'justification of human evil' which occur in the Dionysian state.[34] In contrast with asceticism, Dionysian redemption is 'sacrilegious' (*frevelhaft*): the intoxicated individual is carried away beyond all conventional allegiances, beyond the 'femininity' of Christian conceptions of good and evil.

Despite these differences from Schopenhauer, does *The Birth of Tragedy* remain anchored in Schopenhauerian metaphysics? The main ground for this suspicion is the central role of the primal One, the return to which by the individual is constitutive of Dionysian redemption. Nietzsche's primal One is suspected of being metaphysical because it seems, like Schopenhauer's primal will, to imply a distinction between reality 'in-itself' and 'appearance', a distinction which, it is supposed, Nietzsche is not entitled to in the post-Kantian epoch of philosophy, and which is rejected in his later writings.[35] But the primal One would be a metaphysical posit in the speculative sense criticized by Kant only if it were intended as an object of theoretical knowledge, and this is not the case. Although Nietzsche speaks of 'Dionysian wisdom' and 'Dionysian truth', although he insists that the Dionysian man has 'looked truly into the essence of things' and possesses 'true knowledge, an insight into the horrible truth',[36] the kind of truth, knowledge and insight here implied is very different to the abstract and conceptual knowledge of traditional metaphysics. Nietzsche's critique of Socratic intellectualism, one of his major concerns in *The Birth of Tragedy*, is intended to show that redemption is unattainable through theory. Intuitive insight is something quite different. The primal One is not an object distinct from the knower, who can describe it or delineate its properties. It is much more an 'abyss' (*Abgrund*), not an empty space but an essentially mysterious ground, a life-giving, productive, intoxicating origin to which man returns in Dionysian ecstacy, so that his own individual identity, his own egoistic suffering, his own finite aspirations and goals are swallowed up in the tremendous outflowing of life. Nietzsche himself is prepared to use the term 'metaphysical' in this connection. He speaks of the 'metaphysical comfort' (*metaphysische Trost*) provided by Dionysian tragedy, and of tragic art as the 'truly *metaphysical activity* of man'.[37] But 'metaphysical' here has the meaning of 'redeeming': through the Dionysian man restores his lost unity with the Absolute as primal One. In this latter sense, Nietzsche's critique of Socratism in *The Birth of Tragedy*, as well as his more general anti-Platonism, are indeed 'metaphysical': the theoretical inaccessibility of the Absolute is denied only on the basis of its intuitive accessibility.

In his early writings on the Presocratics, Nietzsche distinguishes the intuitively accessible One of Heraclitus from the conceptually accessible One of Parmenides and Plato: the former is the unity of Becoming, the latter the unity of Being. In *The Birth of Tragedy*, the primal One of Dionysianism is similarly opposed to the theoretical unity of Socratic thought. Nietzsche's Heracliteanism and Dionysianism must be understood together, they are just two expressions of the same fundamental conception. As we read in *Ecce Homo*:

> Before me this transposition of the Dionysian into a philosophical pathos did not exist: *tragic wisdom* was lacking; I have looked in vain for signs of it even among the *great* Greeks in philosophy, those of the two centuries *before* Socrates. I retained some doubt in the case of *Heraclitus*, in whose proximity I feel altogether better and warmer than anywhere else. The affirmation of passing away *and destroying*, which is the decisive feature of a Dionysian philosophy; saying Yes to opposition and war; *Becoming*, along with a radical repudiation of *Being* – all this is clearly more closely related to me than anything else thought to date.[38]

Philosophy in the Tragic Age of the Greeks presents the Heraclitean philosophy as a 'justification of Becoming' (*Rechtfertigung des Werdens*).[39] Prior to Heraclitus the Milesian philosopher Anaximander had anticipated the metaphysical Being of Parmenides and Plato with his doctrine of the *apeiron*, the Indefinite. According to this doctrine (which is distinctly Schopenhauerian in Nietzsche's rendition) all individual existence, as a breach with the primordial unity of the *apeiron* (the Thing-in-itself, in Nietzsche's view) constitutes an 'injustice' for which 'penance' must be payed through destruction.[40] By contrast, Heraclitus teaches that justification does not depend on the flight into another world of metaphysical indefiniteness, but exists in Becoming itself, through the workings of the *logos*. Considered as Becoming, the world is a 'game', i.e. something self-contained and innocent.[41] The equivalence of Heraclitean justification and Dionysian redemption is also indicated by a passage towards the end of *The Birth of Tragedy*:

> For we now understand what it means to wish to see tragedy and at the same time to long to get beyond all seeing....That striving for the infinite, the wing-beat of longing that accompanies the highest delight in clearly perceived reality, reminds us that in both states we must recognize a Dionysian phenomenon: again and again it reveals to us the playful construction and destruction of the individual world as the overflow of a primordial delight. Thus the dark Heraclitus compares the world-building force to a playing child that places stones here and there and builds sand hills only to overthrow them again.[42]

In a note from 1882–83, Nietzsche writes that 'I have always striven to prove to myself the innocence of Becoming (*Unschuld des Werdens*): and probably what I thereby wanted to achieve was the feeling of complete unaccountability – to make myself independent of all praise and blame.'[43] Some five years later, in *Twilight of the Idols*, we find a similar formulation: 'That no one is any longer accountable, that the kind of Being can no longer be traced back to a *causa prima*, that the world is a unity neither as sensorium nor as "spirit", *this alone is the great liberation*, thus alone is the *innocence* of Becoming restored.'[44] The motivation underlying these statements is no different to that which determines the Dionysianism of *The Birth of Tragedy*. What the 'innocence of Becoming' signifies is simply that there is nothing beyond the primal phenomenon of life, that as a living individual being man is not guilty of having 'fallen' from another world.[45] In each case, however, this must be proved through an act of affirmation. Dionysianism is a striving for the infinite, but not for the infinity of a *causa prima* or transcendent metaphysical Being. Nietzsche wants an experience of eternity this side of a metaphysical other world, an experience of eternity within Becoming itself which does not, accordingly, deny the finitude of man. There is no shift in this attitude after *The Birth of Tragedy*, no abandonment of an early 'Schopenhauerian' metaphysic.

Dionysian redemption is achieved through the affirmation of life. But what exactly does Nietzsche mean by 'life'? With this question we run up against the limits of conceptual thinking, for 'life' is a *primitive term* for Nietzsche: it stands for primal reality which as such eludes all description.[46] Nietzsche does attempt to indicate what he means through a variety of metaphors, but when these are taken literally, as they often are in contemporary commentary, the result is a series of comprehensive misunderstandings.[47] For example, Nietzsche sometimes falls into sensualist vocabulary when contrasting the this-worldly character of his philosophy to the other-world-liness of Platonism and Christianity. He repeatedly asserts that the senses have been unjustly maligned by these latter traditions. The slogan of 'inverted Platonism', as well as occasional remarks about the primacy of 'the body', may suggest a version of sensualism. But there are equally many passages in his writings which testify to the inadequacy of any simple opposition between sensuality and spirituality.[48] The famous section 'How the "Real World" at last Became a Myth' from *Twilight of the Idols* ends by saying 'We have abolished the real world: what world is left? the apparent world perhaps? But no! with the real world we have also abolished the apparent world!'. This is Nietzsche's fundamental attitude. Life is neither disembodied spirit nor brute spiritless sense, but is prior to both spirit and sense. Nor can life be identified, in the manner of the postmodernists, with 'multiplicity' and 'difference'. Nietzsche does emphasize the diversity and richness of life, but he insists no less on its unity. Dionysian redemption involves a return to the 'centre' of life. This cannot be positively specified: one can only say what it is not.

Certain clues can be obtained through the manner in which life is affirmed. Dionysian affirmation is not the act of an abstracted intellect set over against an independently existing reality but a holistic state, 'the highest state which a philosopher can attain'.[49] It is a state of intoxication, rapture, forgetfulness of self, ecstacy, enchantment and cheerfulness, of surging power and strength which transports man out of himself. At the same time it is a state of great seriousness, reverence and gratitude. Dionysian affirmation is a kind of 'worship' and 'piety', though of course Nietzsche would insist that these words be understood quite differently than in a Christian context.[50] The Dionysian reveller feels himself in the presence of something tremendous, overpowering and fascinating in the highest degree. This presence is 'self-evident' and 'given', but in the mode of existential rather than epistemological certainty. The Dionysian exemplifies the positivity of mystery, i.e. not mystery as a gap in understanding but as the most fundamental reality.[51] As such, it has a more primordial claim on man than do all intellectually constructed realities. The 'object' of Dionysian affirmation is, in an unmistakable though enigmatic sense, 'godly', and this affirmation is itself a 'participation' in the godly. There are definite resemblances here to Neoplatonic conceptions of divinity. Both the pagan and Christian Neoplatonic traditions speak of God as 'the One' beyond the intellectual deity of Aristotelianism: in analogous manner to Nietzsche they deny that the One can have anything positively predicated of it, and claim that it can be known only through a kind of participatory 'unknowing'.[52] Like the theologians of Neoplatonism, Nietzsche denies any separation between the 'godhead' and the world as such: the divine principle is not situated in a remote other world but manifests itself at every level of reality. Nietzsche does not shrink from the word 'pantheism' in this connection:

> The word 'Dionysian' means: an urge to unity, a reaching out beyond personality, the everyday, society, reality, across the abyss of transitoriness: a passionate-painful overflowing into darker, fuller, more floating states; an ecstatic affirmation of the total character of life as that which remains the same, just as powerful, just as blissful, through all change; the great pantheistic sharing of joy and sorrow that sanctifies and calls good even the most terrible and questionable qualities of life; the eternal will to procreation, to fruitfulness, to recurrence; the feeling of the necessary unity of creation and destruction.[53]

The above passage, from Nietzsche's late period (1888), again indicates how little his idea of the Dionysian changes after *The Birth of Tragedy*. Looking back on this early work in *Ecce Homo*, Nietzsche remarks that 'the cadaverous perfume of Schopenhauer sticks only to a few formulas', and identifies its understanding of the Dionysian phenomenon as one of its two 'decisive innovations', the other being the analysis of Socratism.[54] Actually, the only Schopenhauerian formula which regularly appears in *The Birth of Tragedy* is '*principium individuationis*', and although this disappears in Nietzsche's later writings, the idea itself does not. 'The primal One', which is not even a Schopenhauerian term, also disappears, but once again the idea behind it lives on in such expressions as 'total character of life', and more particularly 'will to power'. Redemption as Dionysian life affirmation does drop out of view in Nietzsche's middle period (see next section), but from *Thus Spoke Zarathustra* onwards (where it is present in fact if not in name) it reappears as a dominant motif. In this later period, Dionysianism remains as Nietzsche's reply to the pessimism of Schopenhauer, i.e. to resignation and renunciation as the road to redemption, to that will to nothingness which turns its back on life. In the light of the considerations at the end of the previous section, I shall later question whether Nietzsche does not pose his opposition to Schopenhauer rather too starkly, and whether he does not read him rather too literally. But it is first necessary to examine the turn of Nietzsche's thought during his 'sceptical' middle period.

THE PSYCHOLOGICAL ANALYSIS OF REDEMPTION

After 1876, Nietzsche reacts against his former Wagnerian 'romanticism' and enters into what is commonly (and rather misleadingly) called his 'positivist' phase. The first book Nietzsche publishes during this period is *Human, All Too Human* (1878), later described in *Ecce Homo* as a 'monument of rigorous self-discipline with which I put a sudden end to all my infections with "higher swindle", "idealism", "beautiful feelings" and other effeminacies.'[55] What lends the label 'positivist' a limited applicability is that for Nietzsche a sobering up is now called for, to be achieved by playing off scientific clear-headedness against the allures of art, metaphysics and religion. Nietzsche's new beginning is partly explicable through his disillusionment with the 1876 Wagner festival in Bayreuth (to which he had contributed much advance publicity, including the essay 'Richard Wagner in Bayreuth'), where what he had originally envisaged as a rebirth of tragedy turned out instead to be an exercise in bourgeois self-intoxication: the 'uplifting' which occurred there had, apparently, little to do with 'Dionysian truth'.[56] But this experience underlined a problem of principle central to *The Birth of Tragedy*, namely what can possibly count as a criterion for the authenticity of Dionysian redemption? The tragic insight had supposedly been given not as an intellectualized content but as a kind of 'intoxication'. What could be said against the objection that this was merely subjective and emotional, with no implications at all for reality? Finding no clear answer to this question, Nietzsche comes to suspect he had been duped by the pretensions of romantic sensibility. Turning away with repugnance from the 'play-acting people' and the 'higher horsemen of the spirit', he writes *Human, All Too Human* as a course in 'anti-romantic self-healing'.[57]

In this book Nietzsche adopts a 'psychological' mode of argumentation, seeking to unmask art, metaphysics and religion as rooted in particular kinds of emotions. He finds that art, metaphysics and religion attempt the amelioration of suffering through 'narcotization': suffering is justified by being narcotically linked with a higher world and a higher truth.[58] In reality, Nietzsche counters, suffering has its origins in mundane psycho-physiological circumstances. Advocating a 'chemistry of moral, religious, aesthetic representations and sensations', he indicates the intended finding, namely that 'in this domain the most glorious colours are derived from base, even from despised materials.'[59] Aphorisms 132–144 apply this technique to the Christian concept of redemption. Through careful consideration, Nietzsche says, it should be possible to obtain an explanation of 'that state of the soul of a Christian called neediness-of-redemption', an explanation 'free of mythology' and 'purely psychological'.[60] Against current theologizing on this matter, in which connection he mentions Friedrich Schleiermacher and his influence, Nietzsche offers an explanation, or the groundwork thereof, himself. Man discovers in himself a tendency to those kinds of actions which stand low in the conventional moral order, together with a longing to perform those actions which stand higher. He feels, however, inadequate to these higher actions, and develops a deep dissatisfaction with himself, together with a yearning for some kind of doctor who could cure this feeling. Now there come moments (perhaps during a Wagner opera or religious ritual) when these feelings of guilt and insufficiency are blown away, and when, despite the persistence of the original deficiencies, a new and elevating self-evaluation is won. The relief thereby experienced is so great that it appears as a 'blessing from above' or proof that 'God is merciful'. According to Nietzsche, what has actually happened is that certain psychological processes are misinterpreted: reacquired self-love is mistaken for godly love. The guilt and sin which are originally experienced are the product of 'errors of reason', from measuring oneself against a fantastic godly standard. It is the idea of God which makes one feel so disturbed and humiliated, and once this is identified as an error the corresponding feelings vanish. The sensation which is experienced as godly redemption has mundane psychological origins, testifying not to 'divine mercy' but to an act of 'self-pardon, self-redemption'.[61]

At first sight, it seems as if Nietzsche in *Human, All Too Human* has completely overturned his previous philosophical position. It also seems that the rough-hewn positivism with which he treats his former romanticism might be more deleterious than the original ailment. On closer inspection, however, it emerges that Nietzsche's new beginning is highly ambiguous. While emotionality and intoxicated subjective states are rejected as possible avenues of truth, other sober and tranquil states are accorded a curiously 'higher' extra-psychological value. Science and reason, it turns out, are not values in themselves, nor are they valued primarily as vehicles of objective knowledge. Instead, the question 'why science?' must find an answer at the level of human subjectivity, an answer just as necessitating as redemption is taken to be to the question 'why religious faith?' In the final aphorism of Section One it is said that the 'influence of cleansing knowledge' shows itself in 'a secure, mild, and basically cheerful soul, which does not need be on guard for tricks and sudden explosions', but which is content 'with that free, fearless hovering over men, customs, laws and the traditional evaluations of things, which is for it the most desirable of states.'[62] Nietzsche quotes these same words in a later *Nachlaß* fragment, as illustrating 'what I at that time experienced and wanted as "health".'[63] The closing aphorism of Section Two states that, with the dawning of scientific consciousness, 'the sun of a new gospel (*eines neuen Evangeliums*) is casting its ray onto the highest mountaintop of the soul.' This new gospel preaches the 'innocence' of human existence, which, when brought to consciousness, amounts to the 'self-illumination' (*Selbsterleuchtung*) and 'self-redemption' (*Selbsterlösung*) of man.[64] Again in the final aphorism of Part Three, immediately after the psychological critique of religion, Nietzsche softens his position to admit that there are 'certain exceptions' among the holy men who are 'attractive in the highest degree'. Only the 'celebrated founder of Christianity' is explicitly mentioned, with Nietzsche referring to Jesus' 'feeling of utter sinlessness, utter freedom from responsibility', and adding that this is a feeling which 'everyone can now attain through science'.[65] From such passages one can wonder whether Nietzsche has really abandoned the concept of redemption, or has only reconsidered its application. The idea that scientific consciousness is to be valued on account of 'feelings' of innocence or freedom from responsibility has a doubtful claim to positivism.[66] In fact, because Nietzsche invokes no criteria by which such existentially significant 'feelings' can be distinguished from the merely psychological sensations (the narcotic effect) allegedly produced by religion, art and metaphysics, the overt critical intention of *Human, All Too Human* is largely thwarted.[67]

Despite Nietzsche's new 'enlightened' attitude, it is noteworthy that he does not explicitly criticize his earlier works. On the tragic Greeks and 'the Dionysian' he remains silent, preferring to direct his attack at Christianity or simply at 'religion' in general. His many sweeping statements would seem to indicate that *The Birth of Tragedy* would fall within the scope of his critique, but he refrains from drawing this conclusion.[68] Rather than reversing his earlier position, Nietzsche pushes it into the background, into a state of suspension. Having seen the dangers of romanticism, he wants temporarily to distance himself from his former enthusiasms, genuinely to feel the strength of that critical intellectualism which he had (as he now suspects) too hastily dismissed in his earlier period. Such taking sides against himself is typical of Nietzsche: it is a method, a strategical device, and by no means a philosophical position in itself. It is that necessary stage in the development of the free spirit when it must turn upon its original 'reverences' and embrace a daring experimentalism.[69] When Nietzsche, through the composition of *Thus Spoke Zarathustra*, fully recovers from his romantic ailment to reach the final 'affirmative' stage of his development, he will reappropriate his early Dionysianism at a higher level, he will understand his original insights to have survived the 'trial' of intellectualism. His 'psychological' suspicions are not cancelled but become more nuanced. The concept of redemption, so 'naively' employed in *The Birth of Tragedy*, and then so summarily 'unmasked' in *Human, All Too Human*, becomes a problem.

Nietzsche continues to have difficulties with the psychology of redemption as late as *The Antichrist* (1888), where he dwells at length on the 'psychological type of the redeemer'. 'The redeemer' is not Paul, who Nietzsche subjects to the familiar *ressentiment* critique, but 'the Nazarene' himself, who, as noted in the previous chapter, is somewhat surprisingly accorded the status of free spirit. In unmistakable tones of approval, Nietzsche describes the 'different Being' (*anderes Sein*) represented by Jesus as an inward life directed against 'every kind of word, formula, law, belief, dogma'.[70] In the associated *Nachlaß* notes, we read that 'Jesus stands for a real life (*ein wirkliches Leben*), a life in the truth (*in der Wahrheit*) as opposed to the normal life.'[71] The kingdom of heaven promised by Jesus is 'a condition of the heart' and a 'meaning change in the individual' (*Sinnes-Änderung im einzelnen*).[72] Rather than turning away from life, Jesus displays 'the profound instinct for how one would have to *live* in order to feel oneself "in heaven", to feel oneself "eternal", while in every other condition one by *no* means feels oneself "in heaven": this alone is the psychological reality of "redemption".'[73]

'Redemption', then, can mean different things. On the one hand it can mean, as a symptom of *ressentiment*, the hope and faith in 'another world' as relief from the burdens of life. On the other hand it can mean the 'psychological reality' attested to by both the Jesus-type and the Dionysian-type. The fact that Nietzsche continues to use the term in his late period, despite its religious connotations and the criticisms of *Human, All Too Human*, indicates that the existential re-orientation which he seeks is something more than a mere perspectival shift, something more than a contingent choice of lifestyles. 'Redemption' continues to belong to Nietzsche's vocabulary of philosophical 'absolutism'.

REDEMPTION AND THE ETERNAL RETURN

In *Ecce Homo*, Nietzsche relates that the idea of eternal recurrence, the 'fundamental conception' of *Zarathustra*, came to him as a 'revelation' in 1881, '6000 feet beyond man and time' in Upper Engadine.[74] Its first public proclamation occurs in the penultimate aphorism 341 of Book Four of *The Gay Science*, under the heading 'the greatest weight'. In *Thus Spoke Zarathustra*, Nietzsche's immediately succeeding book, the idea is approached gradually and at first with mere allusions, coming out into the open towards the end of Part Two, and then dominating the dramatic development of Part Three. There are many passages on eternal return in Nietzsche's later manuscripts. During this period he is preoccupied with the (never actualized) idea of writing a 'philosophy' which would clarify the foundations of his thought: the 'eternal return' frequently appears as the title of such a work in Nietzsche's draft plans.[75] A similar idea can be found in Nietzsche's early writings. It is briefly mentioned, in connection with the Pythagoreans, in the second *Untimely Meditation*.[76] Of particular interest is a passage from *Philosophy in the Tragic Age of the Greeks*:

> Eternal and exclusive Becoming, the impermanence of everything actual, which constantly acts and comes-to-be but never is, as Heraclitus teaches it, is a terrible, paralyzing thought....It takes astonishing strength to transform this reaction into its opposite, into sublimity and the feeling of blessed astonishment.[77]

The relevant passage from *The Gay Science* no. 341 reads as follows:

> Would you not throw yourself down and gnash your teeth and curse the demon who thus spoke? [who announced the eternal return] Or have you once experienced a tremendous moment when you would have answered him: 'You are a god and never have I heard anything more divine'. If this thought gained possession of you, it would change you as you are or perhaps crush you. The question in each and every thing, 'Do you desire this once more and innumerable times more?' would lie upon your actions as the greatest weight. Or how well you would have to be disposed to life to *crave nothing more fervently* than this ultimate eternal affirmation and seal?[78]

Taken together, these passages indicate that the eternal return is at once a Heraclitean and a Dionysian motif, in a sense as the synthesis of the two. While the Heraclitean side gives the reality to be affirmed, the Dionysian side gives the affirmation itself, the required 'attitude' or 'stance' towards reality. The eternal return provides the ultimate test of strength (and thus of truthfulness) in the face of life: this can be seen in *Thus Spoke Zarathustra*, where at the beginning of Part Three Zarathustra prepares himself to think this, his 'most abysmal thought', succeeding at the end only after the most punishing experiences. However, the difference between the two quoted passages should be noted. In the first, Nietzsche speaks simply of eternal Becoming, in the second of eternal return. Now Becoming and eternal return are not equivalent: presumably there could be endless Becoming without repetition. What does this change signify? What does it have to do with the fact that Nietzsche dates his 'revelation' at 1881 rather than some ten years earlier?

We have observed that, in his early period, Nietzsche is Heraclitean in his lectures on the Presocratic philosophers, and Dionysian in *The Birth of Tragedy*. He continues to associate the two in his later works.[79] The conditions of this co-allegiance are not immediately obvious. Heracliteanism appears to be an anti-metaphysical motif, installing Becoming in place of Parmenidean-Platonic Being, while Dionysianism, at least in *The Birth of Tragedy*, is oriented to the 'primal One', which in the view of many commentators is tainted by metaphysics (as noted, Nietzsche does call it a 'metaphysical comfort'). I have previously suggested that, on close examination, no conflict is to be found here: Becoming simply is the primal One, where the latter's oneness is distinct from the logical self-identity of things, and therefore does not involve metaphysics in the sense rejected by Nietzsche. It is noticeable that, after *The Birth of Tragedy*, Nietzsche no longer speaks of the 'primal One', preferring terms like 'life', 'earth' and 'world' to indicate the object of Dionysian-Zarathustrian affirmation. But since in his later period Nietzsche remains faithful to the Heraclitean thesis that 'Becoming is the only reality', all these other terms must mean the same, i.e. life = Becoming, earth = Becoming, world = Becoming. Dionysian affirmation remains the affirmation of Becoming, of the 'impermanence of everything actual, which constantly acts and comes-to-be but never is.'

The idea of eternal return arises in Nietzsche's later philosophy when he comes to consider more closely how Becoming is actually to be affirmed, i.e. how more precisely Heracliteanism and Dionysianism are to be reconciled. Can one really affirm something which never is? Can one affirm the constantly fleeting flux? In particular, can one affirm this in a supreme redeeming act if there is nothing one can hold before oneself as some kind of 'object'? At the time of *The Birth of Tragedy*, Nietzsche could answer these questions by reference to the primal One, which, although not a thing, possesses a quasi-transcendental status behind the Apollinian world of appearance. In his later period Nietzsche becomes uncertain about this solution, and looks for another way out. The flux, he now speculates, can be fixed as an 'object' of affirmation through willing the eternal return of the same things. In this way the unity (self-identity) of the flux is guaranteed by its cyclical character, while no separate realm of eternity, neither 'another world' nor even a 'primal One', need be presupposed. Nietzsche does thereby vouchsafe a kind of eternity, but an immanent this-worldly eternity, both of life as such and of his own being as constantly returning.[80] Through affirming the eternal return, through making this one's most fervent craving, one overcomes the *ressentiment* longing for otherness and nothingness: it is the supreme act of gratitude to life which neither wants things otherwise, nor wishes to enter the 'deep sleep' of nothingness. The eternal return is a doctrine of unbounded finitude, of 'infinite finitude' so to speak, wherein man is fated to exist eternally (i.e. repetitively) in a closed, this-worldly reality. There is no way out of life, and to the extent that one celebrates this with all one's strength, one has redeemed oneself for the gift of life.

What makes the eternal return such a difficult idea is its Dionysian aspect, i.e. the mighty act of affirmation through which it must be appropriated. Lou Salomé and Franz Overbeck testify that, in personal communications of the eternal return, Nietzsche spoke in an uncanny whispering voice, as if in a state of sublime horror.[81] As mentioned, Zarathustra works himself up to his 'most abysmal idea' only through extraordinary resolve, and in the end it almost destroys him: to think this thought, he enters into his 'last solitude' and 'deeper into pain than I have ever descended'.[82] When (in the section 'The Convalescent') the thought finally rises up from his depths, he collapses 'like a dead man' and remains thus stricken for seven days.[83] Upon awakening, the eternal return is proclaimed by his animals, but Zarathustra, 'still sick with my own redemption', dismisses them as 'buffoons and barrel-organs', complaining that they have 'already made a hurdy-gurdy song of it'.[84] At this point Zarathustra ceases all external communication and, encircled by a 'great stillness', converses with his own soul.[85] In the last section of Part Three, he involuntarily breaks into song. The eternal return remains incommunicable as doctrine but is expressed through the pathos of his closing hymn to eternity, 'The Song of Yes and Amen'.

In *Thus Spoke Zarathustra*, the eternal return first appears, albeit without explicit enunciation, in the section 'On Redemption' towards the end of Part Two.[86] Zarathustra proclaims 'To redeem the past and to transform every "it was" into an "I wanted it thus!" – that alone do I call redemption!' That from which man needs redemption is 'the spirit of revenge' (*der Geist der Rache*), understood as 'the will's most lonely affliction' that it cannot will backwards, that it stands helpless before the brute facticity of the past.[87] Man is burdened by the past in a double sense: firstly that he directly suffers from its effects in the present, but more fundamentally, that the past is outside his sphere of willing, that here and only here his will is doomed to defeat.[88] The irrevocability of the past is the last great obstacle to affirmation of life: it is that upon which one takes revenge when one wills differently for the future, as Zarathustra still does (at this stage) when he sees the smallness of modern man. However, Zarathustra does not think of the past just as one dimension of time. The past, as the 'whereto' of the unidirectional flow of time, stands for time itself. To be redeemed from the spirit of revenge is 'reconciliation with time' (*Versöhnung mit der Zeit*) as such, or rather, as Zarathustra says, something 'higher than any reconciliation'.[89] Zarathustra refers to the preaching of 'madness' (Schopenhauer) which yearns for 'redemption from the stream of things and from the punishment "existence".'[90] The reconciliation with time is the annihilation of this yearning and its transformation into the will to eternal Becoming, into that Dionysian will which is a 'liberator and bringer of joy'.[91]

Considered as a cosmological hypothesis, the eternal return is (though perhaps implausible) relatively straight-forward and intelligible. In its redemptive aspect, however, it is ultimately a mystery, to be experienced only in a 'tremendous moment' which Nietzsche calls 'the great midday' (*der große Mittag*).[92] Redemption occurs through the concentration of all 'eternity' into this one moment:

> If we affirm one single moment, we thus affirm not only ourselves but all existence. For nothing is self sufficient, neither in us ourselves nor in things; and if our soul has trembled with happiness and sounded like a harp string just once, all eternity was needed to produce this one event – and in this single moment of affirmation all eternity was called good, redeemed, justified, and affirmed.[93]

Becoming takes on the character of Being (it comes to 'abide' as Heidegger puts it)[94] by the constant return of the self-same, but can only be experienced as such (as 'eternity') through a tremendous act of will. In the 'Song of Yes and Amen', where this act of will has been (or is actually being) accomplished, Zarathustra is in the presence of 'redeeming beams of light' and has himself become 'a grain of that redeeming spice that makes everything mix well together.'[95] Like the Dionysian revellers of *The Birth of Tragedy*, Zarathustra is becoming one with the world, he is placing the 'wedding ring of rings' on the finger of eternity.

The Dionysian aspect of the eternal return, the fulfilling 'moment' (*Augenblick*) of affirmation, has all the characteristics of a mystical experience.[96] It comes as a revelation, at first as a paralysing shock, then immediately goes over to the kinds of feelings of joy and liberation which are traditionally associated with a mystical rebirth. As such, it is not open to discursive examination, proof or disproof.[97] On the other hand, the Heraclitean content of the thought, the idea of time (and therefore reality) as an infinitely recurring cycle of the same things, raises certain problems in relation to Nietzsche's fundamental motivations. It would certainly be perverse to take the eternal return in its apparent cosmological meaning to be Nietzsche's central thought. To understand what Nietzsche is getting at with this idea we must depart from the problem which it is meant to solve. This is the problem of redemption as life affirmation: the eternal return is intended as the 'highest formula of affirmation that is at all attainable'.[98] Now we possess independent knowledge of what Nietzsche means by 'affirmation' from his other writings, and we can therefore ask about the adequacy of this particular formula in a broader context. To be borne in mind are all those aspects of affirmation already encountered, i.e. unity with the primal life force, joy, reverence, gratitude etc. If all these coalesce into a relatively coherent conception, we can ask whether the eternal return adds a further (and decisive) explanatory dimension, or whether, on the contrary, it introduces certain unwarranted difficulties. Such a procedure means that one must refrain from uncritically accepting Nietzsche's own declarations on the supreme importance of the eternal return, and thus from measuring all his other thought against this idea. The hermeneutical principle to be followed is that the clear should be measured against the unclear and not vice versa. And although as a cosmological hypothesis the eternal return may indeed be clear (let us allow this) its suitability as the 'highest formula of affirmation' (thus as the formula for redemption) is open to serious question.

Nietzsche sees the eternal return as the 'object' of a strictly immanent life affirmation. By affirming the return of the same 'things' ('even this spider and this moonlight between the trees, and even this moment and I myself' as the demon in *The Gay Science* says)[99] all recourse to another world or transcendental ground can apparently be avoided. The difficulty with this, however, is that according to Nietzsche's own Heraclitean principles, all 'things' are really 'fictions' which are unfaithful to Becoming. In his lectures on the Presocratics, Nietzsche identifies the supreme object of Heraclitean affirmation as the *logos*, considered as the all-encompassing intelligence ('the One') governing the perpetual flux. Similarly, in *The Birth of Tragedy*, the Apollinian realm of individuation (i.e. of thingliness) is subordinated to the primal One as Dionysian upsurge. Does Nietzsche abandon these conceptions by the time of *Thus Spoke Zarathustra*? But there is no evidence that he moves away from his Heracliteanism: his later manuscripts are full of Heraclitean scepticism concerning the reality of 'things'.[100] Although he no longer speaks explicitly of the primal One, the Dionysianism of his later period involves an affirmation of 'life', 'earth', 'world' etc. which does not easily translate out as an affirmation of 'things'.[101] Deferring for the present the question of whether Nietzsche in fact and contrary to his own stated position does retain a kind of transcendental ground, we must ask how he can see the eternal return of the 'same things' as the content of affirmation.

The answer is to be found in Nietzsche's conception of time. What returns is not just things but things-in-time: this is the whole point of a formula of affirmation which would be strictly this-worldly. More particularly, it is 'moments' of time which recur as thingly events-in-time. For time to 'abide' (i.e. for Becoming to be stamped with the character of Being)[102] it is necessary that all past moments and all future moments not flow away from each other in endless contradiction but link up in the 'ring' of eternal recurrence.[103] Since this ring of recurrence is closed in every 'present moment', each moment of time will be a candidate for the 'great midday' of affirmation, though in each individual case (e.g. Zarathustra's) it will be a question of whether there has been adequate preparation. Seen in this light, the eternal recurrence is the ultimate doctrine of 'seizing the moment': one must live with such an intensity of affirmation that one wills the infinite repetition of every moment. Time as such is affirmed and all other-worldliness banished, but only through the affirmation of every event-in-time, of every 'thing' which comes into being and passes away. Time is not 'detached' and affirmed 'in-itself' but remains inexorably fastened to the events which occur within it. Time is itself 'thingly'. This means, however, that time is defined in terms of what, from a Heraclitean point of view, are nothing more than fictions. In one sense it seems that Nietzsche overcomes the traditional (Aristotelian) sequential conception of time. The supreme act of affirmation looks neither forward nor backward but 'loses itself' in the 'moment', the 'reality' of time is revealed only in the mystical 'now' of Dionysian rapture. Time does not disappear into the mere sequentiality of things but is the original 'revelation' of life itself. On the other hand, by insisting that it is 'things' and 'events' which are affirmed in this mystical moment, Nietzsche reconnects with the sequential conception of time.[104] He fears that, if the 'object' of affirmation were to be anything but such 'things' and 'events', then this would amount to a kind of other-worldliness and transcendentalism. Nietzsche is caught in a bind between his this-worldliness and his

Heracliteanism, and in the end, the idea of eternal return implicitly sacrifices the latter.

It is a curious fact that many contemporary commentators regard the eternal return as a less 'metaphysical' idea than that of the primal One. Of course, such a judgement depends on what one understands as metaphysics. It seems that, implicitly at least, the postmodernist conception of metaphysics as 'closure' or 'centering' is often effective here, and that the primal One is found guilty on this score. Nietzsche's understanding of metaphysics, however, is quite different: for him, metaphysics is the belief in the ultimate reality of 'things'. Whether 'things' are understood as Platonic 'ideas' or as empirically observable objects makes no difference: what Nietzsche's Heracliteanism denies is just the reality of logically self-identical entities. Now the primal One, in *The Birth of Tragedy*, is not such an entity, nor even is will in Schopenhauer's philosophy, because in both cases the 'reality' referred to is not conceptually (logically) determinable. Of metaphysical entities, i.e. of 'things' of every description, it is possible to theorize: this is because their being is constituted through the intersubjective (verbal-conceptual) 'surface-and-sign-world'. The Dionysianism of *The Birth of Tragedy* is meant as an expression, on no account as a theory (which would be Socratism), of that ultimate reality which Nietzsche calls the primal One. When Nietzsche in his later philosophy, still searching for a 'formula of affirmation', embraces the idea of eternal return, he undermines this early position, becoming not less, but more 'metaphysical'. Just why the eternal return exerts so much fascination for the later Nietzsche remains unclear. As indicated, it appeals to him as a principle of 'this-worldliness', but only at the cost of throwing his whole ontology into confusion. Moreover, it is of dubious consistency with his other late motif of 'will to power', which, in analogous manner to the primal One, refers to a quasi-transcendental reality 'behind' those entities which 'eternally recur'. It cannot be said that

Nietzsche attains clarity and consistency on ontological matters in general. Dionysianism, the eternal return, will to power, and Heracliteanism all run parallel with one another in the later writings without Nietzsche properly working out their inter-relations. The envisaged programme of writing a 'philosophy' is never completed, nor even seriously undertaken.

In an important passage from *Beyond Good and Evil*, which Heidegger has called Nietzsche's 'third communication' of the doctrine of return, we read:

> Whoever as a result of some enigmatic craving has, as I have, long endeavored to think pessimism down to its depths...such a one has perhaps, without explicitly willing it, opened his eyes to the opposite ideal: to the ideal of the boldest, most vital, and most world-affirming human being who has not only made his peace and learned to get along with whatever was and is but who wills to have it again *precisely as it was and is* into all eternity, calling insatiably *da capo* not only to himself but to the entire play and spectacle, and not only to the spectacle but at bottom to him who has need of precisely this spectacle – who makes it necessary because he forever has need of himself – and makes himself necessary. – How's that? Would this not be – *circulus vitiosis deus*?[105]

Is the world, considered as eternal recurrence, a kind of god? Whatever the answer (as Heidegger points out, Nietzsche remains deliberately enigmatic on this) the call of *da capo* signifies the redeeming stance of one who has 'made his peace' with the world. But does such a 'pious' attitude towards life (i.e. the Dionysian attitude) necessarily will, as Nietzsche claims, the eternal return of the entire spectacle? Does Nietzsche really show that it is the 'spirit of revenge' to regret any event of the past? Does he show that it is *ressentiment* to will that certain events should not recur, let alone recur an infinite number of times? An affirmative answer in each case depends on identifying time with events-in-time, on giving thingly moments the highest ontological status so that if one does not will them one wills 'nothingness'. Prior to all ontological definitions, this alternative seems artificial. Is it not possible, *contra* Nietzsche, to make one's 'peace with the world' without willing the eternal recurrence of every event-in-time? Is it not possible to look with displeasure and even horror at past events, to wish they never happened and to will with all one's might that they may never happen again, without thereby becoming in the smallest degree less thankful for life, less affirmative in relation to life? Must not ontological definitions be brought into line with our prior intuitions in this area, rather than vice versa? Is not the eternal return in fact a *reductio ad absurdum* of Nietzsche's peculiar synthesis of Dionysianism and the principle of this-worldliness? To answer these questions requires that we take a closer look at this latter principle.

THIS WORLD AND OTHER WORLD

Nietzsche understands himself as a philosopher of immanence, of 'life' rather than an imaginary 'after life', of 'the earth' rather than a fictitious 'beyond'. From *The Birth of Tragedy* through to *Ecce Homo*, he presents himself as a loyal defender of 'this world' against the alleged 'world slander' of the Christian-metaphysical tradition generally, and of Schopenhauerian pessimism in particular. Zarathustra preaches 'I entreat you, my brothers, remain true to the earth, and do not believe those who speak to you of superterrestial hopes!'[106] The crime of the 'afterworldsmen' (*Hinterweltler*) is to have poisoned the springs of life and to have invested all value in its negation:

> If one shifts the centre of gravity of life *out* of life into the 'Beyond' – into *nothingness* – one has deprived life as such of its centre of gravity. The great lie of

personal immortality destroys all rationality, all natu-
ralness of instinct – all that is salutary, all that holds a
guarantee of the future in the instincts henceforth
excites mistrust. *So to live that there is no longer any
meaning in living: that* now becomes the 'meaning' of
life.[107]

Nietzschean redemption, whether expressed in terms of
Dionysianism or the eternal return, is the redemption of
life itself, its reinvestiture with value after a long history of
slander, its cleansing from the poison of *ressentiment*. The
great error has been to seek the justification of individual
existence from outside. To correct this error requires an
existential reorientation of unprecedented difficulty,
indeed one that is beyond the powers of the vast majority.
For the elite free spirits, however, who alone are capable of
reaching the great midday of affirmation, life appears
transfigured in the redeeming stillness of eternity.

Yet Nietzsche is aware that his this-worldly stance
harbours a paradox, to which he draws attention in
connection with the 'psychology' of Zarathustra:

The psychological problem in the type of Zarathustra
is how he that says No and *does* No to an unheard-of
degree, to everything to which one has so far said Yes,
can nevertheless be the opposite of a No-saying spirit;
how the spirit who bears the heaviest fate, a fatality of
a task, can nevertheless be the lightest and most
transcendent.[108]

Nietzsche continues with a reference to the Dionysian and
the 'eternal Yes to all things', which is only to restate the
paradox. Leaving the doctrine of recurrence aside,
Nietzsche's works do not seem to show an 'eternal Yes to all
things' at all, but rather a comprehensive and consistent
saying of No. He affirms 'life', but as previously
observed, this is a peculiarly elusive thing: it is not a

biological phenomenon, nor an 'other-worldly' spiritual force, nor is it human existence in its socio-cultural context. If we take 'world' or 'earth' instead of 'life', the same difficulties arise. What 'world' does Nietzsche affirm? What is the ontological meaning of 'world' in Nietzsche's philosophy? It can hardly mean the 'objective world' of empirical science (Nietzsche rejects this as 'materialism'), nor can it mean the 'sense world' (which is abolished along with the 'higher world'), nor the world of human customs and institutions (which Nietzsche sees as sunk in decadence). But if, acknowledging all this, we say that 'life', 'world' and 'earth' refer to some underlying and hidden reality, are we not forced to question the proclaimed 'this-worldliness' of Nietzsche's fundamental position?

Let us approach the problem the other way around and ask what other-worldliness means for Nietzsche. What does it mean to 'shift the centre of gravity of life' to a 'Beyond'? The first thing to be said is that other-worldliness does not consist in some set of theoretical commitments or beliefs. Nietzsche is quite clear on this: he regards it as his great step forward in the critique of Christianity that he has gone beyond the kind of scientific criticism of the Enlightenment to uncover its moral roots.[109] Nietzsche's rejection of intellectualism means that he sees theoretical beliefs as the expression of existential attitudes rather than vice versa. The content of otherworldly beliefs – whether these relate to heaven, an ideal world, or even nothingness – is a matter of secondary significance, the important point being that they indicate a resentful turning away from life. But this implies that other-worldliness is negatively defined in terms of the elusive concept 'life' (or 'world'), which itself can be explicated only through the existential stance of this-worldliness (life affirmation).

The coherence of Nietzsche's distinction between this-worldliness and other-worldliness depends on whether he can exhibit these as distinct existential attitudes. General formulas such as 'life affirmation' and 'life denial' are by no means adequate for this purpose: one must know what forms of life are thereby implied. However, precisely in this area Nietzsche has difficulties: the difference between this-worldly and other-worldly attitudes is nowhere near as clear cut as it needs to be if Nietzsche's whole philosophy is to be based upon it. To begin with, there is his ambivalence on asceticism in *The Genealogy of Morals* and elsewhere, where he wishes to distinguish a 'virtuous' (world-denying) version from a philosophical (world-affirming) version. Although there may indeed be different kinds of asceticism, it is unclear why these are not more accurately seen as different species of other-worldliness: after all, Nietzsche's philosophical asceticism in some ways involves an even more radical withdrawal from what normally counts as 'world' than is the case with conventional religious asceticism. Nietzsche thinks that the philosophical ascetic is not being weak, resentful and cowardly, that his renunciation is on the contrary an act of strength and 'will to power', but it is not obvious how this makes it any less otherworldly. In *Daybreak*, for example, he is prepared to say the following:

> To forego the world without knowing it, like a *nun* – that leads to a fruitless, perhaps melancholy solitude. It has nothing in common with the solitude of the *vita contemplativa* of the thinker: when he chooses *that* he is renouncing nothing; on the contrary, it would be renunciation, melancholy, destruction of himself if he were obliged to persist in the *vita practica*: he foregoes this because he knows it, because he knows himself. Thus he leaps into *his* element, thus he gains *his* cheerfulness.[110]

The element into which the philosophical ascetic leaps is no doubt 'life', but could not the religious ascetic (e.g. the nun) say something similar? Like the religious ascetic, the thinker has renounced the *vita practica* and is oriented to something removed. One might add that, to judge by Nietzsche's own example, the solitude of the thinker likewise has a distinct 'melancholy' aspect.

We have noticed Nietzsche's problem with the figure of the Nazarene. Nietzsche calls him a 'free spirit', but is he this-worldly or other-worldly? It is difficult to decide, for although Nietzsche emphasizes Jesus' inward life and withdrawal from the world, he also distinguishes him sharply from world-denying *ressentiment*.[111] Can it be that Jesus too is a thinker, who similarly leaps into the element of life? From which world does Jesus withdraw, and which world does he fail to deny? If one presses these questions, the whole this-worldly/other-wordly dichotomy begins to look very shaky indeed: it does not seem adequate for the psychological realities Nietzsche is dealing with. When one considers the matter closely, it emerges that the *ressentiment* type does not 'deny' the world at all, or if he does, it is a confirming kind of denial, in which the world's power over him is all too tellingly attested. Judged from the higher asceticism of Zarathustra and Jesus, the *ressentiment* type is locked in far too close a relationship with the world, with this world concretely here and now, this world with all its enticements, disappointments and pains. The detachment or 'homelessness' of the philosopher is one of the most constantly recurring themes in Nietzsche's writings. By contrast, it is precisely the spiritual pleb who Nietzsche portrays as clinging to the 'things of this world', who is so very interested in the business of this world, who is so utterly at home and secure within it.

Earlier in this chapter I indicated that the Nietzschean formulas 'life affirmation' and 'this-worldliness' originate as a response to Schopenhauer's doctrine of redemption through 'life denial'. I also noted that this Schopenhauerian formula is itself problematic. Although it is supposed to refer to the denial of will as primal life force, it is hard to think of the ascetic type (in which life denial is embodied) as altogether without will: instead, asceticism is usually associated with uncommon strength of will. If the nothingness (*Nirvana*) willed by the ascetic is, as Schopenhauer also admits, only a relative nothingness, can we perhaps conclude that the life thereby denied is only a relative life?[112] The question now suggests itself: is the life denied in Schopenhauerian asceticism really the same life that is affirmed in Nietzschean Dionysianism?

Our doubts on this score are confirmed by a symbol which both philosophers employ for apparently opposite purposes: the symbol of the dance. In the second volume of *The World as Will and Representation*, Schopenhauer refers to the Protestant Shakers of North America – ascetic life deniers on his own account – who celebrate their 'victory' through communal quasi-erotic dancing (the practice continues to the present day and involves convulsive movements of the entire body, especially the pelvis: hence the name 'Shakers'). Schopenhauer comments: 'For whoever has brought the hardest sacrifice may *dance* before the Lord: he is the victor, he has overcome.'[113] For Nietzsche, on the other hand, the dance (similarly erotic in overtones) is an expression of Dionysian life affirmation: 'I would not know what the spirit of a philosopher might wish more to be than a good dancer. For the dance is his ideal, also his art, and finally also his only piety, his "service of God".'[114] Does the dancing of the Shakers deny what Dionysian dancing affirms? Or is it much more that, in both cases, life and world are affirmed in one sense and denied in another? Do the Shakers and the Dionysian revellers evince opposite existential attitudes, or would this conclusion rest on an assimilation of quite different senses of 'life' and 'world'?

These difficulties originate in the fact that neither Schopenhauer nor Nietzsche achieve ontological clarity as to 'life' and 'world'. Although for the most part Schopenhauer rests content with his idea of the world as will, this leaves him with the unresolved problem of accounting for the relative nothingness in which the ascetic resides. For his part, Nietzsche takes the Schopenhauerian will to nothingness rather too literally, as the will to a 'deep sleep' in which all life instincts are extinguished. Schopenhauer does speak of the ascetic redemption as a quietistic state, but the elevated detachment of the Nietzschean philosopher can be similarly described. As we have seen, the true object of Nietzsche's polemics is the attitude of *ressentiment*, but in calling this 'world denial' he obscures rather than clarifies the phenomenon he has in mind. Nietzsche is no doubt repelled by the cowardice and weakness which he sees in so much conventional Christianity, interpreting this as a retreat from the real questions of life, as forfeiture of the intellectual conscience. If this is to be criticized under the heading of 'world denial', however, there must be some stable meaning attaching to 'world'. But this is not the case. Instead, within Nietzsche's polemical discussions there are constant slippages of meaning: not only are the *ressentiment* types world deniers but so are the strong-willed ascetics with whom he has so much in common.

If we look beyond the polemical formulas in Nietzsche's writings to the actual content of his 'psychological' analyses, we can see that he is a world denier in one sense and a world affirmer in another. What he denies is the world of human values, institutions, customs and conceptions: he turns away from the world of politics, the church, business, law, popular culture, education, science, leisure and entertainment, and from the whole system of benefits and honours associated therewith. In this sense Nietzsche is no different from Plato. For too long, Nietzsche's commentators have been prepared to take him at his word with respect to Plato. In fact, Nietzsche's 'anti-Platonism' is largely a self-deception, based on a misinterpretation of Plato as a theoretician of objective-scientific truth. Nietzsche fails to see (or sees but fails to acknowledge it) that the world of Platonic ideas is not 'objective-scientific reality' but a transfigured human world of truth and justice, i.e. of essentially the same values which Nietzsche himself affirms. Nietzsche's basic kinship with Plato can be confirmed by reading the middle books of *The Republic*, where the non-philosophical type is criticized in essentially the same terms as Nietzsche's spiritual plebs: in both cases the emphasis is not on lack of theoretical knowledge but on an attitude of clinging involvement with the things of this world.[115] This is not to say that there are no important differences between Nietzsche and Plato; their differing conceptions of the intellect and thus of the role of art in philosophy is a case in point. But Nietzsche and Plato cannot be contrasted in terms of the this-worldly/other-worldly distinction. Both affirm another 'higher' world than that which is proximally manifested in human existence. And in both cases this other world is, in some sense, divine.

Yet what of the principle of immanence in Nietzsche's philosophy? Does talk of a Nietzschean higher world dismiss this too lightly? The answer is that, without an ontological clarification of 'world' and 'life', we simply cannot know what 'immanence' is supposed to be. To take the example of 'the Nazarene', it turns out that, contrary to initial expectations, Nietzsche regards him as this-worldly rather than other-worldly, as standing for a particular practice of life. Could the same not be said of Plato, and for that matter even of the much-maligned Paul? Nietzsche calls certain kinds of existential attitudes (orientations to life and truth) 'this-worldly' and others 'other-worldly', but these latter designations, rather than adding any explanatory dimension to his discussion, have a polemical function which can be systematically misleading. This is particularly so because Nietzsche takes this polemical opposition seriously as a philosophical explanation of his existential analyses (where his real philosophizing takes place), and attempts to ground it through an ontology of things which eternally recur. If he had remained faithful to his original Heracliteanism he would not have opted for this solution, i.e. he would not have confused 'world' with 'things' or 'time' with 'thingly events'. In sum, the doctrine of eternal return is the clearest indication of Nietzsche's failure to ontologically elucidate the meaning of Heraclitean Becoming, of his failure to articulate a real alternative to metaphysical Being.

All too often, Nietzsche's philosophy continues to be read through the distorting lens of the this-worldly/other-worldly opposition, distorting because relying on vague unexplicated conceptions of 'world'. In fact, the doctrine of return, together with the this-worldly/other-worldly opposition, are at a different level to the concrete existential analyses which form the real substance of Nietzsche's thought. The concept 'redemption' has a crucial function at this existential level, because it indicates that the life affirmation intended by Nietzsche is a releasement, detachment, distancing etc. from what is commonly taken as 'world'. Redemption in this sense is quite different to the anti-dogmatic liberation from authority associated with perspectivist interpretations of Nietzsche, a liberation which, because grounded in 'interest', remains very 'worldly' indeed. Nietzschean redemption is rather the liberation from everything 'worldly' at the same time as it is liberation into the authority of the 'essential' (other-worldly) self.

REDEMPTION AND THE SELF

The journey to redemption traced out in Part Three of *Thus Spoke Zarathustra* is a 'homecoming'. In the first section, 'The Wanderer', Zarathustra reveals 'at last it is coming home to me – my own Self (*mein eigen Selbst*) and those parts of it that have long been scattered among all things and accidents.'[116] Zarathustra then enters his 'last solitude', which gradually intensifies during the course of Part Three, until in the closing sections he is beyond all human contact in a state of Dionysian rapture.[117] In 'The Homecoming' from the middle of Part Three, a distinction is made between 'solitude' (*Einsamkeit*) and 'loneliness' (*Verlassenheit*). Zarathustra had hitherto, in his dealings with men and animals, in his attempts to communicate and teach, been lonely, but now he is coming home to himself: 'O Solitude! Solitude, my home! I have lived too long wildly in wild strange lands to come home to you without tears!'[118] Solitude is the home of Zarathustra's own soul, and when, in 'Of the Great Longing', Zarathustra at last finds himself alone in intimate conversation with his soul, he is again overcome with emotion: 'And truly, O my soul! Who could behold your smile and not dissolve into tears? The angels themselves dissolve into tears through the over-kindness of your smile.'[119]

The meaning of 'self' and 'soul', although in many ways the key to Nietzsche's philosophy, is also the site of the most difficult problems. How are we to reconcile Nietzsche's universalizing and individualizing motifs? On the one hand, Dionysian redemption involves the breaking down of barriers between all things in a 'mystical sensation of unity': it is the becoming one with the primal One and as such the overcoming of the *principium individuationis*. Here it seems that the self is redeemed only by being annihilated. How can it be, then, that in his later writings Nietzsche speaks of selfishness or egoism as a noble virtue, and how are we to understand Zarathustra's redemption as a 'home-coming' to his own self?[120] Why is it that 'the noble soul has reverence for itself' rather than wishing (as Schopenhauer apparently urges) for its own extinction?[121] The easy way out of this difficulty, which is to posit a radical shift in Nietzsche's thinking after *The Birth of Tragedy*, cannot be accepted: as noted, in Nietzsche's later period Dionysianism remains an 'urge to unity'.[122] To put the same problem in a slightly different way, how are we to explain the fact that Zarathustra, and Nietzsche himself, insist on the uniqueness of 'one's own path' and 'one's own truths', while at the same time the Dionysian phenomenon is conceived as possessing supra-individual significance as the 'highest state that a philosopher can reach'?[123] The resolution of these difficulties is of the utmost importance, for a one-sided emphasis on uniqueness and individuality will lead to the 'heterology' of the postmodernist commentators, while a one-sided emphasis on universalism will lose touch with the true 'subject' of Nietzschean redemption and the pervasive theme of solitude.

It is well known that Nietzsche rejects the concept of self as metaphysical 'subject' or 'substance', i.e. as a simple abiding 'thing'. A series of notes to this effect appears in Book Three of *The Will to Power*, e.g:

> The subject: this is the term for our belief in a unity underlying all the different impulses of the highest feeling of reality: we understand this belief as the *effect* of one cause – we believe so firmly in our reality that for its sake we imagine 'truth', 'reality', 'substantiality' in general. 'The subject' is the fiction that many similar states in us are the effect of one substratum: but it is we who first created the 'similarity' of these states; our adjusting them and making them similar is the fact, not their similarity.[124]

Before jumping to conclusions from such passages, it should be asked who the 'we' is that creates the fictional subject. Is Nietzsche saying, as the postmodernist commentators maintain, that the self is a socio-ideological construct, formed through various constellations of 'will to power'? No doubt this is part of the story, but it cannot be the whole. The socially-constructed self is the herd self, and if this were the only kind of self there could be it would be impossible to understand Nietzsche's critique of 'the actor' and of herd life in general. The dictum 'become who you are' does not mean 'become what the herd wants you to be'. Nor is Nietzsche making the 'heterological' point that one should become whatever arbitrary ('different') self which the 'play' of will to power permits. Granted that

Nietzsche rejects the metaphysical 'subject self', he believes nonetheless in some kind of 'essential self' which it is possible to 'become' or to return to in a 'homecoming'. The radical individualism of Nietzsche's philosophy has got nothing to do with 'heterology' as 'being different' for its own sake, but is much more a matter of 'being oneself' in the sense of being faithful to one's own true self: the motif of solitude (ignored by the postmodernist advocates of 'heterology') can be understood in no other way.

In this connection it is significant that Nietzsche retains the concept of 'soul', albeit while rejecting 'soul atomism':

> One must first of all finish off that other and more fateful atomism which Christianity has taught best and longest, the *soul atomism*. Let this expression be allowed to designate that belief which regards the soul as being indestructible, eternal, indivisible, as a monad, as an *atomon*: this belief ought to be ejected from science! Between ourselves, it is not at all necessary by the same act to get rid of 'the soul' itself and thus forego one of the oldest and most venerable of hypotheses: as is often the way with clumsy naturalists, who can hardly touch 'the soul' without losing it.[125]

Leaving aside the question of whether this is indeed a Christian idea, what does Nietzsche have against 'soul atomism'? The answer is suggested in another note from *The Will to Power*, where Nietzsche says that 'all those who are "in the process of becoming" must be furious when they perceive some satisfaction in this area, an impertinent "retiring on one's laurels" or "self-congratulation".'[126] The immediate object of criticism in this passage is 'the Germans', but Nietzsche's point has wider application. Christianity (as Nietzsche understands it) teaches that the immortal soul, as each individual's most precious possession, simply stays as it is one's whole life long: it journeys through this world and then passes over unchanged into the other world. As such, the soul is something which is merely preserved and not at all a project which must be 'worked on' in the process of becoming.[127] The Christian can be complacent and can congratulate himself on his possession of a soul-monad which defines what he 'is' prior to all creative effort. By contrast, Nietzsche sees the self (soul) as a challenge to be either taken up in resolute 'becoming' or forfeited for definition by the herd. Everything depends on whether the self works on itself or whether, on the contrary, it leaves this task to others, to public opinion and the social roles constituted within it. This means that the self is (to anticipate Kierkegaard) a relation of itself to itself: the self does not exist except in the activity of relating.[128] As can be seen from the case of Zarathustra, by thus relating to itself, the self 'comes home' not just to itself, but to 'life' as the supreme object of affirmation. This does not imply that the self is completed or finished and can now rest on its laurels, because life itself is not like this: it is constant movement and overcoming. The self does not attain an end-state because it is not a thing which has states, but it becomes what it essentially is (a never-ending process of becoming and overcoming) through immersion in the element of life.

The self shares with life the character of unknowability. It cannot be pinned down in concepts, it cannot be revealed without residue: '"Everyone is farthest away – from himself"; all who try the reins know this to their chagrin, and the maxim "know thyself!" addressed to human beings by a god, is almost malicious.'[129] Nietzsche makes the delphic maxim his own, he sees himself as following the same road as the solitary Heraclitus who summarized his philosophy in the simple statement 'I searched out myself.'[130] In this sense Nietzsche resembles many religious-mystical thinkers of both the Western and Eastern traditions who see the way to truth (the way to the universal) as the 'inward' way (the way to the individual).

But on the other hand, the expression 'inward' is not strictly applicable in Nietzsche's case, for he pursues neither self nor life in a realm of spiritual interiority, he does not operate with a dualism of inner and outer reality.[131] Instead of inwardness, Nietzsche speaks of 'solitude': a condition pertaining to the whole existing self and not just to the abstracted 'conscious' self. The Nietzschean self has that reflexive character which Heidegger calls 'mineness' (*Jemeinigkeit*), but this is quite different from being closed off from the external world in the manner of the Cartesian ego. Like Heideggerian mineness, Nietzschean solitude defines a sphere of ontological understanding, it is the sphere in which 'Being' (or 'Becoming') discloses itself. Nietzsche resembles traditional mysticism in seeing the return to the true self as the abolition of the empirical self of the *principium individuationis*: the self which remains at the tremendous moment of Dionysian rapture is the greater self which has an eye (or an ear) only for life. Dionysian redemption involves the casting off of everything contingent and socially constructed which still attaches to the self. From the point of view of the herd self, what happens to Zarathustra in 'The Song of Yes and Amen' would amount to a total loss of self, it would seem that no personality is left. From the point of view of Zarathustra, however, it is only in this moment that he has truly become a self, because only now does he finally hold himself out into life with unqualified gratitude.

It is now clear what Nietzsche means when he extolls the value of selfishness. Whoever seeks redemption in Nietzsche's way is indeed selfish, but it is a greater selfishness which has nothing in common with the pursuit of 'interests'. The selfishness which Nietzsche has in mind is simply the condition of philosophical activity, i.e. the strength of self needed to transcend the interests of the herd self (whether conceived heterologically or otherwise) in favour of the 'great problems and question marks':

The lack of personality always takes its revenge: A weakened, thin, extinguished personality that denies itself is no longer fit for anything good – least of all for philosophy. 'Selflessness' has no value either in heaven or on earth. All great problems demand *great love*, and of that only strong, round, secure spirits who have a firm grip on themselves are capable. It makes the most telling difference whether a thinker has a personal relationship to his problems and finds in them his destiny, his distress, and his greatest happiness, or an 'impersonal' one, meaning that he can do no better than touch them and grasp them with the antennae of cold, curious thought. [132]

On this as on other points Nietzsche is not as far from Schopenhauer as he imagines. Schopenhauerian selflessness is likewise a greater selfishness which is rewarded with the bliss of Nirvana, an actual 'psychological' state which can be attained in the ascetic life. The nothingness embraced by the Schopenhauerian ascetic self and the life embraced by Zarathustra are not different: the apparent conflict only indicates that, from the standpoint of the herd self, the truth of redemption is the cancellation of the only reality it knows. In both cases the homecoming to the self is a return to that element of the complex self which partakes of eternity, but which is covered up, suffocated, scorned and mocked by the wisdom of this world. A similar conception is to be found throughout the dialogues of Plato, e.g. in the *Phaedo*, where Socrates says that 'the gods are our keepers, and we men are one of their possessions'. [133] For Nietzsche as for Plato, the way to the universal is the way back to the true individual: the ladder of divine ascent is not the acquisition of many things but the casting off of many things, a process of simplification and purification. Nietzsche would not disagree with Plato when the latter says that 'we men are put in a sort of guard post, from which one must not release oneself or run away'. [134] The self is the unique opening to the divine. It is here that all eternal demands are felt, it is from here that the philosopher experiences 'his destiny, his distress, and his greatest happiness'.

CLEANLINESS AND PURITY

For Nietzsche, Christian redemption is anchored in the poisonous notions of sin and guilt. What he here diagnoses is a *ressentiment* stance towards life, with redemption as a faint-hearted escape rather than a courageous embrace of Dionysian life in all its unfathomability. The Christian conceptions of sin and guilt represent a self-abasement and self-belittling of man, practised by those (nowadays a whole world civilization) who do not have the strength for life, and who bitterly take revenge both on life itself and on their own lives. When the Christians wash away their sins in the ceremony of baptism, Nietzsche can see this only as a washing away of the last vestiges of life, as the symbol of an ultimate capitulation before life, as the expression of a final desperate determination to degrade life and to declare as sacrosanct the inability to live. What Christianity takes as impure Nietzsche takes as the instinct of genuine life; what Christianity takes as cleanliness Nietzsche takes as filth: 'one does well to put gloves on when reading the New Testament' as he says in *The Antichrist*.[135] Like Christianity, Nietzsche sees the 'fallen' state of the soul as one of impurity and uncleanliness, while radically revising (so he considers) what these latter mean:

> That which divides two people most profoundly is a differing sense and degree of cleanliness (*Reinlichkeit*). Of what good is all uprightedness and mutual usefulness, of what good is mutual good will: the fact still remains – they 'cannot bear each other's odour!' The highest instinct of cleanliness places him who is affected with it in the stangest and most perilous isolation, as a saint: for precisely this is

saintliness – the highest spiritualization of the said instinct. To know an indescribable pleasure in bathing, to feel an ardour and thirst which constantly drives the soul out of night into morning, and out of gloom and 'gloominess' into brightness...is a noble inclination – but it also *separates*. The saint's pity is pity for the *dirt* (*Schmutz*) of the human, all too human. [136]

The Nietzschean spiritual aristocrat needs to protect himself against the filth of the spiritual lower orders, he has a 'physiological' reaction to *ressentiment* spirituality in all its manifestations:

And therefore let is have fresh air! fresh air! and keep clear of the madhouses and hospitals of culture! And therefore let us have good company, our company! Or solitude if it must be! But away from the sickening fumes of inner corruption and the hidden rot of disease! [137]

My instinct for cleanliness is characterized by a perfectly uncanny sensitivity so that the proximity or – what am I saying? – the inmost parts, the 'entrails' of every soul are physiologically perceived by me, *smelled*....Extreme cleanliness in relation to me is the presupposition of my existence; I perish under unclean conditions – I constantly swim and bathe and splash, as it were, in some resplendent element. [138]

Such passages suggest that the threat of uncleanliness comes from 'outside', perhaps from mere physical proximity of the spiritual lower orders. But Nietzsche must be read carefully. As pointed out at the beginning of Chapter Two, Nietzsche's different orders of the spirit ultimately stand for different forces within the economy of every spirit. Nietzsche does not think of spiritual cleanliness just as quarantine from external sources of spiritual disease. He does not 'bathe' just in order to remove the pollution arising from his intercourse with those of lesser cleanliness. On the contrary, the 'spiritualization' of the instinct for cleanliness occurs primarily within the self, as self-overcoming, as the overcoming of that instinct of *ressentiment* which rules the herd self. To the extent that this implies a potential uncleanliness even in the spiritual aristocrat, the concepts of guilt and sin are not so foreign to Nietzsche as first appears.[139] The uncleanliness of man is the weakness and cowardice which prevents him from living according to his own higher nature (that of the spiritual aristocrat, the *Übermensch*) and which makes him 'gravitate' towards spiritual plebianism. While the guilt of the spiritual pleb cannot be equated with that of the Christian sinner, there is a structural analogy in that both turn away from the highest reality and thereby forfeit their highest responsibilities.

The whole vocabulary of 'cleanliness', 'purity' and spiritual 'health' is one more indication of the 'absolutism' of Nietzsche's basic philosophical position, more particularly, of the 'absolute' significance of redemption in relation to the self. From the earliest times this kind of language has been associated with 'the sacred', which, as the object of absolute valuation and absolute reverence, must be separated off from everything 'profane'. Whoever (the 'saint') gives himself over to the sacred suffers a heightened sensitivity to any admixture of the profane, to any compromise, discord or *largeur de coeur*, to any hypocrisy or half-heartedness, to any 'relativism', to any weakness of spirit.[140] Precisely this is Nietzsche's attitude to that 'resplendent element' he calls 'life'. Notwithstanding Nietzsche's hostility to the passivity of *ressentiment*, Dionysianism involves an unmistakably 'submissive' dimension, but of a kind which leads to celebration rather than resignation: the overcoming of *ressentiment* submission is made possible by submission to the 'godliness' of life. For one ruled by this kind of submission and reverence, other orientations to life will appear impure and unclean, lacking in respect and self-respect, lacking in valuational proportionality and therefore in a genuine sense perverse. Whoever fails to grasp their own essential nature becomes someone less than himself and thus 'sick' in an ontological sense. However, even the 'highest instinct for cleanliness' can never attain an absolute purity. Nietzsche himself is not altogether untouched by the 'dirt of the human, all too human'. The 'philosopher saint' is 'constantly bathing and splashing' because only thus does he remain properly 'awake' to truth and life.[141] The philosophical life is constantly vigilant against the encroachments of 'the world', it must wash itself clean of the worldly valuations of the herd, it must purify itself of the 'all too human' tendency to hastily resolve the problem of existence, it must courageously hold this problem open and continually refound itself upon it. 'My whole *Zarathustra*', Nietzsche tells us in *Ecce Homo*, 'is a dithyramb on solitude, or, if I have been understood, on *cleanliness*.'[142] The instinct for cleanliness drives the Nietzschean philosopher further and further into solitude, but into the kind of solitude which is also a 'mystical sensation of unity': solitude as purification and cleansing, as obedience to the 'divine element' in man.

4
Nietzsche and Heidegger

Nietzsche's atheism must be liberated from the dubious society of those supercilious atheists who deny God when they fail to find him in their reagent glass, those who replace the renounced God with their 'God' of 'Progress'. We dare not confuse Nietzsche with such 'god-less' ones, who cannot really even be 'god-less' because they have never struggled to find a god, and never can.[1]

With all these pros and cons with respect to humanization, one believes one knows ahead of time what human beings are, the human beings who are responsible for this palpable humanization. One forgets to pose the question that would have to be answered first of all if the suspicions concerning humanization are to be viable or if refutation of these suspicions is to make any sense. To talk of humanization before one has decided – that is to say, before one has asked – who man is, is idle talk indeed.[2]

NIETZSCHE, HEIDEGGER, AND 'POST-METAPHYSICAL' PHILOSOPHY

The problem of 'Nietzsche and Heidegger' has in the last two decades come to the forefront of philosophical controversy, often under the rubric 'the end of metaphysics'. Heidegger's two-volume *Nietzsche*, published in 1961 but based on lectures from the mid-1930s to the early 1940s, has had a major impact, and remains the focus for many discussions.[3] The influence of Heidegger's other writings on the history of metaphysics also makes a comparison with Nietzsche inevitable. Both thinkers seek to break from the tradition of Western philosophy. Both go back to the Presocratic Greeks for inspiration and both seek a 'post-metaphysical' philosophy which would not be bound by the strictures of rational-conceptual knowledge. Both are critical of the 'objectivism' of post-Cartesian philosophy (thus of 'objective truth') and of the consequent domination of epistemological problematics. On the other hand, the projects of Nietzsche and Heidegger do not altogether correspond. To mention just one difference, Nietzsche rejects 'Being' as the 'last cloud of evaporating reality', while Heidegger elevates the 'question of Being' (*Seinsfrage*) to the status of the first and last question of his own philosophy, indeed of philosophy in general.

The postmodernist commentators have an ambiguous attitude to Heidegger.[4] They acknowledge his importance for the 'deconstruction' of the tradition, but consider that his own *Seinsfrage* (which makes this deconstruction possible) is itself a metaphysical residue indicating Heidegger's 'nostalgia' for a superseded *primum signatum*. Derrida has stated that 'Heideggerian thought would reinstate rather than destroy the instance of the *logos* and of the truth of Being as *primum signatum*.'[5] By contrast, Derrida sees Nietzsche as having 'contributed a great deal to the liberation of the signifier from its dependence or derivation with respect to the *logos* and the related concept of truth or the primary signified, in whatever sense that is understood.'[6] Derrida and many other postmodernist writers are critical of Heidegger for reviving a kind of 'first philosophy' and thus falling back into what is allegedly a pre-Nietzschean position, while Nietzsche is celebrated as a 'liberating' thinker on account of his 'perspectivist' rejection of absolute truth (the *primum signatum*). The postmodernists are also critical of Heidegger's thesis of Nietzsche as the 'last metaphysician', which, they believe, involves an imposition on Nietzsche of Heidegger's own metaphysical nostalgia.

It is not the purpose of the present chapter to specifically analyse the postmodernist discussion of the Nietzsche–Heidegger nexus. Implicitly, the terms of this discussion have already been criticized in the preceeding chapters: in essence, the postmodernists contrast a perspectivist and pluralist Nietzsche with an absolutist and dogmatic Heidegger. If 'Nietzsche and Heidegger' is a context in which 'truth' becomes problematic, perspectivist commentary turns this into a complex of epistemological problems about the rights and entitlements of varied discourses. Nor is it just postmodernist authors who interrogate the 'end of metaphysics' in epistemological terms: this is the unquestioned methodological presupposition of most writers on the subject.[7] The postmodernist literature should be understood in this wider context: it is one of many epistemological expressions of the basic quandary of post-metaphysical philosophy: how can dogmatism be given up without lapsing into an essentially arbitrary subjectivism?

In considering the relation between Heidegger and Nietzsche, it is important to distinguish Heidegger's interpretation of Nietzsche from Heidegger's philosophy more generally. Heidegger interprets Nietzsche in terms of his own conception of metaphysics and ultimately in terms of his own *Seinsfrage*. But it would be wrong to conclude that Heidegger's general philosophical position necessitates the specific thesis of Nietzsche as the 'last metaphysician'. Nor would it be correct to suppose that everything of interest which Heidegger has to say on Nietzsche can be subsumed under this latter thesis. Heidegger's attitude to Nietzsche is complex and multi-dimensional, as well as constantly changing, even within the various materials included in the *Nietzsche* book. The fundamental problem is not Heidegger's interpretation of Nietzsche, but the relation between Heidegger's philosophy and that of Nietzsche. As I shall argue, there are good reasons for thinking that Nietzsche is far more closely related to Heidegger than Heidegger himself acknowledges, and that as philosophers, i.e. as occupied with the *Sache* of philosophy, they both stand in irreconcilable opposition to every species of relativism. The 'last metaphysician' thesis is only the most well known aspect of Heidegger's considerations on Nietzsche, and when superficially understood (i.e. without seriously attending to Heidegger's wider philosophy) provides the postmodernists with the contraposition which they are in any case determined to find.

In the following section Heidegger's 'last metaphysician' thesis will be examined. This has been widely misunderstood, because what Heidegger means by metaphysics is misconstrued. As regards critical assessment, we shall find that Heidegger's thesis is distinctly one-sided. Heidegger seizes upon the weaknesses of Nietzsche's explicit ontological conceptions, particularly eternal return and will to power, and accentuates them, seemingly in order that his own *Seinsfrage* may stand out more prominently. Although Heidegger reveals the absolutism of Nietzsche's philosophical position, he is over hasty in assimilating Nietzsche to the Aristotelian 'onto-theological' tradition of absolutism. At the same time, Heidegger is not insensitive to the complexities of Nietzsche's philosophy, and the limitations of the 'last metaphysician' thesis are discernible within his own wider discussions. The third section attempts to reveal the fundamental affinity between Nietzsche and Heidegger by means of the latter's idea of the '*Sache*' of thought. Considered in this context, Nietzsche and Heidegger are concerned with the same 'phenomenon', but look at it from different angles: Heidegger is more occupied with explicit ontological articulation, with the way in which Being has been 'forgotten' by the metaphysical tradition from Plato and Aristotle onwards, while Nietzsche is occupied with the situation of the individual, by the challenge of living in the 'terrible' truth. Both thinkers, however, are perpetually 'on the way' to this *Sache* and within this *Sache*. Finally, in the fourth section, I shall briefly canvass the enigmatic character of this *Sache* as a sphere of 'nothingness'.

NIETZSCHE AS THE 'LAST METAPHYSICIAN'
First of all, what does Heidegger mean by metaphysics? A fundamental difference from Nietzsche is that Heidegger

proceeds not from the Platonic dichotomy between a real and an apparent world, but by reference to Aristotle's 'onto-theological constitution of metaphysics'. It is well known that Aristotle himself does not use the expression 'metaphysics': a later editor gave this title to a series of treatises on 'first philosophy' (*prote philosophia*), i.e. a science of 'first principles' relating not to any special region of beings, but to beings in general, beings *qua* beings.[8] Aristotelian 'ontology' (another word the Stagirite does not use himself, but which means the science of *ta onta*, of things *qua* things) gains its unity by reference to a *theos*, which Heidegger translates as 'highest being' (*höchste Seiende*).[9] Departing from these Aristotelian definitions, Heidegger understands metaphysics as the science of all beings whatsoever, grounding the totality of beings in a first being, e.g. in the case of Aristotle *ousia* (substance, ultimately 'divine' substance). Metaphysics is concerned with the 'way of Being of beings'.[10] It asks about 'what everything is' and in the course of its history has given various answers: everything is 'substance', everything is 'mathematical', everything is 'spiritual', everything is 'physical' et al. As such – this is Heidegger's basic thesis – metaphysics overlooks the more primordial question of Being (*Sein*) itself, of the prior 'is-ness' of all beings, regardless of their nature: the onto-theological constitution of metaphysics is, as he puts it, an expression of the 'oblivion of Being' (*Seinsvergessenheit*).[11]

Heidegger finds Nietzsche's metaphysics primarily in the doctrines of will to power and eternal return. Before proceeding to systematic questions some preliminary comments are needed on this choice. It is well known that Heidegger attributes great importance to the posthumously published fragments from Nietzsche's late period, particularly those appearing in *The Will to Power*: in Heidegger's view these contain Nietzsche's 'philosophy proper', while the published works are mere 'foreground'.[12] He supports this by reference to Nietzsche's repeatedly stated intention, in the years beginning with the composition of *Thus Spoke Zarathustra*, to write a 'philosophy' which would bring order and unity to his earlier thought, and provide it with proper foundations. Since will to power and eternal return are frequently recurring motifs in the notebooks of this period, appearing as headings and subheadings of the projected philosophical work, Heidegger feels justified in focusing on them. Now, while attention to Nietzsche's *Nachlaß* is of course not objectionable in itself, the priority Heidegger gives to this calls for some misgivings. Nietzsche's practice was to write voluminously, but often only experimentally, in his notebooks, then to sift this material and rework it for publication. In his late published books (and in those prepared for publication), many of the ideas from the notebooks play a comparatively minor role, e.g. will to power is mentioned quite rarely, while the early Dionysian motif continues to figure prominently.[13] *The Will to Power*, compiled and published after Nietzsche's death by his sister Elizabeth and Peter Gast, provides scenes from his literary workshop over a period of years, with the individual fragments (some of which were retrieved from waste-paper baskets and from the bottom of cupboards in the hotel rooms Nietzsche had occupied) ordered according to the editors' own assumptions about what the author intended. Around 1886 Nietzsche did develop plans for writing a 'book' called 'The Will to Power', which would be his 'main work'. He announces at the end of *The Genealogy of Morals* that he is preparing such a work. But this 'preparation', when seen in the context of Nietzsche entire *Nachlaß* of the period, is confined to tentative jottings with no attempt at systematization.[14]

Nietzsche apparently had great hopes for both will to power and eternal return which never materialized. Lou Salomé reports that at one stage he intended to undertake extensive research in the natural sciences to verify these principles.[15] Many fragments of *The Will to Power* show that, at least for a time, Nietzsche was interested in the possible 'explanatory' function of these principles for natural physical phenomena.[16] Yet if will to power and eternal return are meant as quasi-scientific hypotheses, or even as metaphysical hypotheses about 'everything', they remain at an extremely crude level of development, incomparably inferior to Schopenhauer's metaphysic of nature in Book Two of *The World as Will and Representation*. In many of their formulations, will to power and eternal return constitute more an embarrassment than anything else: they cannot be ignored, but their pretentions are out of all proportion to their ill-defined contours. Under such circumstances, Heidegger's identification of just these ideas as the 'essence' of Nietzsche's thought is puzzling: can it be that Heidegger is over eager to fit Nietzsche into his definition of metaphysics? In the 1937 lecture course on Nietzsche, Heidegger, apparently responding to students' queries about his neglect of Dionysus, says that:

> *What* the words *Dionysus* and *Dionysian* mean to Nietzsche will be heard and understood only if the 'eternal return of the same' is thought.…The mythic name *Dionysus* will become an epithet that has been *thought through* in the sense intended by Nietzsche the thinker only when we try to think the *coherence* of will to power' and 'eternal return of the same'.[17]

The question is, however, whether will to power and eternal return are really, as Heidegger supposes, clearer and more satisfactory conceptions that Dionysian affirmation. In respect of eternal return, I have already suggested (Chapter Three) that this is not the case. I shall now pursue this same question in respect of will to power. How does Heidegger understand this Nietzschean idea?

Early on in the 1936/37 lectures on Nietzsche, Heidegger announces the thesis: 'The expression "will to power" designates the basic character of beings; any being which is, insofar as it is, is will to power. The expression stipulates the character that beings have as beings.'[18] This makes will to power a metaphysical (onto-theological) doctrine in Heidegger's terms, for it comprehends everything (all 'beings') under a single principle. As an ontological principle, will to power cannot be explained in terms of psychological willing; rather, all psychological phenomena must be explained through will to power.[19] Although Nietzsche does refer to will as an 'affect', a 'passion', a 'feeling' and a 'command', Heidegger insists that all these terms must be understood ontologically.[20] The same point applies to power: will to power is not a psychological willing which happens to be directed to power rather than to happiness, pleasure or some other end, but power belongs to the essence of will itself.[21] Nietzsche's psychological examples are helpful only insofar as they indicate the essential (ontological) structure of will, which Heidegger specifies thus: 'Willing always brings the self to itself (*ein Sich-zu-sich-selbst bringen*); it thereby finds itself out beyond itself (*Über-sich-hinweg*). It maintains itself within the thrust away from one thing toward something else.'[22] This means that 'will is in itself simultaneously creative and destructive. Being master out beyond oneself (*das Über-sich-hinaus-Herrsein*) is always also annihilation. All the designated moments of will – the out beyond itself, enhancement, the character of command, creation, self-assertion – speak clearly enough for us to know that will in itself is already will to power.'[23] Drawing from Book Three, Part IV, of *The Will to Power*, Heidegger goes on to consider 'the will to power as art'. Art is the highest expression of will to power because it is creative-destructive in the indicated sense. Nietzsche's basic (though inadequately articulated) idea is that:

Art, thought in the broadest sense as the creative, constitutes the basic character of beings. Accordingly, art in the narrower sense is that activity in which

creation emerges for itself and becomes most per-
spicuous; it is not merely one configuration of will to
power among others but the *supreme* configuration'.[24]

To this conception of art as the genuine *metaphysical* activity
of man, Nietzsche opposes the Platonic valuation of truth.
Nietzsche's statement that 'art is worth more than truth'
means, on Heidegger's reading, that:

> Art, as "sensuous", is more in being (*ist seiender*) than
> the supersensuous. Granted that supersensuous being
> served heretofore as what is highest, if art is more in
> being, then it proves to be the being most in being (*das
> Seiendste im Seienden*), the basic occurrence within
> beings as a whole.'[25]

Heidegger acknowledges that these ideas remain
'unthought' within Nietzsche's own texts. But in his
opinion they can be extracted from a close reading of the
Nachlaß fragments: the fundamental tendency of
Nietzsche's philosophy, only obscurely grasped by the
thinker himself, can be recognized. A crucial statement
which Heidegger relies on in this respect occurs in the well-
known section 617 of *The Will to Power*: 'To impose upon
Becoming the character of Being – that is the supreme will
to power (*Dem Werden den Charakter des Seins aufzuprägen –
das ist der höchste Wille zur Macht*).'[26] In the 1937 lectures,
Heidegger comments as follows:

> The sense is not that one must brush aside and replace
> Becoming as the impermanent – for impermanence is
> what Becoming implies – with beings (*das Seiende*) as
> the permanent. The sense is that one must shape
> Becoming as beings (*zum Seienden*) in such a way that
> *as something becoming* (*als Werdendes*) it is preserved, has
> subsistence, in a word, *is*. Such stamping, that is, the
> recoining of Becoming as beings (*zum Seienden*), is the

supreme will to power. In such recoining the will to power comes to prevail most purely in its essence.[27]

Nietzsche is revealed as a 'metaphysician' because he sees will to power as the principle of all 'beings' whatsoever, more precisely (in its 'supreme' expression) as giving Becoming the character of 'beings'. Heidegger makes the same point in regard to Nietzsche's further statement (in the same section of *The Will to Power*): 'that everything (*alles*) recurs is the closest approximation of a world of Becoming to a world of Being (*extremste Annäherung einer Welt des Werdens an die des Seins*).'[28] Now up to a point Heidegger's interpretation here does indeed accord with my own earlier findings in respect of the eternal return: as will be recalled, I argued that with this latter doctrine Nietzsche falls back into an ontology of 'things' (i.e. 'beings'). However, the difference is that Heidegger rushes to judgement on Nietzsche's philosophy as a whole. While I took the view that eternal return is an experimental (and overestimated) solution to the problem of Dionysian affirmation, Heidegger has no hestitation in elevating both eternal return and will to power to the status of metaphysical principles, and in identifying them without further ado as the essence of Nietzsche's thought.

Other passages from Nietzsche's *Nachlaß* could easily bring Heidegger's general thesis into question. Even a close scrutiny of the quoted statements from *The Will to Power* no. 617 is sufficient to cast doubts. For Nietzsche does not literally say what Heidegger paraphrases him as saying, i.e. that will to power shapes Becoming as 'beings' (*Seienden*); what he says is that will to power shapes Becoming as 'Being' (*Sein*). Since Heidegger's whole argument depends on the 'ontological difference' between Being and beings, it is somewhat surprising that he passes over Nietzsche's terminology with such apparent indifference. He simply assumes that Nietzsche never means anything by 'Being' except 'beings'. But we have seen that Nietzsche equivocates on 'Being' quite regularly, as if he thinks that a 'non-metaphysical' (i.e. non-Platonic) concept of Being would be equivalent to his own (Heraclitean) concept of Becoming. With respect to 'beings', on the other hand, Nietzsche is entirely consistent from his earliest writings to his last: it is the thing-ification of Becoming which is the original sin of abstract (metaphysical) thought. For example, we read in another passage from *The Will to Power* that 'one must admit nothing which is a being (*man darf nichts Seiendes überhaupt zulassen*) – because then Becoming would lose its value and actually appear meaningless and super-fluous...one realizes that this hypothesis of beings (*Hypothese des Seienden*) is the source of all world-defamation'. This seems to mean approximately the opposite of what Heidegger, by equating 'Being' with 'beings', takes the statement from no. 617 to mean, and makes it difficult to maintain, as Heidegger does, that Nietzsche's philosophy is all about 'beings as a whole' (*das Seiende im Ganzen*).[29]

But there is a further problem of principle for Heidegger's account. For it is not at all clear why 'shaping Becoming as beings' should be the 'supreme' will to power, i.e. should be that which occurs in Dionysian affirmation or 'artistic-metaphysical' activity. On the contrary, this is what routinely happens in 'sub-Dionysian' life preservation, i.e. in scientific knowledge and every kind of instrumental activity. Heidegger does say that 'supreme' will to power does not 'brush aside and replace Becoming as the impermanent' but rather 'preserves' Becoming 'as something becoming'. But what can this mean except that – contrary to Heidegger's thesis – Becoming gets preserved as Being? On the other hand, if we drop Heidegger's condition that will to power is the principle of 'beings', and take seriously the word which Nietzsche actually uses, namely 'Being', the statement from no. 617 is readily comprehensible: to 'impose upon Becoming the character of Being' means that Becoming is affirmed as the Absolute, i.e. as the supreme repository of value. What Nietzsche is saying in this late fragment would then not be essentially different from what he says of Heraclitus in *Philosophy in the Tragic Age of the Greeks*:

> Eternal and exclusive Becoming, the impermanence of everything actual, which constantly comes to be and never is, as Heraclitus teaches it, is a terrible paralyzing thought....It takes astonishing strength to transform this reaction into its opposite, into sublimity and the feeling of blessed astonishment.[30]

As earlier indicated, there is a tendency in Nietzsche (particularly in the *Nachlaß*) to consider will to power and eternal return as quasi-scientific hypotheses, thus as 'metaphysics' in Heidegger's sense (a 'theory of beings'). But this is only a tendency, a very tentative one at that, which is offset by the more characteristic and anti-metaphysical Dionysian motif. One does not take Nietzsche the thinker seriously by taking every one of his proclaimed 'theses' as of equal import, but one must look to the unity and organic development of his thought. Heidegger's 'Nietzsche as metaphysician' thesis does not observe this methodological maxim. It is a dogmatic thesis because it takes will to power and eternal return out of context, and appears to be governed by Heidegger's prejudice that no one before himself has risen to *Seinsdenken*. There is ample evidence that Heidegger's renewed study of Nietzsche in the 1930s (in connection with the project of a new edition of Nietzsche's works, never completed) was a decisive event for his own philosophical development.[31] Can it be that Heidegger came to feel swamped by Nietzsche, as if Nietzsche had 'already said' what Heidegger all along had wanted to say? Such a fear would not be justified – Heidegger is too original and resolute a thinker for that – but it might explain the 'Nietzsche as metaphysician' thesis as an artificial 'rearguard action', as an attempt by Heidegger to gain some distance from Nietzsche, and thus to secure the future direction of his own *Denkweg*.

From the beginning of the Second World War, Heidegger links the history of metaphysics more and more closely with the 'essence of technology'. In the 1940 lecture course on 'European Nihilism', will to power emerges as the most advanced formula of a subjectivism which would make 'man the measure of all things'. From the position of Heidegger's 'reversal', wherein Being must be thought out of itself rather than from the human being, will to power becomes the supreme expression of that challenging and commanding relation to the world which is the essence of metaphysical subjectivity:

> Nietzsche's doctrine, which makes everything that is, and as it is, into the 'property and product of man', merely carries out the final development of Descartes' doctrine, according to which truth is grounded on the self-certainty of the human subject. If we recall here that in Greek philosophy before Plato another thinker, namely Protagoras, was teaching that man was the measure of all things, it appears as if all metaphysics – not just modern metaphysics – is in fact built on the standard-giving role of man within beings as a whole.[32]

Heidegger takes will to power as the concealed essence of metaphysics from the beginning of its history. Coming to a new level of self-consciousness in the Cartesian principle of subjective certitude, it attains its final clarity only in Nietzsche's philosophy, where subjectivity is stripped of all inessential determinations to reveal itself as pure domination.[33] As Heidegger now sees it, the metaphysics of will to power proclaims that the being-ness of beings (i.e. what counts as 'reality') is determined only through the projects of human control, intervention and utilization.

This new turn to Heidegger's critique is influenced by the Nazi appropriation of Nietzsche in the 1930s, while reversing the Nazi's positive evaluation of the *Übermensch*.

But once again, although textual evidence for Heidegger's interpretation is not entirely lacking (the Nazis too could readily call upon it), when considered in the context of Nietzsche's total corpus it appears as a one-sided reading, determined above all by Heidegger's conception of the history of metaphysics. Will to power as technological overlordship does not do justice to Nietzsche's original (and continuing) Dionysian motif, and Heidegger's insistence that the latter must itself be understood from will to power cannot be justified from Nietzsche's texts. Nietzsche's primitive phenomenon of 'life' cannot plausibly be interpreted as a field of technical domination. There are many aspects of Nietzsche's thought, discussed by Heidegger in other contexts, which would rather indicate a non-metaphysical outlook, even within Heidegger's own terms. For example, Heidegger sees metaphysics as 'fixing and grasping' reality, whereas Nietzsche sees philosophy as 'wooing' an essentially ungraspable and elusive reality (life is a 'woman', as Nietzsche sometimes says). The reverence and thankfulness for life, upon which Nietzsche lays so much stress, do not seem consistent with the stance of domination. Stillness, silence and solitude also seem at odds with a metaphysics of subjectivity. The list of such anomalies could be extended.

It is true that will to power, and Nietzschean 'affirmation' more generally, often seem to involve an irreverent kind of 'self-assertion'. To assimilate this with technological subjectivity, however, is no more justified than to treat Heideggerian *Seinsverständnis* (which proceeds from human *Dasein*) in like manner. The crucial question concerns the 'object' of affirmation and, as already demonstrated, this is quite unlike the sphere of 'things' susceptible to instrumental control. No doubt the 'power' and 'strength' so lauded by Nazi ideologists would have seemed to Nietzsche as just one more example of the timidity of herd consciousness, oriented as it always is to tangible benefits, terrified as it always is by the unfathomable 'abyss' of 'life'. In respect of will to power as 'self-assertion', our earlier differentiation between herd self and essential self must be borne in mind. If will to power, considered as Dionysian affirmation, is a kind of self-deification, this applies to the self which is already divine and which asserts itself ever more resolutely as divine (i.e. progressively frees itself from the herd self). By contrast, the self which is on no account divine asserts itself by reference to non-divine reality (i.e. 'things') in a project which, when taken to the ultimate limits (as the Nazis attempted, but as our modern world continues to attempt, in less violent ways) founders on the fact of finitude. The difference between metaphysical subjectivity (as Heidegger understands it) and Nietzschean affirmation is that the former culminates in an act of self-destruction, the latter in an act (e.g. Zarathustra's 'Song of Yes and Amen') of self-redemption.

If Heidegger's thesis of Nietzsche as the 'last metaphysician' is thus revealed as untenable, this corroborates the critique of the postmodernist commentators only in a formal sense. What they object to is Heidegger's 'dogmatism' in attempting to 'centre' a body a thought which supposedly repudiates all universal values, universal projects and especially a universal concept of truth. However, if Nietzsche is not a 'metaphysician' in Heidegger's sense, this by no means implies that he abjures all philosophical 'centering'. The preceding chapters have shown that the question for Nietzsche is not whether there is an Absolute (or 'centre', if this word is preferred) but what kind of Absolute there is. Accordingly, Heidegger's 'last metaphysician' thesis is unacceptable not because it 'centres' Nietzsche's thought but because it does so in the wrong way: it attributes to Nietzsche an onto-theological conception of the Absolute when it is precisely this that Nietzsche attempts to overcome. Such is also Heidegger's project. What makes Heidegger's treatment of Nietzsche so puzzling is that Nietzsche's overcoming of metaphysics bears such deep resemblances to Heidegger's own. The sprawling two-volume *Nietzsche* brings many of these resemblances to light, but the 'Nietzsche as metaphysician' thesis covers them over again. It is necessary, therefore, to take a broader view of the two philosophers.

SACHE AND TRUTH IN NIETZSCHE AND HEIDEGGER

For a long time it has been a cliché in discussions of Nietzsche to say that he rejects the philosophical 'system'. Just what 'system' means in philosophy is rarely reflected upon. In the case of Nietzsche, the aphoristic and 'fragmentary' mode of presentation is frequently held up as the decisive matter, as indicating the 'de-centred' and 'undogmatic' nature of his thinking. Alexander Nehamas' view, typical of the postmodernist authors, is that 'Nietzsche's textual fragments are for him sentences that essentially lack a context, a whole to which they belong, and to which appeal is necessary if we are to interpret them.'[34] The traditional approach of ransacking Nietzsche's work for assertions, and then attempting to identify the centre of his philosophy, is rejected by the postmodernists in favour of a conception of Nietzschean 'fragmentary writing', explained by Ernst Behler as 'first of all, refusal of a system, passion for incompletion, and voyage of thought.'[35] Nietzsche's rejection of system is taken as tantamount to rejection of truth, in particular (under the influence of Jacques Derrida) as displacement of truth by 'style'.[36] The novelty of Nietzsche's method is understood as the affirmation of a stylistic pluralism and experimentalism which liberates discourse from dogmatism.

The postmodernists were not the first to notice that Nietzsche rejects the traditional academic treatise as a suitable medium for presenting his thoughts. Major studies by Karl Jaspers and Karl Löwith, both from the 1930s, pay special attention to Nietzsche's style and investigate its significance for his concept of philosophy. Löwith maintains that a 'system in aphorisms' can be found in

Nietzsche.[37] Jaspers advocates searching out Nietzsche for his contradictions, and never being satisfied with an X till one has discovered the corresponding not-X, a technique similarly oriented to a unitary understanding of his writings.[38] What is specific to the postmodernist commentators is not their concern with Nietzsche's style as such, but their perspectivist rejection of any unitary *Sache* underlying this style, their haste to equate Nietzsche's plurality of styles with a plurality of truths. Thus Nehamas writes that:

> We must thoroughly reject the view that Nietzsche's many styles reflect his effort to find a single 'adequate means of expression'....Far from being directed toward getting to 'the things themselves', the very idea of which Nietzsche radically repudiates, his many modes of writing are directly connected with his view that 'facts are precisely what there is not, only interpretations'.[39]

Now it is correct that Nietzsche believes neither in 'facts' (as basic states of affairs which can be accurately described) nor in a final 'adequate means of expression', but this does not at all imply disbelief in 'the things themselves' as the *Sache* of thought, i.e. as the source of the 'great problems and question marks' which occupy the philosopher. Heidegger puts the matter in the following terms:

> Those who posit the uppermost values, the creators, the new philosophers at the forefront, must according to Nietzsche be experimenters; they must tread paths and break trails in the knowledge that they do not have *the* truth. But from such knowledge it does not at all follow that they have to view their concepts as mere playing chips (*Spielmarken*) that can be exchanged at any time for any currency. What does follow is just the opposite: the solidity and binding quality of thought must undergo a grounding in the

things themselves (*die Härte und Verbindlichkeit des Denkens muß eine Gründung in den Sachen selbst erfahren*) in a way that prior philosophy does not know.[40]

The difference between Nietzsche and Heidegger on the one hand, and the postmodernists on the other, can be clearly read from this statement: although there is agreement on both sides that philosophy must be experimental and can never 'have the truth', the postmodernists do not believe in the 'solidity and binding quality of thought', nor in *die Sache selbst*. In the end, this is the difference between philosophy and sophistry: the ideas of 'fragmentary writing' and of 'stylistic pluralism' (however innocuous in themselves) in fact function to discredit the rigour of truth: what one writes becomes 'justified' when one 'gets away with it', when one 'gets read'.

For Heidegger, 'because in philosophical thought there rules the highest possible rigour, all great thinkers think the Same. This Same, however, is so essential and so rich that a single thinker never exhausts it.'[41] What is this Same? Heidegger calls it 'Being'. Nietzsche's preferred expressions are 'life', 'world', 'earth' etc. From this difference in terminology, it cannot be assumed that Nietzsche and Heidegger are talking about different things.[42] Neither believes that the *Sache* of philosophical thought can be 'signified' to ensure the kind of intersubjective negotiability required for theoretical discourse. Both consider that the *Sache* must first of all be 'seen', and only then will the thinker realize the essential inadequacy of all verbal representations, indispensable as they are.[43] This is what Nietzsche is getting at with his emphasis on the 'intuitive' nature of philosophical thought, and it is what Heidegger intends with his 'phenomenological' method. In *The Genealogy of Morals*, Nietzsche writes:

Whoever thinks in *words* thinks as an orator and not as a thinker – it shows that fundamentally he does not think facts, nor factually, but only in relation to facts (*daß er im Grunde nicht Sachen, nicht sachlich denkt, sondern nur in Hinsicht auf Sachen*), that he is really thinking of *himself* and his listeners.[44]

Similarly, although Heidegger is well known for his statement that 'language is the house of Being', he does not mean language as written or spoken words, nor that Being is in any sense a linguistic phenomenon. On the contrary, he considers that the *Sache* of philosophy is 'genuinely preserved' only in an 'active silence' (*Erschweigen*). As he puts it at the end of his 1937 Nietzsche lectures:

> Wherever that sphere is not incessantly called by name, called aloud, wherever it is held silently in the most interior questioning, it is thought most purely and profoundly. For what is held in silence is genuinely preserved; as preserved it is most intimate and actual....Supremely thoughtful utterance does not consist simply in growing taciturn when it is a matter of saying what is properly to be said; it consists in saying the matter in such a way that it is named in non-saying. The utterance of thinking is an active silence. Such utterance corresponds to the most profound essence of language, which has its origins in silence.[45]

It is true that, for both Nietzsche and Heidegger, the 'event' of philosophical understanding can occur in language, but only on condition that the *Sache* is already comprehended prior to verbalization. This 'event' is not the original acquisition of knowledge, nor is it the consolidation of pre-theoretical knowledge in 'determinate conceptual form', but is much more what Plato alludes to in the *Phaedrus* and the *Seventh Letter*, the 'remembrance' of what is already known, the 'bringing to mind' of that which must always exceed and elude conceptual-linguistic determinations.[46] The objections brought by Derrida and other postmodernists to Heidegger's alleged espousal of a 'master name' ('Being', but for consistency Nietzsche should be charged with the same thing in respect of 'life') are thus misplaced, for they reduce language to its significatory or naming function. In essence, Derrida's whole argument against Heidegger begs the question on the 'ontological difference' between Being and beings: since for Heidegger it is only beings which can be signified, objections to the 'privilege' of Being (its 'master' status), based on considerations about practices of signification in the realm of beings, just miss the point.[47]

As for the mode of 'given-ness' of the *Sache*, there is a close structural parallel between Nietzsche and Heidegger. In Nietzsche's view, life can be appropriated only through a process of radical individualization (the attainment of philosophical solitude), while for Heidegger, especially in *Being and Time*, Being can only be understood through the 'existence' (*Existenz*) of the human being (*Dasein*). Heidegger's conception of the 'mineness' (*Jemeinigkeit*) of existence has the same meaning as Nietzschean solitude: the most 'absolute' reality is also the most 'personal'.[48] Even after Heidegger's so-called 'reversal', this remains the case: although Being is now to be thought out of Being itself, human existence is still the privileged 'site' of Being's self-revealing. The difference between this and perspectivism is indicated in Heidegger's 1937 lectures, when he takes up the problem of Nietzsche's 'standpoint'. Quoting from aphorism 374 of *The Gay Science* (also much referred to in postmodernist commentary) where Nietzsche says that 'we cannot see around our own corner', Heidegger writes:

We are thinking of this fundamental relation in the decisive disposition of human beings in general when we say that the Being of human being – and, as far as we know, of human being alone – is grounded in *Dasein*: the *Da* is the sole possible site for the necessary location of its Being at any time. From this essential

connection we also derive the insight that humanization becomes less destructive of truth as human beings
relate themselves more originally to the location of
their essential corner, that is to say, as they recognize
and ground *Da-sein* as such. Yet the essentiality of the
corner is defined by the originality and the breadth in
which Being as a whole is experienced and grasped –
with a view to its sole decisive aspect, that of Being.[49]

The *Da* of *Dasein*, as the 'essential corner' from which
philosophical thinking takes place, is not what the
postmodernists would call a perspective.[50] It is the unique
site of philosophical thought because only here do human
beings understand themselves as 'who' they are, only here
do they understand themselves out of Being (Heidegger) or
out of life (Nietzsche). This is possible only through
holding at a distance all definitions of self which are
determined by what Heidegger calls '*Das Man*' (the anonymous 'One') and what Nietzsche calls 'the herd'.

Heidegger thinks of his own philosophy as a new kind of
(non–onto–theological) ontology. Can Nietzsche be seen in
the same way? In *The Gay Science*, we read:

As we thus reject the Christian interpretation and
condemn its 'meaning' like counterfeit, *Schopenhauer's*
question immediately comes to us in a terrifying way:
Has existence any meaning at all? It will require a few
centuries before this question can even be heard
completely and in its full depth. What Schopenhauer
himself said in answer to this question was – forgive
me – hasty, youthful, only a compromise....But he
posed the question.[51]

Nietzsche's question, the *Sache* of Nietzsche's philosophical thought, is 'the meaning of existence'. This is a question
which Schopenhauer asks before him and Heidegger asks
after him. It is an ontological question because it does not

ask about any particular form of existence, i.e. not about any contingent social role or perspective on existence, but about existence as such, the bare phenomenon of existence.[52] The basic concepts of Nietzsche's philosophy – the Dionysian, life, world, eternal return, and will to power – are ontological concepts which attempt to think Being as Becoming. As argued earlier, however, Nietzsche has difficulties in this area: when he attempts to resolve his particular existential analyses into ontological formulas, he is unable to overcome the metaphysical conceptions implicit in his favoured 'this-world/other-world' distinction. Being (as Becoming) gets interpreted as a sphere of 'beings' and states-of-affairs, so that philosophical 'life affirmation' cannot be ontologically distinguished from mundane, pre-philosophical activity, nor can the 'detachment' of the philosopher be accounted for. Heidegger's conception of the 'ontological difference', which defines Being in a strictly transcendental manner, allows him to break more radically from metaphysics: Being is transcendent not because it is 'another world', but because it is not a 'being' of any kind. The great difficulty of Heidegger's philosophy, and the stumbling block which it represents for all traditional ontology, is that Being is irreducible to 'things', thus possessing no determinate 'content'. Being is the original 'giving' (*'es gibt Sein'* as Heidegger says) of the openness in which beings can be. It is an 'event' (*Ereignis*) which is ontologically prior to all thingly manifestations and occurrences.[53] In *Being and Time*, Heidegger attempts to show in detail how this elusive 'phenomenon' of Being is the prime determinant for human self and world understanding. To be human is first of all to know that one exists, to understand the difference, therefore, between existence and non-existence. Such understanding can never be obtained from 'things' themselves because, as Kant already knew (though failing to draw the necessary conclusions), existence is not a 'predicate' of any kind.[54] Only to the extent that human beings transcend from the thing world (the world of *Vorhandensein*, presence-at-hand) to Being are they able to distinguish themselves from animals, only thus do they understand their own existence as 'being-towards-death' rather than as an enduring 'presence' which is 'terminated' by death.[55]

It was noted earlier that Nietzschean life affirmation is a stance of 'thankfulness' (*Dankbarkeit*). The primordial 'giving' for which the Dionysian philosopher is thankful is not some particular thing, nor even the totality of things, but the 'event' of life itself. To be sure, not everything which Nietzsche says about 'life' can in this way be assimilated to Heidegger's Being. Particularly in connection with will to power, Nietzsche sometimes falls back into what Heidegger would call an 'ontic' level of analysis, wherein some kind of quasi-scientific theory of beings is seemingly in question. But the main tendency of Nietzsche's thought, which takes life as an essentially unfathomable and indeterminable mystery, is not in this direction. Thankfulness for life, understood as the 'piety' of the Dionysian 'dancing' philosopher, is not directed towards reality under such-and-such descriptions, but to a phenomenon which is prior to any descriptive content.[56] Rather than propounding a theory of this phenomenon, the Dionysian philosopher testifies to it: this is his spontaneous sense of gratitude, his fundamental 'taste' for a reverential relation to life. Heidegger means the same thing when he says that 'thinking is thanking', and that philosophical questioning is 'the piety of thought' (*die Frömmigkeit des Denkens*).[57] Philosophical thinking is directed to '*das Frag-würdige*' in a double sense, i.e. to that which is most 'worthy of thought' but which at the same time is most 'doubtful' and 'questionable'. It is this dual nature of *das Frag-würdige* which constitutes the necessary risk of philosophical activity.

The postmodernists seem to fear that too close an association between Nietzsche and Heidegger would subvert the 'literary' quality of Nietzsche's works. True enough, the Heideggerian idea of *Sache* does indeed relativize the importance of any particular literary style, however brilliant it may be. Nietzsche himself has a fine sense for detecting mere brilliance in a writer, and always expresses profound contempt for the 'men of letters' who, lacking all relation to the 'great problems and question marks', stand for everything which is artificial and mere semblance in the realm of the spirit. On the other hand, if Nietzsche's thought is governed by the same *Sache* as that of Heidegger, this does not mean that Nietzsche's style is irrelevant, nor that he would have to be reproached for speaking in his own language rather than in Heidegger's. For both thinkers, philosophical discourse is the most extreme possibility of language: it is the self-transcendence of language wherein its ontic function is superseded by the power of ontological recognition. There are no rules which govern this and which could specify in advance what form of language is adequate. Heidegger does not insist that the *Sache* can only be articulated through the word 'Being' or through any kind of limited technical vocabulary. He stresses that the point of his writings is not to develop a 'Heideggerian philosophy' but just to think the *Sache* itself, something which can also be done along other 'thought paths' (*Denkwege*) within the same *Sache*. Nietzsche takes an identical attitude. Acutely conscious of the questionability of language, acutely aware of the dangers inherent in any rigidification or standardization of philosophical discourse, Nietzsche experiments with different styles. Always, however, just 'one thing' is at stake.

It cannot be sufficiently emphasized that, for both Nietzsche and Heidegger, the *Sache* of philosophy is a phenomenon and not at all a 'theoretical posit'. That the *Sache* thus 'shows itself', that man lives within the 'self-revealing' of this *Sache*, is nothing else but its 'truth'. This conception of truth is explicitly enunciated only by Heidegger (the 'truth of Being'), but is implicit in Nietzsche as well (Dionysian truth). It is a non-epistemological and non-linguistic conception which has nothing to do with the adequacy or decidability of discourses.[58] Before any discourse arises, before any theoretical judgements can be made concerning beings of whatever kind, these beings must first be brought into view, they must first be brought out into the 'openness' (even if as 'theoretical posits') of the 'event' of Being's (or life's, in Nietzsche's case) self-revealing. Nietzsche and Heidegger both acknowledge that 'truth' also has a second-order meaning, pertaining to propositions, assertions, conventions and 'perspectives'. But truth in the fundamental philosophical sense is, for both thinkers, the truth of the *Sache* itself. The philosopher does not 'propound' the truth but 'exists in the truth': this means that he is open to the openness of the *Sache*.

Because this kind of truth is not bound by the rules of discursive thought (particularly not by the structure of the assertion) neither does it obey the law of non-contradiction. The *Sache's* self-revealing is at the same time a self-concealing, while openness to the *Sache* can take the deficient form of a 'turning away'. In *Being and Time*, Heidegger expresses this by saying that '*Dasein* is equiprimordially both in the truth and in the untruth', while Nietzsche, in *Human, All Too Human*, remarks that 'the whole of human life is sunk deeply in untruth.'[59] It does not follow, just because the *Sache* (Being, life) is a phenomenon, that it is unproblematically available to every 'observer'. Precisely because this phenomenon is no kind of 'thing', precisely because it cannot be made present-to-hand for theory or ready-to-hand for practical utilization, it is by no means accessible through 'observation' but only through existential reorientation (with all the difficulties this implies). Nietzsche and Heidegger both consider that a tendency to 'fall away' from truth is an ontological structure of human existence, but also that this testifies to a certain consciousness of the *Sache* rather than to the sheer obliviousness of animals and other non-human entities.[60] Nietzsche's spiritual plebs are weak not because they are completely non-cognizant of the *Sache* but because they seek to avoid it: they turn away from life out of cowardice before this phenomenon, and because they do not enter into it (i.e. do not take up the Dionysian stance) they do not come to 'know' it more profoundly. In similar vein, Heidegger speaks in *Being and Time* of the anxious falling from Being into the familiar world of beings as a 'fleeing' from the perceived 'uncanniness' (*Unheimlichkeit*) of Being.[61]

The philosophies of Nietzsche and Heidegger will always be found deficient on epistemological criteria. How, it will be asked, do they know what they claim to know? What in any case do they claim to know? Is not their 'knowing' in the last resort mere 'speculation'? Are not their writings in the last resort mere 'literature'? These questions can only be asked by those who do not have the phenomenon of Being/life in view. This phenomenon can be encountered, and indeed must be encountered before any theorization or practice takes place. The question is not whether one cognitively 'admits' it, but what 'attitude' or 'stance' one takes towards it. It is a question of 'attitude' because the phenomenon 'gives itself' not as a theoretical but as an existential challenge: it says 'know me' only in the sense of 'enter into me'. Human existence is philosophically 'truthful' when it is *sachgemäß*, i.e. fitting and proper in respect of the *Sache*. By the same token, when one says that, because this *Sache* cannot be captured within the confines of rational cognition, its 'reality' cannot be admitted, one is making an existential decision. The same applies to those postmodernists who, wary of epistemological 'closures', might prefer to say that the purported *Sache* is 'uninteresting'. This would be like saying that the existence of God is an 'uninteresting' hypothesis. Judged by their actual lives, even many 'believers' find the existence of God relatively 'uninteresting': does this say more about God or about themselves and their 'interests'?

The bulk of Heidegger's writings consists of a detailed examination of the ontological problematics of Western philosophy. He attempts to trace the career of onto-theology and to analyse the specific modes of metaphysical *Seinsvergessenheit* since Plato and Aristotle. Nietzsche, on the other hand, does not possess the historical erudition, nor indeed the inclination, for such an analytical task. As observed in connection with his treatment of the Presocratics, Nietzsche is a very subjective thinker, who reads the great philosophers (to the extent that he reads them at all) only to confirm his own basic intuitions. It is significant that Heidegger, with all his historical and analytical fastidiousness, nevertheless takes Nietzsche as the most important philosopher of modern times. The reason lies in Nietzsche's phenomenological method: his very naivety is what allows him to focus on the *Sache* itself and to philosophize out of it. For Heidegger, this is exactly what is called for at the end of metaphysics, where the ontological preconceptions of more than two thousand years are no longer capable of guiding philosophical thinking. Although Nietzsche's grasp of the contours of traditional ontology is faulty, although his own endeavours to articulate new ontological formulas are inadequate, his faithfulness to the *Sache* makes his thought ontological in a more profound sense. Nietzsche's writings (as well as his life) exhibit rather than analyse the situation of the truthful individual in an age where the guarantees of metaphysics are no longer available. In this sense Nietzsche's philosophy is complementary, even a corrective, to Heidegger's emphasis on more overarching ontological structures. Nietzsche recognizes that the problem of truth is first and foremost a problem for the individual and not for 'history', 'society' or 'the epoch'. Heidegger is also aware of this, but his fear of 'subjectivism' (especially in his later writings) leads him in the direction of a 'history of Being' in which the centrality of the individual often seems compromised, i.e. wherein the problem of truth seems more like a problem for Being itself than a problem for man.

The common statement that Nietzsche and Heidegger are 'post-metaphysical' philosophers harbours an ambiguity which is often overlooked. It is true that both philosophers have to come to terms with modern nihilism and the exhaustion of the metaphysical tradition. They respond to the spiritual situation of the present age and not, for example, to the spiritual situation of medieval Christianity. But this fact (a truism really, however much it is taken as a revelation in some quarters) does not mean that the underlying *Sache* of their thought is peculiarly modern. The 'great problems and question marks' which occupy Nietzsche and Heidegger do not have their origin in any particular historical epoch, but in a phenomenon which remains the same throughout all epochs.[62] For both thinkers, historical consciousness is necessary in order to get back to the *Sache*, in order to recognize the same *Sache* underneath its many historical guises and to avoid the pitfalls of historically relative perspectives. In this sense Nietzsche and Heidegger affirm philosophy as an eternal possibility for man, indeed as an eternal necessity (a command of conscience) if man is to be what he authentically is.[63] Both consider that philosophy as it has hitherto been practised is no longer viable. But when one looks closely, this 'as it has hitherto been practised' is not so monolithic as it first appears. Despite their sweeping critiques of the tradition, Nietzsche and Heidegger are prepared to acknowledge isolated figures of what could be called a counter-tradition. It is arguable that they could, and should, have been more open on this score, and that the impression of novelty hinders more than it aids in the comprehension of their thought. Novelty is a time-bound concept which pertains to the trends and fashions of thought rather than to the *Sache*: only when the latter is obscured do these trends become the main focus of interest. Heidegger often points out that philosophy, unlike the sciences, does not make 'progress'. This is because philosophy can never be reduced to a reified body

of theory, but exists as an activity, as a particular individual's involvement with the *Sache*: progress is meaningful
only in respect of the individual philosopher, as the *Sache* is
entered into ever more profoundly and steadfastly.
Nietzsche would not disagree: for him, the philosopher's
progress is nothing else but his own solitary pilgrimage.

In an age obsessed by novelty, in a garrulous age in which
opinions, information, so-called communication, points
of view, theories and perspectives are accorded extraordinary importance, it is difficult to understand the simplicity
of what Nietzsche and Heidegger want in their philosophies. It is difficult to accept that all they want, as
philosophers, is to bring a certain phenomenon into view.
In this context, however, simplicity cannot be equated with
ease of access: the simple is also what is most 'hidden'. It is
hidden, not just because of the encrustations of metaphysical conceptuality, but because of its own very nature and
the nature of human beings. The writings of Nietzsche and
Heidegger are complex, but not because their *Sache* is
complex. Rather, the way to the *Sache* is complex, because
it is a way through the complexities of human world and
self understanding. Nietzsche says in his early lectures on
the Presocratics that the Heraclitean One 'cannot appear in
any other way' than through the flux of Becoming.[64] It
similarly holds that Nietzschean life and Heideggerian
Being, simple as they are, 'cannot appear in any other way'
than through the complex phenomena of human existence.
The idea of *Sache*, therefore, is no kind of reductionism or
'closure'. On the contrary, it is precisely the *Sache* which
opens up the phenomena in their complexity, which is the
source of this complexity and its condition of existence.

REDEMPTION AND NOTHINGNESS
Nietzsche's post-metaphysical thinking aims not at the
dissolution of philosophy but at its reconstitution, through
new conceptions of the Absolute and of philosophical
truth. Fundamental to this project is a new way of thinking

of the subjective value of truth. Nietzsche finds the realities defined by metaphysics subjectively unsatisfying because they relate to the abstracted knowing subject rather than to the existing human being. In his view, metaphysics has determined the basic character of Western culture by defining the nature of reality in terms of a truncated intellectual (Socratic) subjectivity oriented to things and objective states-of-affairs. Within this framework, the question 'why do we want truth?' finds an answer only at the intellectual level: we want truth simply because we want to know, because we have come to think of ourselves as in essence 'knowers'.[65] As long as philosophy moves within an unproblematized metaphysical self understanding, this answer will seem entirely obvious and adequate, while Nietzsche's queries, if they are not dismissed as idiosyncratic, will be interpreted in epistemological terms. At the same time, notwithstanding the deep-rootedness of metaphysical presuppositions, despite the integration of these within so-called 'common sense', the phenomena of life and of the human self are never altogether obscured. As absolute realities, life and self make absolute demands. This is why philosophy comes into being.

For Nietzsche, the absolute truth sought by philosophy must be absolutely satisfying at the subjective level. This subjective satisfaction is that of redemption: through the appropriate stance towards the phenomenon of life, human beings become who and what they are. Heidegger, with his *Seinsfrage*, wants the same kind of truth. Like Nietzsche, Heidegger considers that human beings are proximally what they are not, that for the most part they confuse their own 'is-ness' with the objective 'presence' of things. Although Heidegger does not use the term redemption, the 'truth of Being' has the redemptive function of liberating the human being into his own essence, into an essence which, because it is no kind of thing, does not suffer from the thingly preoccupations of the false self. In fact, the *Gelassenheit* ('releasement') of which Heidegger

speaks in his later period has strong resemblances to
Schopenhauerian as well as to Nietzschean redemption: as
Hannah Arendt says, it is a kind of 'will not to will', a will
which releases itself from beings so as to allow Being to
show itself.[66] Like Nietzsche's Dionysian truth, the
Heideggerian truth of Being involves an unburdening
from that which normally counts as reality, but not as an
escape, not as a flight from the hardships and difficulties of
life. On the contrary, for both Nietzsche and Heidegger, it
is precisely the ordinary man, the non-philosopher, who
takes it easy in life by clinging to and remaining secure in
the thing-world, who refuses to risk his fragile pseudo-self
by opening up to an Absolute which reduces his egoistic
claims to nought.

Does this mean that Nietzsche and Heidegger are 'religious' thinkers? This question is overhasty as long as the
meaning of 'religion', 'God' and related concepts is not
subjected to the kind of radical reconsideration both
thinkers make of the metaphysical tradition. Nietzsche and
Heidegger employ religious vocabulary and draw inspiration from religious sources, but hold all mainstream
religious movements at arm's length. They both consider
that the God of orthodox Christianity is a metaphysical
God, i.e. a supreme 'being', which as such is the very
antithesis of what is sought in Dionysian affirmation and
Seinsdenken. The same kind of interest in the mystical
dimension of religion which I have identified in Nietzsche
is also to be found in Heidegger, with the same kind of
ambivalence and unwillingness to make a decision. This
attitude does not point to a deficiency in their thinking, but
reflects the circumstance that, at the end of metaphysics,
the problem of religion is reopened.[67] The common and
complacent dismissal of stereotypical conceptions of 'religion' and 'God' is no more acceptable to Nietzsche and
Heidegger than is the vulgar Church conformism bereft of
an intellectual conscience. To call the thought of Nietzsche
and Heidegger either religious or non-religious reveals

nothing about their *Sache*. In respect of particular figures and tendencies both within and without the traditions conventionally called religious, the only question is whether they think the same *Sache* as Nietzsche and Heidegger, and this cannot be determined by the presence or absence of a certain restricted vocabulary. As both conceive it, the task of thought is no more to pass a judgement on the 'theologies' of Aquinas, Eckhart and Luther than it is to pass a judgement on the 'philosophies' of Plato, Kant and Hegel. It may be expected that, just as Heidegger is enabled to enter into the *Sache* through the interpretation of metaphysical philosophers such as those just mentioned, the same would be possible through the interpretation of theologians. That Heidegger does not pursue this possibility (at least not on anything like the same scale as his interpretations of the metaphysical tradition) does not justify the conclusion that he 'rejects theology'.[68] The same can be said of Nietzsche who, while dismissing the conceptually articulated theologies of Christianity, relies heavily in his writings on a religious 'pathos'.[69]

It was previously noticed that Nietzsche's philosophy of affirmation has a peculiarly negative character which, when superficially understood, might justify the relativistic interpretations of the postmodernist commentators. Such relativism insinuates itself all the more to the degree that Nietzsche's religious pathos is ignored or regarded as a stylistic device, for it is precisely this pathos which is attuned to an Absolute which cannot be encapsulated in words and concepts. Notwithstanding his 'Nietzsche as metaphysician' thesis, Heidegger recognizes this 'negative absolutism' of Nietzsche's standpoint:

> Thus the world as a whole becomes something we fundamentally cannot address, something ineffable – an *arreton*. What Nietzsche is practicing here with regard to the world totality is a kind of 'negative theology', which tries to grasp the Absolute as purely

as possible by holding at a distance all 'relative' determinations, that is, all those that relate to human beings. Except that Nietzsche's determination of the world is a negative theology without the Christian God. [70]

The label 'negative theology' has also been applied to Heidegger's own thought, and as long as it is not too narrowly understood, aptly conveys the common stance of Nietzsche and Heidegger: it indicates that the 'negativity' of both philosophers is oriented to, and has its rationale in, an Absolute. Only because this Absolute is phenomenologically evident, only because it and it alone presents itself as the proper object of reverence and gratitude, can the relativity of the thing-world, of knowledge and conceptuality, be maintained.

This enigma of the 'negative Absolute' is what the postmodernists and relativists of every description fail to see. For them, negativism in philosophy has the opposite meaning to absolutism: it is the refusal of the 'pretentiousness' of truth, the escape from the discipline and obligatoriness of truth. For Nietzsche and Heidegger, however, real pretentiousness is to be found in that enormous self-overestimation wherein one's own 'perspectival' interests are substituted for the claim of the Absolute. At first sight relativism can seem, and is often presented as, a modest attitude, but in fact it is the reverse. Capitulation and retreat are not modesty, nor is the claim to 'know' that there is no Absolute particularly unpretentious. What could be more arrogant than bringing the Absolute before the tribunal of the 'interested' intellect, to ask what can be done with it, what strategical significance it has for contemporary writers and readers? Such an attitude amounts to nothing but hubris, impiety and pitiable blindness. In truth, as both Nietzsche and Heidegger realize, the Absolute is testified to as much by fear and flight as by the over-confident claims of metaphysics to have determined its nature. 'Negative theology' does not believe in such determinations, but is not so immodest as to make determinability the criterion of reality.

Nietzsche hopes for future philosophers who become adept at maintaining themselves 'on light ropes and possibilities, and even at dancing around abysses.'[71] Similarly, Heidegger wants a 'new beginning' of philosophy in which the thinker experiences the 'nearness of the Nothing in the Being of beings.'[72] In a manner reminiscent of the negative theologian Meister Eckhart, both thinkers consider that the original philosophical act is one of emptying out from the self everything which does not pertain to truth. If one does this resolutely, rather than in the half-hearted and compromising fashion of metaphysics (e.g. of Descartes) one is left with that which common sense will not tolerate, with what seems like a total void. Therefore, says common sense, let us not do this, let us instead make presuppositions and get on with securing our 'interests'. However, what if our essential 'interests' are to be found precisely in this apparent void? What if our essential selfhood can only be discovered by entering into the unfathomable mystery which is the 'event' of Being? Let those who dismiss this as impractical look around the world today and congratulate themselves on its progress, let them call for renewed efforts in the creation of perspectives. Nietzsche and Heidegger, on the other hand, do not consider that any more perspectives are necessary. For both thinkers, what is needed is simplicity: no easy nostalgia, no innocent return to the past, but the difficult and rigorous simplicity which lets go of so much which has filled up and puffed up human beings for many centuries. Neither Nietzsche nor Heidegger propound new philosophies, neither seeks to light up the road ahead or to provide a vision of the future (except by way of warning, of showing where the progressive decline of man is heading). What they want us to realize is that, before speaking of the 'way forward', we must stop dead and abide for a very long while in the problems of who and what we are, on what it means for human beings 'to be'.

CONCLUSION
How to Read Nietzsche

From the considerations adduced in the present study it might be thought that advice on how to read Nietzsche is either superfluous or futile: superfluous for those who already possess the requisite intuition and who will always find their own way to Nietzsche's philosophical meaning, futile for those whose 'interests' are other than philosophical and who will always make of Nietzsche whatever they please. With respect to these latter 'interested' readers, I readily concede the futility of communication, but for readers in the former category a 'reminder' of what they already do will perhaps not be out of place. In fundamental respects, of course, Nietzsche should be read in the same manner as any other philosopher. What I attempt here, briefly and by way of conclusion, is an integration of universal principles of philosophical reading with principles pertaining to the specific characteristics of Nietzsche's writings.

Firstly and most fundamentally, the *Sache* of Nietzsche's thought must be brought into view. The purpose of philosophical reading is not to ascertain the 'opinions' of the author, but to think the *Sache* through and with the author, to think about those very same things which the author thinks about. How often this seemingly obvious principle is transgressed, and how ludicrous is the result: a 'philosophical education' which consists in the collected summary reports of what various philosophers have said. When the *Sache* recedes from view, or when (as with the postmodernists) it is denied outright, the author's words and concepts provide abundant material for castles in the air. Among those who believe in nothing but words, philosophy degenerates into an endless cycle of 'readings' which, for lack of substance, resort to ever more artificial, ever more convoluted and decorative techniques. The *Sache*, on the other hand, has no need of make-up, which is why *sachliches Denken* expresses itself plainly and without contortions. To be sure, *sachliches Denken* is really an ideal, which is only ever approximately achieved by fallible writers and readers. One must strive to see behind the author's language, to sense when the author's words and phrases provide genuine guidance and when they might lead one astray. This applies to Nietzsche as much as to anyone else. We have seen in the present study that Nietzsche has his pet phrases and pet formulas, which do not always succeed in conveying his basic meaning. He has an overly schematized conception of the history of Western ontology, and he also has his prejudices, particularly on the subject of Christianity. If one hangs on every phrase and formula, one is certainly lost, but awareness of this is also no licence for being overly 'creative' with Nietzsche's texts: the control and discipline of philosophical reading is always the *Sache* itself. As Schopenhauer once said, to follow an author's words alone is like following footprints in the sand: to see where the author has gone one must open one's own eyes.

Secondly, the philosopher himself must be brought into view. Some people are irritated by the fact that in his writings Nietzsche speaks so much about himself, that he pushes himself into the foreground and makes himself part of his own subject matter. Does this indicate personal arrogance and self-preoccupation on Nietzsche's part? Is he unable to resist the constant insinuation of 'autobiographical remarks'? Does it follow that Nietzsche's writings must be understood as literature rather than as philosophy? Such queries fail to appreciate the existential character of

Nietzsche's philosophical activity: he speaks of 'himself' because, as I have attempted to show, this is inseparable from the *Sache* itself. On the other hand, this 'himself' is not exactly 'Herr Nietzsche', the man born in Röcken in 1844 and who died in Weimar in 1900. What Nietzsche pushes into the foreground is his 'philosophical' or 'essential' self: on contingent features of his life he is, with few exceptions, properly reticent. It is this distinction which is overlooked by the current slogan 'death of the author'. While it is certainly true that texts have a value and meaning independent of authorial idiosyncrasies, philosophical texts are strictly valueless and meaningless except in relation to the essential self-reflection that underlies them: this statement applies to dry and turgid philosophers like Aristotle as much as to 'artistic' philosophers like Nietzsche. A philosophical reading of Nietzsche brings one's 'very own self' into view equiprimordially with that of Nietzsche, for they are the same self. This is impossible for those who are estranged from themselves and for whom self-reflection is thwarted by group identity. But those in touch with themselves will know very well how to read the autobiographical dimension of Nietzsche's writings, including the valuable materials contained in the *Nachlaß* and letters. They will not always be fascinated by his love affairs and quarrels with his family, but what they will see reflected is his philosophical self-development.

Thirdly, and following on from these considerations on self, Nietzsche's writings must be read in the context of his philosophical 'pilgrimage'. It is standard practice to periodize an author's works: in Nietzsche's case one recognizes the inevitable 'early', 'middle' and 'late' phases. One also understands that, as for all important thinkers, changes in Nietzsche's thought are prompted by internal philosophical problems rather than being arbitrary shifts of opinion. On the other hand, the character of these changes and developments is distorted when they are treated in an abstracted intellectual fashion, entirely at the level of text. For

Nietzsche, since philosophy pertains to the stance of the
existing self, it is a path, a journey to be undertaken along
which, like life itself, there are necessary stages. It is not
necessary, though it is certainly useful, to read Nietzsche's
writings in chronological order. What is essential, in respect
of any particular text, is to locate it within Nietzsche's
philosophical 'journey', to grasp what existential decisions
and problems he has already endured, and what others still
await him. To do this, one must be 'on the way' oneself:
only then will one recognize the milestones and signposts
which Nietzsche encounters, which every philosopher, as
someone who by no means 'stays at home', must
encounter.

Fourthly, a philosophical reading of Nietzsche must be
'ruminative'. Nietzsche emphasized himself that the pace
of modern intellectual life mitigates against the proper
assimilation and 'digestion' of his ideas. It pertains to the
nature of the 'great problems and question marks' that they
cannot be hurried along, cannot be conquered by storm,
cannot be brought to submission by the kind of journalistic
Blitzkrieg one so often encounters today. How absurd an
impression it makes when one hears, from the postmodernists and others, that the greatest advances in philosophy
have occurred very recently, in a few European and
American universities, and that, armed with such concepts
as 'logocentrism' and 'phallocentrism' one can
'deconstruct' the whole of philosophy from Plato to
Heidegger. There is, apparently, much to do in haste, there
are so many scores to settle, wrongs to be righted, lost time
to be recouped. By contrast, Nietzsche's thought can be
fruitfully approached only when one lets it firmly sink in
that all the essential problems of philosophy were already
well understood two and a half thousand years ago, which
is not to say that they were settled at that date or ever can be
settled. In reading Nietzsche one must take a long view,
which means one must settle down and quieten down: one
must want and expect must less from 'today' at the same

time as wanting and expecting much more from philosophy itself.

Fifthly, Nietzsche's writings require a 'presuppositionless' reading. Of course, the postmodernists would regard this as a hermeneutically uninformed demand: do not presuppositions first of all enable a reading to be undertaken? Indeed they do, but in the case of philosophical reading it is precisely presuppositionlessness which is the presupposition. Among the postmodernists it has become standard practice to make any presuppositions they like, under the excuse that these are in any case 'unavoidable': the result is not philosophy but advocacy. Philosophy, and especially the philosophy of Nietzsche, is methodologically presuppositionless in the sense that it positively seeks to undermine its own presuppositions, it continually attempts to deprive itself of its own foundations. This has nothing whatever to do with the phony enterprise of 'deconstructionism', which, far from being genuinely presuppositionless, is guided by the anti-philosophical presupposition, to be found nowadays on every street corner, that 'there is no truth'. Nietzsche, on the other hand, does not need to 'presuppose truth', because he realizes that truth is the condition of making any presuppositions at all. He attempts in his writings to suspend all presuppositions of what truth is so that its nature will be forced upon him: this is the meaning of his search for primordiality. Nietzsche's readers must follow the same method if they are to avoid becoming entangled in theoretical constructions and conflicting 'points of view'. In this sense too one must be content with 'less' from Nietzsche if one wants 'more': one must dispense with handy 'tools' and 'views' if one wants truth.

What emerges from each of the above points is that Nietzsche's philosophy must be freed from the domesticating influence of postmodernism, an influence which in recent years has become all pervasive in the academy. The postmodernist processing of university undergraduates is a

painful spectacle to behold. The youthful soul has somehow come to question itself, from somewhere it has gained
an inkling that the world is questionable, that there is a
depth dimension to existence to be explored and ventured.
But what does it hear from the postmodernist proponents
of 'correctness', what nourishment and encouragement is
provided for the journey it wants to undertake? As a matter
of principle, nothing but discouragement, nothing but the
constant assurance that the very idea of philosophical depth
is a piece of arrogance, that there is no 'journey' here at all.
An education in postmodernism is a coaxing out of
philosophy, a bringing back to something familiar,
unthreatening, unchallenging, tranquillizing. Of those
intuitions which are the original spark of all genuine
philosophy, it is explained that these are 'epistemologically'
untrustworthy, and that it is better to believe in words,
phrases and texts. What postmodernism teaches is little
more than what Nietzsche called the 'intellectual masquer-
ade': the means of ornamentation and self-flattery for an
outlook on life which is 'generally accepted'. It is an irony,
but one which Nietzsche himself foresaw, that this movement should speak in his name, that it should make of the
greatest critic of anti-philosophical resentment a mere
conduit for the smooth flow of this self-same resentment
into today's academies.

What are the conditions for understanding the writings
of Nietzsche? He knew he would not be understood by the
'idling reader', who does not even seek understanding but is
content to pull out quotations for suitable occasions and
causes. Neither would he be understood by an ever so
thorough 'philological' reading unless accompanied and
guided by that philosophical intuition which provides
original access to his problems. Nietzsche does not put his
writings forward for academic discussion and debate, he
does not seek to lay the foundations for new programmes
of 'research'. He does not want to convert or liberate
anyone, nor even to inform anyone of anything essential

they do not already know. The printing press may have created the 'reading public', but it has no power to create the kind of readership Nietzsche wants. Like Plato's dialogues, Nietzsche's writings are directed to his 'companions in philosophy', to those lovers of wisdom and truth who never tire of 'bringing to mind' the richness and depth of the 'great problems'. This book has also been written for such readers, as a 'reminder' of the Nietzsche they 'already know'.

Notes

INTRODUCTION

1 GS no. 378, pp. 340-41 [KGW V.2: p. 313].
2 BGE no. 292, p. 198 [KGW VI.2: p. 245].
3 BGE no. 212, p. 124 [KGW VI.2: p. 149].
4 Contributions to this literature can be found in the following anthologies (among others): David Allison (ed.), *The New Nietzsche*, MIT Press, Cambridge, Massachusetts, 1985; Clayton Koelb (ed.), *Nietzsche as Postmodernist*, State University of New York Press, Albany, 1990; Laurence Rickels (ed.) *Looking After Nietzsche*, State University of New York Press, Albany, 1990; Volker Dürr et al. (eds), *Nietzsche: Literature and Values*, University of Wisconsin Press, Madison and London, 1988. Much of this literature shows a general indebtedness to Jacques Derrida, although the degree to which Derrida approves of it remains unclear. There are many short considerations of Nietzsche in Derrida's writings, but his most sustained and influential discussion is *Spurs. Nietzsche's Styles*, University of Chicago Press, Chicago and London, 1979. A systematic and supportive discussion of Derrida's attitude to Nietzsche is Ernst Behler, *Derrida–Nietzsche: Nietzsche–Derrida*, Ferdinand Schöningh, Munich, 1988; of similar tendency is Alan Schrift, *Nietzsche and the Question of Interpretation*, Routledge, London, 1990. An especially influential study has been Alexander Nehamas, *Nietzsche: Life as Literature*, Harvard University Press, Cambridge, Massachusetts, 1985. Nehamas is a 'soft' postmodernist who attempts to build bridges between the Derrideans and revisionist Anglo-American epistemologists. A book which brings out the often unstated political dimension of postmodernism's interest in Nietzsche is Mark Warren, *Nietzsche and Political Thought*, MIT Press, Cambridge, Massachusetts, 1988. Gilles Deleuze's *Nietzsche and Philosophy*, Athlone Press, London, 1983, although predating the rise of postmodernism (the original French edition was published in 1962) continues to exercise influence.

Anyone familiar with this literature (and countless contributions of allied tendency) is aware that it is not a perfectly homogeneous bloc. It is also true that some of these writers would be reluctant to accept the label 'postmodernist'. Nevertheless, this study accepts the risk of speaking of 'postmodernism' as an identifiable trend of modern academic philosophy in general, and of Nietzsche commentary in particular, a trend the significance of which exceeds that of any individual author. As to the plane on which I criticize this phenomenon, there will naturally be objections from those sympathetic to postmodernism that I do not take into account this or that subtlety, this or that turn of argumentation. I contend, however, that this would be a very 'un-postmodern' response to what could be seen (in the present text) as a 'deconstructive reading'. It is characteristic of many of these writers that the interpretative liberty with which they approach other ('metaphysical', 'logocentric', 'phallocentric') authors is met with indignation when applied to themselves. As a matter of fact I do not believe I am 'taking liberties' on anything essential. The significance of postmodernism as a cultural-ideological tendency does not consist in a few recondite points buried somewhere in the texts of Derrida, but in its general orientation to philosophy. It is only the latter which concerns me here.

At this level, I believe, postmodernism is most appropriately criticized under the heading of 'sophistry', not in the trivial sense which this word is often given today, but in the original and differentiated sense indicated by Plato and Aristotle. The words of Plato in *The Republic* (493a) are highly pertinent: 'All those individuals who make their living by teaching, and whom the public call "sophists", and envy for their skill, in fact teach nothing but the conventional views held and expressed by the mass of the people they meet; and this they call a science.' Nietzsche is just as conscious as Plato that public opinion is continually being dressed up and refined as the semblance of philosophy: the sophists do this not only because their incomes and reputations depend on the paying public, but because they share in the non-philosophical life of the vast majority. Referring in *The Theaetetus* to the teaching of the sophist Protagoras (of whom echoes within contemporary postmodernism are unmistakable) that each person is the measure of his own wisdom, Socrates remarks (161e): 'Must we not think that Protagoras was "playing to the gallery" in saying this?' As sophistry, postmodernism 'plays to the gallery': e.g. consider the fact that university undergraduates become convinced postmodernists after a few semesters of study, and that postmodernist authors have become *de rigueur* within contemporary feminism. Plato stresses that the success of sophistry depends on the ignorance and gullibility of its audience, which becomes dazzled and befuddled by an extravagent terminology, at the same time being confirmed in its pre-philosophical opinions. In the nature of the case it is impossible to 'engage' with sophists at a philosophical level: 'If you ask one of them a question, he pulls out puzzling little phrases, like arrows from a quiver, and shoots them off; and if you try to get hold of an explanation of what he has said, you will be struck with another phrase of novel and distorted wording, and you will never make any progress whatsoever with any of them, nor do they themselves with one another, for that matter, but they take very good care to allow nothing to be settled either in an argument or in their own minds, thinking, I suppose, that this is being stationary' (*Theaetetus* 180ab). Among modern philosophers, no one is more aware of the ever-present danger of sophistry than Heidegger: 'Everything essential, however, which has decisive meaning without being conspicuous, is always attended by what looks like the genuine and real thing, the semblance. This is why, in every period, philosophy must bring in its wake something that looks like philosophy and imitates it in manner and behaviour, and even outdoes it – and yet at bottom poses an embarrassment. The semblance of the *philosophos* is the *sophistes* [sophist]. The latter does not strive for genuine understanding, has no perseverence, but only nibbles on everything, always just the newest and usually on what is genuinely worthwhile, but he only nibbles on it and is seduced into mere curiosity and bluffing' (*The Metaphysical Foundations of Logic*, Indiana University Press, Bloomington, 1984, p. 12). The diagnosis of postmodernism as sophistry is not to deny that the major authors of this tendency have some valuable things to offer (as Plato recognized too, in respect of Protagoras and other leading sophists). As stated, however, I consider the main significance of postmodernism to be its cultivation of a certain attitude to philosophy rather than its contributions in various areas of specialized research. In line with Aristotle's remark 'A man is a "sophist" because he has a certain kind of moral purpose' (*Rhetoric* 1355b20) I will restrict myself to this level of discussion. Whether my ongoing remarks on the 'postmodernist commentators' are directed at a chimera, must be left for the reader to decide. In the final analysis, however, the present study seeks to stand under the dictum mentioned by Plato in *The Sophist* (246d): 'it is not these men we care about; we merely seek the truth.' My major argument concerns Nietzsche, not the postmodernists.

As far as philosophical methodology is concerned, I dispense with any lengthy preliminary statement. There may still be some people who believe that philosophical positions can be 'proved'. In rejecting this view, I am in the company of such philosophers as Plato, Aristotle, Schopenhauer, Nietzsche and Heidegger. Nothing is 'proved' in the present book; however, something may be 'shown' for those who have eyes to see. Purported 'proving' in philosophy always comes back to what is 'generally accepted', i.e. to certain 'opinions'. For example, a philosophical position on morality will be taken as 'refuted' if it is shown to be in conflict with the axiom of 'equal rights' or to imply 'elitism' of any sort. This is the manner of the postmodernists, and is why they cannot even enter into the region of Nietzsche's philosophical questioning, which dares to be 'immoral'. The present text is obviously not directed to those members of the worldwide church of postmodernism of whom it could be said that 'Lynceus himself could not make them see.' Instead, it is directed to the very large number of Nietzsche readers who, in my experience, have become averse to, and suspicious of, this new intellectual orthodoxy, as well as to those happy souls who have never encountered it.

5 This statement needs qualification. I shall be arguing that the 'pluralism' and 'anti-dogmatism' of the postmodernists fundamentally reflect the anti-philosophical instinct. Strictly speaking it is incorrect to represent this as a 'political view'. In the final analysis, the postmodernists are not really 'pluralists' at all: the conformism of their political correctness testifies to that. Instead, they have given 'pluralism' a bad name by founding it on resentment. What I mean will become clear in the course of the following chapters.

6 The common opinion that nihilism is a peculiarly modern phenomenon is historically uninformed. The 'flight of the gods' was in full force at the time of Socrates and Plato, and was an important impetus for their philosophical activity. Historians are aware that nihilism was endemic in Mediterranean culture in the centuries preceding the establishment of the Christian Church. There were also regular 'outbreaks' of nihilism during the long reign of Christendom.

7 It is possible to see Nietzsche as effecting an 'existential radicalization' of Cartesian doubt. Because Descartes limited his doubt to the sphere of reason, Nietzsche regards him as 'superficial' (BGE no. 191, p. 96; KGW VI.2: p. 115).

8 See e.g. TI '"Reason" in Philosophy' no. 1, p. 35 [KGW VI.3: p. 68].

9 See e.g. BGE no. 20, pp. 31–32 [KGW VI.2: pp. 28–29].

CHAPTER ONE: PERSPECTIVISM AND ITS LIMITS

1 HAH II, no. 20, p. 218 [KGW IV.3: p. 23].

2 EH 'Preface' no. 3, p. 219 [KGW VI.3: p. 257].

3 GM 'Preface' no. 2, p. 16 [KGW VI.2: pp. 261–62].

4 Jean Granier, 'Perspectivism and Interpretation', in David B. Allison (ed.), *The New Nietzsche*, MIT Press, Cambridge, Massachusetts, 1977, p. 191.

5 Alan Schrift, *Nietzsche and the Question of Interpretation*, Routledge, London, 1990, pp. 124 and 131.

6 Debra B. Bergoffen, 'Nietzsche's Madman: Perspectivism Without Nihilism', in Clayton Koelb (ed.) *Nietzsche as Postmodernist: Essays Pro and Contra*, State University of New York Press, Albany, 1990, p. 68.

7 Babette E. Babich, 'Nietzsche and the Condition of Postmodern Thought: Post-Nietzschean Postmodernism', in Koelb, *Nietzsche as Postmodernist* (op. cit.) p. 259.

8 Alexander Nehamas, *Nietzsche: Life as Literature*, Harvard University Press, Cambridge, Massachusetts, 1985, p. 68.

9 Gilles Deleuze, *Nietzsche and Philosophy*, Athlone Press, London, 1983, p. 95.

10 The Heideggerian term '*Sache*' will be employed throughout this study. Its nearest English equivalent, for the sense here intended, would be something like 'subject matter'. The maxim '*zu den Sachen selbst*' (sometimes translated 'to the things themselves') is taken over by Heidegger from Edmund Husserl, and in both thinkers indicates a desire to get back from 'theoretical constructions' to the 'substance' of philosophy. I speak of the '*Sache*' of philosophy to avoid the misleading connotations of the term 'object', i.e. to avoid 'objectivistic' assumptions about the nature of philosophy.

11 George Stack, *Lange and Nietzsche*, Walter de Gruyter, Berlin and New York, 1983, p. 204.

12 GS no. 354, pp. 299–300 [KGW V.2: p. 275].

13 See also GS no. 357, pp. 305–306 [KGW V.2: pp. 280–81] where Nietzsche says that 'what we call consciousness constitutes only one state of our spiritual and psychic world (perhaps a pathological state) and *not by any means the whole of it.*'

14 GS no. 373, p. 335 [KGW V.2: p. 307].

15 Walter Kaufmann's translation is inaccurate in rendering 'über' in this passage as 'beyond' rather than as 'over'.

16 On Nietzsche's relation to the Kantian critique of metaphysics, see Keith Ansell-Pearson, 'Nietzsche's Overcoming of Kant and Metaphysics: From Tragedy to Nihilism, *Nietzsche-Studien* 16 (1987) pp. 310–339; and Josef Simon, 'Die Krise des Wahrheitsbegriffs als Krise der Metaphysik', *Nietzsche-Studien* 18 (1989), pp. 242–259.

17 PT pp. 11–12 [KGW III.4: pp. 15-16]. In UM III no. 3, pp. 140–41 [KGW III.1: pp. 351–52] Nietzsche quotes with sympathy Heinrich Kleist's reaction to Kant: 'We cannot decide whether what we call

truth really is truth....My one great goal has failed me, and I have no other.'

18 PT p. 13 [KGW III.4: p. 17].

19 For Schopenhauer, the way beyond Kant is given by 'that other truth that we are not merely the *knowing subject*, but that *we ourselves* are also among those realities or entities we require to know, that *we ourselves are the Thing-in-itself.* Consequently, a way *from within* stands open to us to that real inner nature of things to which we cannot penetrate *from without*' (*The World as Will and Representation* Vol. II, The Falcon's Wing Press, Indian Hills, Colorado, p. 195). Kant, allegedly blinded by an adherence to abstract-conceptual thinking, cut himself off from this realm of inner-awareness and thus from the true path of metaphysics. The Kantian critique remains valid for Schopenhauer if this is understood as ruling out the production of new knowledge (especially of 'absolute knowledge') through mere ratiocination. But metaphysics, as Schopenhauer understands it, must open its eyes to the totality of human experience. In no sense can abstraction/conceptualization add any new content to the original knowledge derived from inner and outer intuition. Although it is possible to catalogue and order what is already given by intuition, these procedures can never lead to a new dimension of truth. In one of Schopenhauer's favourite analogies, concepts relate to intuition as cheques relate to hard cash: although the former are in many ways convenient, an element of uncertainty always attaches to them, and the suspicion of fraud is never entirely absent. A frenzied trading in words is possible without there being any intuitions in the bank to cover them. Nietzsche is in profound sympathy with these views. On Schopenhauer's relation to the Kantian critique of metaphysics, see Martin Morgenstern, 'Schopenhauers Grundlegung der Metaphysik', *Schopenhauer Jahrbuch* 69 (1988), pp. 57–66. On Nietzsche's relation to Schopenhauer, see Georges Goedert, 'Nietzsche und Schopenhauer', *Nietzsche-Studien* 7 (1978), pp. 1–26; and Jörg Salaquarda, 'Zur gegenseitigen Verdrängung von Schopenhauer und Nietzsche', *Schopenhauer Jahrbuch* 65 (1984), pp. 13–30.

20 Schopenhauer, *The World as Will and Representation* II (op. cit.), Ch. 17.

21 BT no. 5, p. 52 [KGW III.1: p. 43].

22 KGW III.3 (*Nachlaß*): p. 207: 'The visions of the primal One can only be adequate mirrorings of Being (*Spiegelungen des Seins*).'

23 Maudemarie Clark's book, *Nietzsche: On Truth and Philosophy*, Cambridge University Press, Cambridge, 1990, also challenges postmodernist readings of 'Truth and lies'. However, in ascribing to Nietzsche a 'metaphysical correspondence theory' of truth (see

esp. pp. 85–90), Clark remains within an epistemological frame of reference which is inadequate to Nietzsche's intentions.

24 PT p. 80 [KGW III.2: p. 370].

25 PT p. 81 [KGW III.2: p. 372].

26 Among the postmodernist commentators, the idea of 'style' (as a substitute for truth) has gained much currency. See e.g. Jacques Derrida, *Spurs: Nietzsche's Styles*, University of Chicago Press, Chicago, 1978; and Alexander Nehamas, *Nietzsche: Life as Literature* (op. cit.), Ch. 1.

27 PT p. 90 [KGW III.2: p. 383].

28 KGW III.4 (*Nachlaß*): p. 8.

29 KGW III.4 (*Nachlaß*): p. 22.

30 KGW IV.1 (*Nachlaß*): p. 108.

31 I have been unable to locate this important statement in the KGW. It appears in Karl Schlecta's edition of Nietzsche's *Werke*, Ullstein, Frankfurt am Main, 1969, Vol. III, p. 1037.

32 PT p. 129 [KGW IV.1: p. 175].

33 Other critics of relativistic interpretations include Katherine Higgins, 'Nietzsche and Postmodern Subjectivity', and Robert C. Solomon 'Nietzsche, Postmodernism, and Resentment: A Genealogical Hypothesis', both in Clayton Koelb, *Nietzsche as Postmodernist* (op. cit.). The present study fully concurs with Solomon's views that 'perspectivism was never itself the key to Nietzsche's outlook or method' (p. 70) and that postmodernism has its origins in resentment, as 'an expression of disappointment, a retreat, a purely negative thesis' (p. 282). However, Solomon fails to situate Nietzsche's perspectivism with respect to supra-perspectival truth, and thus does not provide a real alternative to the postmodernist position. Correspondingly, he fails to give sufficient attention to Nietzsche's crucial opposition between the 'individual' and the 'herd'. See also Berndt Magnus, 'Nietzsche and Postmodern Criticism', *Nietzsche-Studien* 18 (1989), pp. 301–316.

34 BGE Preface, pp. 13–14 [KGW VI.2: p. 4].

35 D Preface no. 4, p. 4 [KGW V.1: p. 8].

36 PTAG no. 5, p. 51 [KGW III.2: p. 316].

37 GA XIX: p. 173.

38 GA XIX: p. 177.

39 GA XIX: p. 177.

40 PTAG no. 11, p. 82 [KGW III.2: p. 339].

41 PTAG no. 11, p. 83 [KGW III.2: p. 340].

42 PTAG no. 10, p. 79 [KGW III.2: p. 337].

43 PTAG no. 10, p. 79 [KGW III.2: p. 337].

44 PTAG no. 10, p. 80 [KGW III.2: p. 338].

45 BT no. 18, p. 112 [KGW III.1: p. 114]: 'The extraordinary courage and wisdom of *Kant and Schopenhauer* have succeeded in gaining the

most difficult victory, the victory over the optimism concealed in the essence of logic – an optimism that is the basis of our culture.'

46 GA XIX: p. 186.

47 GA XIX: p. 186.

48 Diels–Kranz Fragment 101, in G. S. Kirk, J. E. Raven, and M. Schofield, *The Presocratic Philosophers*, Cambridge University Press, Cambridge, 1983, p. 211.

49 GA XIX: p. 169.

50 On Nietzsche's relation to Heraclitus, see Tilman Borsche, 'Nietzsches Erfindung der Vorsokratiker', in Josef Simon (ed.) *Nietzsche und die philosophische Tradition* I, Königshausen & Neumann, 1985, pp. 62–87; Jackson P. Hersbell and Stephen A. Nimis, 'Nietzsche and Heraclitus', *Nietzsche-Studien* 8 (1979), pp. 17–38; and Sarah Kofman, 'Nietzsche und die Dunkelheit des Heraklit', in Sigrid Bauschinger, Susan Cocalis and Sara Lennox (eds) *Nietzsche Heute: Die Rezeption seines Werks nach 1968*, Francke Verlag, Bern and Stuttgart, 1988, pp. 75–104.

51 PT p. 83 [KGW III.2: pp. 373–74].

52 PT p. 86 [KGW III.2: p. 378].

53 PT p. 90 [KGW III.2: p. 383].

54 Eugen Fink, *Nietzsches Philosophie*, Kohlhammer Verlag, Stuttgart, 1960, p. 38.

55 Heidegger's stronger claim that Nietzsche's whole philosophy is determined by a misunderstanding of Parmenides is an exaggeration. Nietzsche's polemical opposition between Being and Becoming may well be grounded in such a misunderstanding, but as I hope to show, this opposition is far from encapsulating Nietzsche's total thought.

56 PTAG no. 5, p. 56 [KGW III.2: p. 320].

57 PTAG no. 11, p. 83 [KGW III.2: p. 340].

58 BT no. 4, p. 45 [KGW III.1: p. 34].

59 BT no. 5, p. 49 [KGW III.1: p. 40].

60 BT no. 7, p. 60 [KGW III.1: p. 53].

61 WP no. 553, p. 300.

62 See John Sallis, *Crossings*, University of Chicago Press, Chicago, 1991, pp. 61–68. Sallis (pp. 67–68) is troubled by the fact 'that Nietzsche himself, despite the critique [of Schopenhauer's doctrine of Will] invokes the metaphysical axis at several major junctures in *The Birth of Tragedy*'. However, Sallis misunderstands the basic tendency of Schopenhauer's critique of Kant. Nietzsche realizes that the 'determinations' which Schopenhauer gives to Will run counter to this basic tendency. On the other hand, Schopenhauer's failings in this respect are not entirely avoided by Nietzsche himself, especially in his later notes on 'will to power'.

63 WP no. 555, p. 301.
64 WP no. 556, p. 301.
65 WP no. 560, pp. 302–303.
66 UM III no. 5, p. 159 [KGW III.1: p. 376].
67 WP no. 715, p. 380.
68 Eugen Fink puts the matter as follows (*Nietzsches Philosophie*, op. cit., pp. 164–65): 'One misjudges the scope of Nietzsche's polemic against the categories if one conceives it merely as a fictionalist theory of knowledge. Nietzsche does not proceed from a critical investigation of the faculty of knowledge to arrive at a rejection of categorial forms of thought...but proceeds from the primordial intuition (*Ur-Intuition*) of his Heraclitean philosophy, which takes Becoming as the sole reality....Nietzsche's fictionalist theory of knowledge, which conceives the will to power as the falsifying, distorting power of the intellect, is in its essential meaning a negative ontology of the thing: there are no things. His critique is not directed against all knowledge whatsoever, but only against knowledge of things, the empirical, above all against the *a priori* knowledge which gives a categorial interpretation of thing-hood as such. His intuition, the philosophical awareness of Becoming, is *not* affected by this critique of knowledge; it is much more the presupposition which in the first place makes this critique possible and valid.' The fact that Nietzsche's 'perspectivism' applies to 'things' rather than to Becoming as 'primordial reality', is what allows connections to be drawn between Nietzsche and Heidegger, who likewise distinguishes between 'ontic' and 'ontological' knowledge.
69 PTAG no. 9, p. 69 [KGW III.2: p. 329].
70 UM III no. 4, p. 155 [KGW III.1: p. 370].
71 GS no. 370, p. 329 [KGW V.2: pp. 303–304].
72 WP no. 617, p. 330.
73 TI 'Expeditions of an Untimely Man' no. 26, pp. 82–83 [KGW VI.3: p. 122]. The incommunicability of his philosophy is a prominent theme of Nietzsche's later correspondence. See e.g. the letter to Overbeck of 2 July 1885, in which he plainly states that 'my "philosophy" – if I have the right to call it by the name of something which has maltreated me down to the very roots of my being – is no longer communicable, at least not in print' (*Briefwechsel* III.3: p. 62).
74 BGE no. 289, p. 197 [KGW VI.2: p. 244].
75 Alan Schrift, *Nietzsche and the Question of Interpretation* (op. cit.) pp. 181–94.
76 Jacques Derrida, *Spurs: Nietzsche's Styles* (op. cit.) p. 139.
77 Alexander Nehamas, *Nietzsche: Life as Literature* (op. cit.) p. 67.

78 WP no. 481, p. 267.

79 Nehamas, *Nietzsche: Life as Literature* (op. cit.) p. 29.

80 E.g. EH 'Why I am so clever' no. 3, p. 243 [KGW VI.3: pp. 282–83]: 'I almost always seek refuge with the same books – actually a small number – books proved to me. Perhaps it is not my way to read much, or diverse things: a reading room makes me sick. Nor is it my way to love much, or diverse things. Caution, even hostility against new books comes closer to my instincts than "tolerance", "largeur du coeur" and other "neighbour love".'

81 Quoted by K. P. Janz, 'Nietzsche's Verhältnis zur Musik seiner Zeit', *Nietzsche-Studien* 7 (1978), p. 309.

82 BT 'Attempt at Self-Criticism', no. 3, p. 20 [KGW III.1: p. 9].

83 GS no. 383, pp. 347–48 [KGW V.2: p. 319].

84 CW no. 1, p. 158 [KGW VI.3: p. 8]. Cf. UM IV, p. 15 [KGW IV.1: pp. 27–28]: 'As soon as men seek to come to an understanding with one another, and to unite for a common work, they are seized by the madness of universal concepts, indeed even by the mere sounds of words, and, as a consequence of this incapacity to communicate, everything they do together bears the mark of this lack of mutual understanding....Now when the music of our German masters resounds in the ears of mankind injured to this extent, what is it really that here becomes audible? Precisely this *right feeling (richtige Empfindung)*, the enemy of all convention, all artificial alienation and incomprehension between man and man.' In his late period, Nietzsche comes to consider that Wagner, with his concept of the 'music-drama', had compromised himself as musician. E.g. CW no. 8, pp. 172–73 [KGW VI.3: p. 24]: 'Wagner was *not* a musician by instinct. He showed this by abandoning all lawfulness and, more precisely, all style in music in order to turn it into what he required, theatrical rhetoric, a means of expression, of underscoring gestures, of suggestion, of the psychologically picturesque. Here we may consider Wagner an inventor and innovator of the first rank – *he has immeasurably increased music's capacity for language*: he is the Victor Hugo of music as language. Always presupposing that one first allows that under certain circumstances music may not be music but language, instrument, *ancilla dramaturgica*.'

85 EH 'Thus spoke Zarathustra' no. 6, p. 305 [KGW VI.3: p. 342] and 'Why I am so wise' no. 8, p. 234 [KGW VI.3: p. 274].

86 EH 'Why I Write Such Good Books' no. 4, p. 265 [KGW VI.3: p. 302].

87 Martin Heidegger, *Being and Time*, Basil Blackwell, Oxford, 1962, p. 175.

88 E.g. HAH 2nd 'Preface' no. 1, p. 209 [KGW IV.3: p. 3]: 'My writings speak *only* of my overcomings: "I" am in them, together

with everything which was inimical to me, *ego ipsissimus* [my very own self], indeed, if a yet prouder expression be permitted, *ego ipsissimum* [my innermost self].'

89 In D 'Preface' no. 5, p. 5 [KGW V.1: p. 9] Nietzsche calls for the kind of 'slow reading' in which philologists are trained. It must be remembered, however, that Nietzsche frequently admonishes philologists for remaining entangled in language, and thus failing to address the 'great problems and question marks'. Further to this, see the third section of Chapter Two, below.

90 BGE no. 296, pp. 201–202 [KGW VI.2: pp. 249–50]. Nietzsche's view of the philosophical inadequacy of writing has strong resemblances to Plato's attitude in the *Phaedrus* (274–79) and the *Seventh Letter* (342–44). In his early lectures on the Platonic dialogues, Nietzsche opposes Friedrich Schleiermacher's 'literary' interpretation of Plato: 'The whole hypothesis [of Schleiermacher] is in contradiction with the explanation which is found in the *Phaedrus*....In fact Plato says that writing has its meaning only for those who already know, as a means for bringing it back to mind....Instead for Schleiermacher writing must be the means, which is the best of a poor lot, to bring those who do not know to knowledge. The whole of the writings therefore has the general function of teaching and education. But according to Plato writing in general does not have the function of teaching and educating, but only the function of bringing to mind for those who are already educated and possess knowledge.' This passage was brought to my attention by Giovanni Reale, one of the foremost spokesmen for the 'esoteric' Plato (*Plato and Aristotle*, State University of New York Press, Albany, 1990, p. 10). It appears in GA XIX pp. 239–40 and is quoted here as per Reale. There are many passages from the *Phaedrus* and the *Seventh Letter* which Nietzsche would subscribe to without reservation. Just two examples: 'Once a thing is committed to writing it circulates equally among those who understand the subject and those who have no business with it; a writing cannot distinguish between suitable and unsuitable readers. And if it is ill-treated or unfairly abused it always needs its parent to come to its rescue; it is quite incapable of defending or helping itself.' (*Phaedrus* 275, compare with the first quote from Nietzsche heading the Introduction of this book); 'When one sees a written composition, whether it be on law by a legislator or on any other subject, one can be sure, if the writer is a serious man, that his book does not represent his most serious thoughts; they remain stored up in the noblest region of his personality.' (*Seventh Letter* 344, compare with the second quote from Nietzsche in the present section).

91 Jean-Luc Nancy, "'Our Probity!'": On Truth in the Moral Sense in Nietzsche', in Laurence Rickels (ed.) *Looking After Nietzsche*, State University of New York Press, Albany, 1990, p. 70.

92 Jacques Derrida, *Margins of Philosophy*, Harvester, Brighton, 1982, p. 111.

93 One may see in the postmodernists' 'strategical' conception of discourse yet another confirmation of the maxim that 'truth is the first casualty of war'.

94 Mark Warren, *Nietzsche and Political Thought* (op. cit.) p. 3.

95 EH 'Why I Am a Destiny' no. 1, p. 326 [KGW VI.3: p. 363-64].

96 EH 'Why I Am a Destiny' no. 5, p. 330 [KGW VI.3: p. 368].

97 GM I, no. 2, p. 26 [KGW VI.2: p. 273].

98 GS no. 3, p. 77 [KGW V.2: p. 48].

99 BGE no. 5, p. 18 [KGW VI.2: p. 13].

100 GS no. 371, p. 331 [KGW V.2: p. 304].

101 BGE no. 34, p. 47 [KGW VI.2: p. 49].

102 Warren, *Nietzsche and Political Thought* (op. cit.) p. 9.

103 Warren, *Nietzsche and Political Thought* (op. cit.) pp. 11 and 17.

104 Gilles Deleuze, 'Nomad Thought', in David Allison (ed.) *The New Nietzsche* (op. cit.) p. 149.

105 Jacques Derrida, *Spurs: Nietzsche's Styles* (op. cit.) p. 53.

106 BGE no. 260, p. 178 [KGW VI.2: p. 222].

107 BGE no. 202, p. 107 [KGW VI.2: p. 127].

108 See also 'Of the Way of the Creator' in Z I, p. 89 [KGW VI.1: p. 77]: 'Do you call yourself free? I want to hear your ruling idea, and not that you have escaped from a yoke.'

109 HAH I, no. 438, p. 161 [KGW IV.2: pp. 295–96].

110 GS no. 270, p. 219 [KGW V.2: p. 197].

111 For Nietzsche's distinction between the intellectual and the moral conscience, see GS no. 335, p. 263 [KGW V.2: pp. 240–44].

112 GS no. 2, p. 76 [KGW V.2: p. 47].

113 Nehamas, *Nietzsche: Life as Literature* (op. cit.) p. 68.

114 GS no. 3, p. 78 [KGW V.2: p. 49].

115 GS no. 380, p. 342 [KGW V.2: p. 315].

116 GS no. 359, p. 314 [KGW V.2: p. 287].

117 BGE no. 204, p. 112 [KGW VI.2: pp. 135–36].

118 D no. 543, pp. 216–17 [KGW V.1: pp. 317–18].

119 Preface to Jacques Derrida, *Of Grammatology*, John Hopkins University Press, Baltimore, 1974, p. 19.

CHAPTER TWO: HIERARCHY OF THE SPIRIT

1 HAH 1st 'Preface' no. 7, p. 10 [KGW IV.2: p. 15].

2 AC no. 57, p. 177 [KGW VI.3: p. 240].

3 GM I, Concluding 'Note', p. 56 [KGW VI.2: p. 303].

4 WP no. 886, p. 472.

5 BGE no. 263, p. 183 [KGW VI.2: p. 227].

6 BGE no. 213, p. 126 [KGW VI.2: p. 152].

7 BGE no. 270, pp. 189–90 [KGW VI.2: p. 235].

8 EH 'Why I am a Destiny' no. 3, p. 328 [KGW VI.3: p. 365].

9 EH 'Preface' no. 3, p. 218 [KGW VI.3: p. 257].

10 UM II no. 6, p. 89 [KGW III.1: p. 283]: 'The truth is that few serve truth because few possess the pure will to justice, and of these few only a few possess the strength actually to be just.'

11 UM II no. 6, p. 89 [KGW III.1: p. 283].

12 Nehamas makes no attempt to disguise the banality of his position: 'In order to be motivated to produce a new view, interpretation, painting, theory, novel, or morality, one must not think that it is simply one among many equally good alternatives; one must believe that it is a very good, perhaps the best, view, interpretation, painting, theory, novel, or morality' (*Nietzsche: Life as Literature*, Harvard University Press, Cambridge, Massachusetts, 1985, p. 59). Bravo! This as a summary of Nietzsche's philosophy! Those postmodernists with more 'literary talent' would express the same shallow idea in more convoluted terminology.

13 See e.g. GM III no. 14, pp. 121–25 [KGW VI.2: pp. 385–90].

14 On 'the great health' see GS no. 382, pp. 346–47 [KGW V.2: pp. 317–319].

15 BGE no. 44, pp. 53–54 [KGW VI.2: pp. 56–57].

16 WP no. 864, p. 460: 'all men, especially the most healthy, are sick at certain periods of their lives.' BGE no. 260, pp. 175–76 [KGW VI.2: p. 218]: 'There is *master morality* and *slave morality*. I add at once that in all higher and mixed cultures attempts at mediation between the two are apparent and more frequently confusion and mutual misunderstanding between them, indeed sometimes their harsh juxtaposition – even within the same man, within *one* soul.'

17 Zarathustra's main enemy is the 'spirit of gravity': see Z III 'Of the Spirit of Gravity', pp. 210–13 [KGW VI.1: pp. 237–41].

18 Leslie Thiele, *Friedrich Nietzsche and The Politics of the Soul*, Princeton University Press, Princeton, New Jersey, 1990, p. 52.

19 BGE no. 43, p. 53 [KGW VI.2: p. 56].

20 Plato, *The Republic* 412b–449a; Aristotle, *Nichomachean Ethics*, 1177a–1179a.

21 Pseudo-Dionysius, *The Ecclestiastical Hierarchy*, in *Pseudo-Dionysius: The Complete Works*, Paulist Press, Mahwah, New Jersey, 1987, pp. 193–259; John Climacus, *The Ladder of Divine Ascent*, Paulist Press, Ramsey, New Jersey, 1982.

22 AC no. 4, p. 116 [KGW VI.3: p. 169]: 'There are cases of individual success constantly appearing in the most various parts of the earth

and from the most various cultures in which a *higher type* does manifest itself: something which in relation to collective mankind is a sort of superman. Such chance occurrences of great success have always been possible and perhaps always will be possible. And even entire races, tribes, nations can under certain circumstances represent such a *lucky hit.*'

23 BGE no. 26, p. 39 [KGW VI.2: p. 40]: 'The study of the *average* human being, protracted, serious, and with much dissembling, self-overcoming, intimacy, bad company...this constitutes a necessary part of the life-story of every philosopher, perhaps the most unpleasant and malodorous part and the part most full of disappointments.'

24 Plato indicates as much in his dialogue *The Sophist* (253c): 'Have we unwittingly stumbled upon the science that belongs to free men and perhaps found the philosopher while we were looking for the sophist?'

25 GS 'Preface' no. 4, p. 37 [KGW V.2: p. 19]. Nietzsche is sometimes regarded as an unreserved champion of the sexual pleasures. That this is not the case can be seen from Z I, 'Of Chastity' and 'Of Marriage and Children' (pp. 81–82 and 95–96; KGW VI.1: pp. 65–66 and 86–88).

26 The shallowness of modern educational institutions is a major theme of UM I on David Strauß and of Nietzsche's Basel lectures 'Über die Zukunft unserer Bildungsanstalten' [KGW III.2: pp. 133–244].

27 BT no. 17, p. 109 [KGW III.1: p. 110].

28 BT no. 18, pp. 112–13 [KGW III.1: p. 115].

29 PTAG no. 11, p. 81 [KGW III.2: p. 339]: '"Grant me, ye gods, but one certainty", runs Parmenides' prayer, "and if it be but a log's breadth on which to lie, on which to ride on the sea of uncertainty".'

30 EH 'The Birth of Tragedy' no. 2, p. 272 [KGW VI.3: p. 309].

31 GM III no. 14, p. 123 [KGW VI.2: p. 387].

32 D no. 105, p. 61 [KGW V.1: pp. 90–91]. On the same point WP no. 873, p. 467: 'In ordinary "egoism" it is precisely the "non-ego", the profoundly average creature, the species man, who desires to preserve himself.'

33 GS no. 270, p. 219 [KGW V.2: p. 197] consists of the single question and answer: 'What does your conscience say? "You shall become the person you are".'

34 WP no. 962, p. 505: 'A great man...knows he is incommunicable: he finds it tasteless to be familiar; and when one thinks he is, he usually is not. When not speaking to himself, he wears a mask'; GS no. 365, p. 321 [KGW V.2: p. 295]: 'We, too, associate with "people"; we, too, modestly don the dress in which (as which) others know us,

respect us, look for us – and then we appear in company, meaning among people who are disguised without wanting to admit it. We, too, do what all prudent masks do, and in response to every curiosity which does not concern our "dress" we politely place a chair against the door.'

35 As Kathleen Higgins ('Nietzsche and postmodern subjectivity', in Clayton Koelb (ed.) *Nietzsche as Postmodernist*, State University of New York Press, Albany, 1990, p. 192) comments, Nietzsche 'aims at direct and personal encounter', while 'the postmodernists, by contrast, do not seem particularly concerned with personal subjectivity.'

36 D 'Preface' no.1, p. 1 [KGW V.1: p. 3].

37 In his later period, Nietzsche, reversing his earlier opinion, comes to think of Wagner as a spiritual pleb, e.g. CW no. 9, p. 176 [KGW VI.3: p. 28]; 'Wagner does not seem to have been interested in any problems except those that now preoccupy the little decadents of Paris. Always five steps from the hospital. All of them entirely *metropolitan* problems.' It seems that, already at the Bayreuth festival of 1876, Nietzsche was struck by the horrifying thought that Wagner had come to believe in his own mask.

38 Z III 'The Convalescent', p. 236 [KGW VI.1: p. 270].

39 GS no. 276, p. 223 [KGW V.2: p. 201].

40 AC no. 6, p. 117 [KGW VI.3: p. 170].

41 GS no. 50, pp. 114–115 [KGW V.2: p. 89].

42 BGE no. 202, p. 106 [KGW VI.2: p. 126].

43 Plato, *The Republic* 496ab.

44 AC no. 6, p. 117 [KGW VI.3: p. 170].

45 BGE no. 61, pp. 67–68 [KGW VI.2: p. 61].

46 GS no. 2, pp. 76–77 [KGW V.2: pp. 47–48].

47 GS no. 366, p. 323 [KGW V.2: p. 297]: 'No, my scholarly friends, I bless you even for your hunched backs. And for despising, as I do, the "men of letters" and culture parasites....And because your sole aim is to become masters of your craft, with reverence for every kind of mastery and competence, and with uncompromising opposition to everything that is semblance, half-genuine, dressed up, virtuosolike, demagogical, or histrionic in *litteris et artibus* – to everything which cannot prove to you its unconditional probity in discipline and prior training.'

48 On the reception of *The Birth of Tragedy*, see Ronald Hayman, *Nietzsche: A Critical Life*, Weidenfeld and Nicolson, London, 1980, pp. 156–57, and Werner Ross, *Der ängstliche Adler: Friedrich Nietzsches Leben*, Deutscher Taschenbuch Verlag, Stuttgart, 1980, pp. 298–307.

49 In his translator's notes to GS no. 381 (pp. 344–45), Walter Kaufmann quotes a letter to Overbeck from 1886: 'In this

university atmosphere the best people degenerate: I continually feel that the background and ultimate power even in such types as Rhode is a damned general indifference and a total lack of faith in their own stuff. That someone like I has been living among problems *diu noctuque incubando* and has his distress and happiness there alone – who could have any empathy for that? R. Wagner, as I've mentioned, did; and that is why Tribschen was such a recreation for me, while now I no longer have any place or people who are recreation for me.' Nietzsche's difficult relationship with Jacob Burckhardt, who much to Nietzsche's consternation (he admired Burckhardt greatly) also remained doggedly 'middle class' in his scholarly life, is treated in Karl Löwith's *Jacob Burckhardt, Sämtliche Schriften* 7, J. B. Metzlersche Verlagsbuchhandlung, Stuttgart, 1984, pp. 44–90. See also the third essay 'Burckhardt and Nietzsche' in Erich Heller's *The Importance of Nietzsche: Ten Essays*, The University of Chicago Press, Chicago and London, 1988.

50 GM III no. 23, p. 147 [KGW VI.2: p. 415]. Cf. BT 'Attempt at self criticism' no. 1, p. 18 [KGW III.1: pp. 6–7]: 'Is not the resolve to be scientific about everything perhaps a kind of fear of, an escape from, pessimism? A subtle last resort against – *truth*? And, morally speaking, a sort of cowardice and falseness?'

51 GS no. 373, p. 334 [KGW V.2: pp. 307–308].

52 BGE no. 204, p. 110 [KGW VI.2: pp. 133–34]: 'I should like to venture to combat a harmful and improper displacement of the order of rank between science and philosophy which is today, quite unnoticed and as if with a perfect good conscience, threatening to become established.... The Declaration of Independence of the man of science, his emancipation from philosophy, is one of the more subtle after-effects of the democratic form and formlessness of life.... "Away with all masters" – that is what the plebian instinct desires here too.'

53 BGE no. 207, p. 115 [KGW VI.2: p. 139].

54 GA XIX: p. 227; TI 'The Problem of Socrates' no. 3, p. 30 [KGW VI.3: p. 62].

55 EH 'Why I am so Clever' no. 2, p. 241 [KGW VI.3: p. 281]: 'During my Basel period my whole spiritual diet, including the way I divided up my day, was a completely senseless abuse of extraordinary resources, without any new supply to cover this consumption in any way, without even any thought about consumption and replenishment'; EH 'Human, all too Human' no. 3, p. 286 [KGW VI.3: p. 323]: 'Ten years lay behind me in which the nourishment of my spirit had really come to a stop; I had not learned anything new which was useful.' On Nietzsche's Basel years, see Werner Ross, *Der ängstliche Adler: Friedrich Nietzsches Leben* (op. cit.) pp. 188–383.

56 Z II 'Of Scholars', p. 147 [KGW VI.1: p. 156]: 'Too long did my soul sit hungry at their table.'

57 Nietzsche's attitude to the university is highly reminiscent of that of Arthur Schopenhauer, also an academic outsider. No doubt he was familiar with Schopenhauer's polemical essay 'Über die Universitätsphilosophie' (in *Parerga und Paralipomena*, *Sämtliche Werke* IV, Suhrkamp, Stuttgart, 1986, pp. 171–242) and would have approved of most of it.

58 At the same time, it is only the 'universal' in the individual which is valued by Nietzsche. Further to this, see Chapter Three, 'Redemption and the self.'

59 PTAG 'Preface', p. 24 [KGW III.2: pp. 295–96].

60 PTAG no 8, p. 66 [KGW III.2: p. 328].

61 Z I 'Of the Bestowing Virtue' no. 3, p. 103 [KGW VI.1: p. 97].

62 BGE no. 287, p. 196 [KGW VI.2: pp. 242–43].

63 WP no. 919, p. 486: 'I wish men would begin by *respecting* themselves: everything else follows from that. To be sure, as soon as one does this one is finished for others: for this is what they forgive last: "What? A man who respects himself?"'

64 GM III nos. 7–8, pp. 107–108 [KGW VI.2: pp. 369–70].

65 Z II 'Of the rabble', p. 120 [KGW VI.1: p. 120].

66 WP no. 876, p. 468.

67 UM III no. 1, p. 129 [KGW III.1: p. 336]: 'But how can we find ourselves again? How can man know himself? He is a thing dark and veiled; and if the hare has seven skins, man can slough off seventy times seven and still not be able to say: "this is really you, this is no longer outer shell."'

68 GS no. 283, p. 228 [KGW V.2: p. 206]; 'For believe me: the secret for harvesting from existence the greatest fruitfulness and the greatest enjoyment is – to *live dangerously*! Build your cities on the slopes of Vesuvius! Send your ships into unchartered seas!'

69 BGE no. 39, p. 50 [KGW VI.2: pp. 52–53]: 'It could pertain to the fundamental nature of existence that a complete knowledge of it would destroy one – so that the strength of a spirit could be measured by how much "truth" it could take.'

70 GS no. 346, pp. 285–86 [KGW V.2: pp. 261–62].

71 See AC no. 4, p. 16 [KGW VI.3: p. 169].

72 TI 'What I Owe to the Ancients' no. 4, pp. 108–109 [KGW VI.3: p. 152].

73 TI 'What I Owe to the Ancients' no. 2, p. 106 [KGW VI.3: p. 150]: 'It has cost us dearly that this Athenian [Plato] went to school with the Egyptians.' Here Nietzsche accepts the view of Schopenhauer and of the nineteenth century in general that all 'wisdom' has Eastern origins.

74 BT no. 11, p. 78 [KGW III.1: p. 74].

75 UM III no. 2, p. 135 [KGW III.1: p. 345].

76 BGE no. 49, p. 60 [KGW VI.2: p. 68].

77 BT nos. 10–11, pp. 75–79 [KGW III.1: pp. 70–75].

78 BT no. 12, p. 82 [KGW III.1: p. 79].

79 BT no. 13, p. 87 [KGW III.1: p. 85]: '"Only by instinct": with this phrase we touch upon the heart of the Socratic tendency. With it Socratism condemns existing art as well as existing ethics. Wherever Socratism turns its searching eyes it sees lack of insight and the power of illusion; and from this it infers the essential perversity and reprehensibility of what exists.'

80 TI 'The Problem of Socrates' no. 1, p. 29 [KGW VI.3: p. 61].

81 BT no. 17, p. 104 [KGW III.1: p. 105].

82 TI 'What I Owe to the Ancients' no. 5, p. 110 [KGW VI.3: p. 154].

83 Walter Kaufmann, *Nietzsche: Philosopher, Psychologist, Antichrist*, Princeton University Press, Princeton, New Jersey, 1974, pp. 391–411.

84 BT no. 15, p. 95 [KGW III.1: p. 95].

85 BT no. 15, p. 98 [KGW III.1: p. 97].

86 Nietzsche's most sustained discussion of Plato's thought occurs in the early Basel lectures 'Introduction to the study of the Platonic Dialogues' (GA XIX, pp. 125–304). The interpretation developed therein remains the foundation for all his subsequent polemics on the topic. Crucial for Nietzsche's interpretation is the assumption that the Platonic Ideas are *super-sensory objects* known through corresponding *concepts* (GA XIX: p. 263). On this view, the Ideas are Plato's solution to the epistemological scepticism implied by Heraclitus' doctrine of the eternal flux: since this flux pertains to the whole realm of sensory experience, true knowledge must refer to the super-sensory. Nietzsche is emphatic in opposing Schopenhauer's *aesthetic* interpretation of the Ideas (GA XIX: pp. 273–74). Such a view is wrong, Nietzsche insists, because Plato proceeds from *abstract* concepts such as justice, beauty, the good etc. Affirming a general division between artistic and scientific-mathematical temperaments, Nietzsche puts Plato unequivocally into the latter category.

87 On Nietzsche's ambivalent attitude to Plato, see Dieter Bremer, 'Platonisches, Antiplatonisches', *Nietzsche-Studien* 8 (1979) pp. 39–103, and Stanley Rosen, *The Question of Being: A Reversal of Heidegger*, Yale University Press, New Haven and London, 1993, Chapter Four. Rosen comments (p. 139) that 'by retaining the Platonic conception of the synoptic vision of the philosopher with respect to human nature, or historical possibility, Nietzsche preserves the key feature of Platonism.'

88 In comparison with Plato, Nietzsche's writings contain little on Aristotle. There is a brief consideration in the early lectures on the 'History of Greek Literature' (GA XVIII: pp. 77–88), but this consists mainly of biographical and philological information. Nietzsche is more interested in Aristotle's lost dialogues than in the extant systematic works, because the former testify to the artistic and literary side of the Stagirite. He claims that, in the systematic works, Aristotle 'shrivels up to a thinker totally enclosed within rigorous speculation' (GA XVIII: p. 85). In *The Birth of Tragedy*, Nietzsche briefly engages with Aristotle's doctrine of *catharsis*, developed in the *Poetics* to explain the effect of tragic art. Counterposing his own idea of tragedy as a stimulant to life, Nietzsche comments that the theory of *catharsis* reflects 'no experience of tragedy as a supreme *art*' (BT no. 22, p. 132, KGW III.1: p. 138). The same point is made in later writings and in general seems to exhaust Nietzsche's interest in Aristotle. This is not surprising, for the severe analytical style of the Stagirite is perhaps the antithesis not only of Nietzsche's youthful 'romanticism' but of all 'intuitive' philosophy. Nietzsche does not see Aristotle as adding anything essentially new to Plato, who remains the primary seducer to the cold world of abstractions.

89 WP no. 251, p. 145.

90 D no. 68, p. 40 [KGW V.1: p. 61].

91 D no. 68, p. 41 [KGW V.1: p. 63].

92 AC no. 42, p. 154 and no. 45, p. 161 [KGW VI.3: pp. 213 and 221].

93 But see the passing comments on 'the Hebrew' in Z I 'Of voluntary death', p. 98 [KGW VI.1: p. 90]. For a summary discussion of Nietzsche's attitude to Jesus, see Uwe Kühneweg, 'Nietzsche und Jesus – Jesus bei Nietzsche', *Nietzsche-Studien* 15 (1986), pp. 382–97. A more ambitious treatment is Karl Jaspers' *Nietzsche und das Christentum*, Piper, Munich, 1952.

94 AC no. 32, p. 144 [KGW VI.3: p. 202].

95 AC no. 34, p. 147 [KGW VI.3: p. 205].

96 AC nos. 31 and 28, pp. 143 and 141 [KGW VI.3: pp. 200 and 198].

97 The resemblances between Jesus and Zarathustra are also noticed by Thomas Altizer, 'Eternal Recurrence and the Kingdom of God', in David Allison (ed.) *The New Nietzsche*, MIT Press, Cambridge, Massachusetts, 1977, pp. 232–46. Altizer comments (p. 239) that 'Nietzsche portrays Jesus as a kind of innocent forerunner of Zarathustra.'

98 GS no. 350, p. 292 [KGW V.2: p. 268].

99 BGE no. 58, p. 66 [KGW VI.2: p. 75].

100 This begins already with Nietzsche's friend Franz Overbeck, a professor of church history, whose *Über die Christlichkeit unserer*

heutigen Theologie appeared in 1873 bound together in one volume (C. G. Naumann Verlag, Leipzig) with Nietzsche's first 'Untimely Meditation' against Strauß. For a survey of the 'theological reception' of Nietzsche in the twentieth century, see Peter Köster, 'Nietzsche-Kritik und Nietzsche-Rezeption in der Theologie des 20 Jahrhunderts', *Nietzsche-Studien* 10/11 (1981/82), pp. 615–685.

101 Paul Tillich, *A History of Christian Thought*, Simon & Schuster, New York, 1967, p. 503.

102 AC no. 38, p. 149 [KGW VI.3: pp. 207–208].

103 GS no. 357, p. 307 [KGW V.2: p. 282]: 'You see what it was that really triumphed over the Christian god: Christian morality itself, the concept of truthfulness that was understood ever more rigorously, the father confessor's refinement of the Christian conscience, translated and sublimated into a scientific conscience, into intellectual cleanliness at any price.' Despite this statement, Nietzsche thinks that 'intellectual cleanliness' is the last thing to be expected from 'modern men'.

104 E.g. WP no. 22, p. 17.

105 BGE no. 262, p. 182 [KGW VI.2: pp. 226–27].

106 BGE 'Preface' p. 13 [KGW VI.2: p. 3]: 'Today every kind of dogmatism stands sad and discouraged. *If* it continues to stand at all! For there are scoffers who assert it has fallen down, that dogmatism lies on the floor, more, that dogmatism is at its last gasp'; AC no. 1, p. 115 [KGW VI.3: p. 167]: '"I know not which way to turn; I am everything that knows not which way to turn" sighs modern man. It was from this modernity that we were ill, from lazy peace, from cowardly compromise, from the whole virtuous cleanliness of modern Yes and No.'

107 BGE no. 44, p. 54 [KGW VI.2: p. 57].

108 UM III no. 1, p. 128 [KGW III.1: p. 334].

109 The thesis that Nietzsche misidentifies Christianity as the source of modern *ressentiment* is maintained by Max Scheler in his profound study *Das Ressentiment im Aufbau der Moralen*, Klostermann, Frankfurt am Main, 1978 (first published 1912). Scheler sees *ressentiment* not in Christian values but in the autonomous values of modern 'bourgeois' man (see pp. 68–69).

CHAPTER THREE: REDEMPTION AND LIFE AFFIRMATION

1 GM II, no. 24, p. 96 [KGW VI.2: p. 352].

2 BGE no. 295, p. 200 [KGW VI. 2: p. 248].

3 GS no. 125, pp. 181–82 [KGW V.2: pp. 158–60].

4 Cf. GS no. 2, pp. 76–77 [KGW V.2: pp. 47–48]: 'I keep having the same experience and keep resisting it every time. I do not want to believe it although it is palpable: *the great majority of people lacks an intellectual conscience.*'

5 Lou Salomé comments (*Friedrich Nietzsche in seinen Werken*, Carl Konegan, Vienna, 1911, p. 147): 'Not until the beginnings of Nietzsche's late philosophy does it become fully clear to what degree it is the fundamental religious drive which governs Nietzsche's nature and outlook....And just for this reason do we encounter in these late works such a passionate struggle with religion, with belief in God and the neediness-for-redemption, i.e. because he was so dangerously drawn to them himself.' See also Manfred Kaempfert, *Säkularisation und neue Heiligkeit*, Erich Schmidt Verlag, Berlin, 1971, pp. 17–27, which documents a variety of opinions on Nietzsche's 'religiosity'.

6 AC no. 47, pp. 162–63 [KGW VI.3: p. 223].

7 AC no. 44, p. 158 [KGW VI.3: p. 218].

8 Of course, it is a question of how Nietzsche's texts are to be read. In this study, I have proceeded from the presupposition that the kind of 'slow reading' (D 'Preface' no. 5, p. 5; KGW V.1: p. 9) Nietzsche wants is above all a philosophical reading, in which every particular passage is understood in the context of the unitary whole of philosophical meaning.

9 BGE no. 1, p. 15 [KGW VI.2: p. 9].

10 In a letter to his friend Carl von Gersdorff on 7 April, 1866, the twenty-one year old Nietzsche writes that 'if Christianity means belief in an historical event or in an historical person then I have nothing to do with it. But if it means neediness for redemption I can value it very highly' (*Briefwechsel* II.3: p. 122). This remains Nietzsche's basic attitude right through to *The Antichrist*.

11 GS no. 357, p. 307 [KGW V.2: pp. 281–82].

12 Schopenhauer considers this as the philosophical meaning of the Christian doctrine of 'original sin'; see e.g. *The World as Will and Representation* I, The Falcon's Wing Press, Indian Hills, Colorado, 1958, p. 405f.

13 In a survey of the various spheres of art, Schopenhauer indicates the Platonic Ideas which belong respectively to them. However, Schopenhauer's idiosyncratic employment of the Platonic Ideas is a secondary matter. The main point of his discussion (in *The World as Will and Representation* I, Book Three) is to show the disinterested, and therefore redemptive, character of aesthetic experience. For a discussion of this aspect of his thought, see Georg Simmel, *Schopenhauer and Nietzsche*, University of Illinois Press, Urbana and Chicago, 1986, Ch. 5; and Thomas Mann's essay 'Schopenhauer', in Mann's *Essays: Musik und Philosophie*, Fischer Verlag, Frankfurt am Main, 1978, pp. 193–234.

14 Schopenhauer, *The World as Will and Representation* I, p. 176.

15 *The World as Will and Representation* I, pp. 178–79.

16 *The World as Will and Representation* I, p. 379.
17 *The World as Will and Representation* I, p. 385.
18 *The World as Will and Representation* I, p. 390.
19 *The World as Will and Representation* II, p. 606.
20 *The World as Will and Representation* I, p. 319.
21 *The World as Will and Representation* I, p. 403.
22 *The World as Will and Representation* I, p. 409.
23 *The World as Will and Representation* I, pp. 411–12.
24 *Aphorismen zur Lebensweisheit*, in *Sämtliche Werke IV*, Suhrkamp, Frankfurt am Main, 1986, pp. 373–592.
25 Walter Burkert, in *Greek Religion*, Basil Blackwell, Oxford, 1985, pp. 161–62, describes the Dionysian phenomenon as follows: 'Dionysus can seemingly be defined quite simply as the god of wine and of intoxicated ecstacy. Intoxication as change in consciousness is interpreted as the irruption of something divine. But the experience of Dionysus goes far beyond that of alcohol and may be entirely independent of it; madness becomes an end in itself. *Mania*, the Greek word, denotes frenzy, not as the ravings of delusion, but, as its etymological connection with *menos* would suggest, as an experience of intensified mental power. Nevertheless, Dionysian ecstacy is not something achieved by an individual on his own; it is a mass phenomenon and spreads almost infectiously. This is expressed in mythological terms by the fact that the god is always surrounded by the swarm of his frenzied male and female votaries. Everyone who surrenders to this god must risk abandoning his everyday identity and becoming mad; this is both divine and wholesome. An outward symbol and instrument of the transformation brought by the god is the mask. The merging of god and votary which occurs in this metamorphosis is without parallel in the rest of Greek religion: both votary and god are called Bacchus.' See also M. L. Baeumler, 'Das moderne Phänomen des Dionysischen und seine "Entdeckung" durch Nietzsche', *Nietzsche-Studien* 6 (1977), pp. 123–53.
26 BT no. 7, p. 59 [KGW III.1: p. 52].
27 TI 'What I Owe to the Ancients' no. 4, p. 110 [KGW VI.3: p. 153].
28 BT no. 2, pp. 40 and 38 [KGW III.1: pp. 28 and 26].
29 BT no. 5, p. 52 [KGW III.1: p. 43].
30 BT no. 10, p. 74 [KGW III.1: p. 69].
31 BT no. 4, p. 45 [KGW III.1: p. 35].
32 BT no. 3, p. 41 [KGW III.1: pp. 30–31].
33 BT 'Attempt at a Self-Criticism' no. 5, p. 23 [KGW III.1: p. 12].
34 BT no. 9, p. 71 [KGW III.1: p. 65].
35 See e.g. John Sallis, *Crossings: Nietzsche and the Space of Tragedy*, University of Chicago Press, Chicago and London, 1991, pp. 67–68.

36 BT no. 7, p. 60 [KGW III.1: p. 53].

37 BT no. 7, p. 59 [KGW III.1: p. 52]; BT 'Attempt at a Self-Criticism' no. 5, p. 22 [KGW III.1: p. 15].

38 EH 'The Birth of Tragedy' no. 3, p. 273 [KGW VI.3: pp. 310–11].

39 PTAG no. 5, p. 51 [KGW III.2: p. 316].

40 PTAG no. 4, p. 46 [KGW III.2: p. 313].

41 PTAG no. 7, p. 62 [KGW III.2: p. 324].

42 BT no. 24, pp. 141–42 [KGW III.1: p. 149].

43 KGW VII.1 (*Nachlaß*): p. 246.

44 TI 'The Four Great Errors' no. 8, p. 54 [KGW VI.3: p. 62].

45 See the discussion by Karl Jaspers, *Nietzsche: An Introduction to the Understanding of his Philosophical Activity*, Gateway, South Bend, Indiana, 1965, pp. 149–151.

46 Before the First World War, Nietzsche was principally known as a *Lebensphilosoph* (philosopher of life). See e.g. George Simmel, *Schopenhauer and Nietzsche* (op. cit.) Ch. 1. Simmel states (p. 6): 'Life in its primary sense, beyond the opposition of corporeal and spiritual existence, is seen here as an immeasurable sum of powers and potentials which, in themselves, are aimed at the augmentation, intensification, and increased effectiveness of the life process. It is impossible to describe this process through an analysis.' In Simmel's opinion, Nietzsche gives life a 'Darwinian' (self-overcoming) dimension which is absent in the Schopenhauerian concept.

47 Jaspers (*Nietzsche: An Introduction to the Understanding of his Philosophical Activity*, op. cit., p. 294) comments: 'But "life" and "will to power" are expressions that, whether taken in their direct and customary sense or in their definite biological and psychological sense, fail to hit upon what Nietzsche has in mind. Since they are used to refer to being itself, what they really are remains "unfathomable".' To distinguish them from concepts in the proper cognitive sense, Jaspers calls Nietzsche's fundamental expressions 'ciphers'. To be noted, in connection with Nietzsche's 'Heracliteanism', is Heraclitus' saying 'The lord whose oracle is in Delphi neither speaks out nor conceals, but gives a sign' (Diels-Kranz Fr. 93, in *The Presocratic Philosophers*, ed. G. S. Kirk, J. E. Raven and M. Schofield, Cambridge University Press, Cambridge, 1983, p. 209). Nietzsche thinks of his own utterances as similarly 'delphic'.

48 E.g. BGE no. 10, p. 22 [KGW VI.2: p. 17]: 'In the case of stronger, livelier thinkers who are still thirsty for life...when they take sides *against* appearance and speak even of "perspective" with arrogant disdain, when they rank the credibility of their own body about as low as the ocular evidence which says "the earth stands still" and thus with apparent good humour let slip their firmest possession (for what is believed in more firmly today than the body?) – who

knows whether they are not at bottom trying to win back something which was formerly an even *firmer* possession, some part or other of the old domain of the faith of former times, perhaps the "immortal soul", perhaps "the old God", in short ideas by which one could live better, that is to say more vigorously and joyfully, than by "modern ideas"?'

49 WP no. 1041, p. 536.

50 Some commentators, however, see distinct Christian elements in Nietzsche's Dionysianism: for documentation and discussion see Kaempfert, *Säkularisation und neue Heiligkeit* (op. cit.) p. 154.

51 On the positivity of mystery (something altogether different to the positive determinability of mystery, which is a contradiction in terms), see the classic study by Rudolf Otto, *The Idea of the Holy*, translated by J. W. Harvey, Oxford University Press, 1923.

52 See e.g. R. T. Wallis, *Neoplatonism*, Duckworth, London, 1972; and Andrew Louth, *The Origins of the Christian Mystical Tradition*, Clarendon, Oxford, 1981.

53 WP no. 1050, p. 539.

54 EH 'The Birth of Tragedy' no. 1, p. 271 [KGW VI.3: p. 308].

55 EH 'Human, All Too Human' no. 5, p. 288 [KGW VI.3: p. 325].

56 For a discussion of Nietzsche's Bayreuth experience, see Werner Ross, *Der ängstliche Adler: Friedrich Nietzsches Leben*, Deutsche Taschenbuch Verlag, Stuttgart, 1980, pp. 416–74.

57 HAH 2nd 'Preface' no. 2, p. 210 [KGW IV.3: p. 5].

58 HAH I no. 108, p. 60 [KGW IV.2: p. 107].

59 HAH I no. 1, p. 12 [KGW IV.2: p. 20].

60 HAH I no. 132, p. 70 [KGW IV.2: p. 124].

61 HAH I no. 134, pp. 72–73 [KGW IV.2: pp. 128–29].

62 HAH I no. 34, p. 30 [KGW IV.2: p. 51].

63 *Die Unschuld des Werdens* (Selections from Nietzsche's *Nachlaß*), ed. Alfred Baeumler, Kröner Verlag, Stuttgart, 1978, Vol. I, p. 405.

64 HAH I no. 107, p. 58 [KGW IV.2: p. 103].

65 HAH I no. 144, p. 79 [KGW IV.2: p. 140].

66 Nietzsche's 'psychological' analysis of religion in HAH is in some respects reminiscent of Ludwig Feuerbach's 'anthropological' critique, while the thesis of 'narcotization' has affinities with Karl Marx's well-known diagnosis of religion as the 'opiate of the people'. These latter authors, however, are far more resolute in their 'positivism' than is Nietzsche, who wants the 'tragic pathos' to survive the psychological 'demasking' of conventional religiosity. For the broader context of Nietzsche's critique of Christianity, see Karl Löwith, 'Die philosophische Kritik der christlichen Religion im 19. Jahrhundert', in Löwith's *Sämtliche Schriften* 3, J. B. Metzlersche Verlagsbuchhandlung, Stuttgart, 1985, pp. 96–162.

67 Although in HAH I Nietzsche highlights the opposition between intellect and emotions, his discussions continually indicate that these are not adequate terms for the formulation of his problem. If art, metaphysics and religion are reduced to emotionality, how should we understand the stated 'tragic' implications of their loss in scientifically enlightened culture? E.g. 'Won't our philosophy turn into tragedy? Won't truth become inimical to life and to the best among us? A question weighs upon our tongue and yet not wishes to be voiced: if one can consciously remain in the untruth? or, if one *must*, whether death is not to be preferred?' (HAH I no. 34, p. 29, KGW IV.2: pp. 49–50). What is the force of this 'must'? Is it the psychological circumstance that human beings need the 'untruth' of the whole apparatus of consolation which has now been intellectually discredited, and that in the last resort no adaptation to 'actual truth' can be expected? But if this is so, why will truth be inimical precisely to the 'best'? Further, why, as Nietzsche maintains (HAH I no. 20, p. 23, KGW IV.2: p. 37), can metaphysics be overcome only through a 'retrospective movement' in which one 'recognizes that the greatest advance has come from here'?

68 E.g. HAH I no. 110, p. 62 [KGW IV.2: p.110]: 'A religion has never yet, either directly or indirectly, either as dogma or as parable, contained a truth.' This statement is directed against Schopenhauer's thesis of the 'allegorical truth' of religion, but whereas Nietzsche in this aphorism refers to Jewish, Christian and Indian religion, he is curiously silent about the Greeks.

69 The stages passed through by the free spirit are indicated in a formula from Nietzsche's *Nachlaß* as 1) the stage of 'I should' (*Ich soll*), 2) the stage of 'I want' (*Ich will*), and 3) the stage of 'I am' (*Ich bin*). This schema is discussed by Karl Löwith, *Nietzsches Philosophie der ewigen Wiederkehr des Gleichen* (in Löwith's *Sämtliche Schriften* 6, J. B. Metzlersche Verlag, Stuttgart, 1987) pp. 123–30. It can also be seen in BGE no. 31, p. 44 [KGW VI.2: pp. 45–46]: 'In our youthful years we respect and despise without that art of nuance which constitutes the best thing we gain from life, and, as is only fair, we have to pay dearly for having assailed men and things with Yes and No in such a fashion....The anger and reverence characteristic of youth seem to allow themselves no peace until they have falsified men and things in such a way that they can vent themselves on them – youth as such is something which falsifies and deceives. Later when the youthful soul, tormented by disappointments, finally turns suspiciously upon itself, still hot and savage even in its suspicion and pangs of conscience: how angry it is with itself now, how it impatiently rends itself....A decade later: and one grasps that all this too – was still youth!' On the transition from 'I should' to 'I

want' ('the great liberation'), see HAH 1st 'Preface' no. 3, pp. 6–7 [KGW IV.2: pp. 9–11]. Nietzsche's middle period is more accurately characterized as 'experimental' or 'demystificatory' than 'positivist' or 'scientific' in the strict sense.' As Eugen Fink comments (*Nietzsches Philosophie*, Kohlhammer, Stuttgart, 1960, p. 45): 'It is remarkable in what a vague sense Nietzsche speaks here [HAH] of "science"; strictly speaking it is none of the positive sciences; it is much more a broad kind of critical questioning and procedure.'

70 AC no. 39, p. 151 and no. 32, p. 144 [KGW VI.3: pp. 209 and 202].

71 WP no. 166, p. 100.

72 WP no. 161, pp. 98–99.

73 AC no. 33, p. 146 [KGW VI.3: p. 204].

74 EH 'Thus Spoke Zarathustra' no. 1, p. 295 [KGW VI.3: p. 333].

75 See the section 'Systementwürfe und Pläne 1883–1887' in Baeumler's *Nachlaß* collection *Die Unschuld des Werdens* (op. cit.) Vol. 2, pp. 271–313.

76 UM II no. 2, p. 70 [KGW III.1: p. 257].

77 PTAG no. 5, p. 54 [KGW III.2: pp. 318–19].

78 GS no. 341, pp. 273–74 [KGW V.2: p. 250].

79 E.g. EH 'The Birth of Tragedy' no. 3, pp. 273–74 [KGW VI.3: pp. 310–11].

80 Z III 'The Convalescent' no 2, p. 237 [KGW VI.1: p. 272].

81 Kaempfert, *Säkularisation und neue Heiligkeit* (op. cit.) p. 166.

82 Z III 'The Wanderer' pp. 174–75 [KGW VI.1: pp. 190–91].

83 Z III 'The Convalescent' no. 1, pp. 232–33 [KGW VI.1: pp. 266–67].

84 Z III 'The Convalescent' no. 2, pp. 234–35 [KGW VI.1: pp. 268–69]. Zarathustra had earlier reacted similarly to the dwarf in Z III 'Of the Vision and the Riddle' no. 2, p. 178 [KGW VI.1: p. 195].

85 Z III 'Of the Great Longing' pp. 238–40 [KGW VI.1: pp. 274–77].

86 Karl Löwith comments (*Nietzsches Philosophie der ewigen Wiederkehr des Gleichen*, op. cit., p. 334) that 'the whole of *Zarathustra*, from his first appearance to the final ass-festival, is the prolonged history of an ever-delayed redemption.'

87 Z II 'Of Redemption' p. 162 [KGW VI.1: p. 176].

88 Z II 'Of Redemption' p. 161 [KGW VI.1: p. 175].

89 Z II 'Of Redemption' p. 163 [KGW VI.1: p. 177].

90 Z II 'Of Redemption' p. 162 [KGW VI.1: p. 177].

91 Z II 'Of Redemption' p. 161 [KGW VI.1: p. 175].

92 The coming of the great midday is presaged in Z III 'On the Virtue Which Makes Small' no. 3, p. 192; 'Of Passing By', p. 198; 'Of the Three Evil Things' no. 2, p. 209; 'Of Old and New Law-Tables' no. 3, p. 125 and no. 30, p. 231 [KGW VI.1: pp. 213, 221, 236, 244, 265]; it finally arrives at the end of Book Three. See also the section 'At Midday' from Z IV and aphorism 308 'At Midday' in HAH. On this

motif, see Otto Bollnow, *Das Wesen der Stimmungen*, Vittorio Klostermann, Frankfurt am Main, 1956, Ch. XIII.

93 WP. no. 1032, pp. 532–33.

94 Heidegger, 'Who is Nietzsche's Zarathustra?', in David Allison (ed.), The New Nietzsche, MIT Press, Cambridge, Mass., 1977, p. 74.

95 Z III 'The Seven Seals' pp. 244 and 246 [KGW VI.1: pp. 283 and 285].

96 On Nietzsche as 'mystic', see Jörg Salaquarda, 'Der ungeheure Augenblick', *Nietzsche-Studien* 18 (1989) pp. 317–37.

97 Heidegger, 'Who is Nietzsche's Zarathustra?' (op. cit., p. 75): 'The Eternal Recurrence of the same remains a vision for him, but also an enigma. It can be neither verified nor refuted logically or empirically. At bottom, this is true of every thinker's essential thought: envisioned, but enigma – worthy of questioning.'

98 EH 'Thus Spoke Zarathustra' no. 1, p. 295 [KGW VI.3: p. 333].

99 GS no. 341, p. 273 [KGW V.2: p. 250].

100 See e.g. WP nos 553–69, pp. 300–307.

101 Eugen Fink comments that 'The concept of earth in Nietzsche's thought is difficult to grasp. At this point we can only indicate that Nietzsche does not think of earth as something simply present at hand (*Bloß*= *Vorhandenes*) but as the breaking open (*Aufgehenlassen*), as the womb of all things, as the movement of bringing-forth' (*Nietzsches Philosophie*, op. cit., p. 77). The same could be said of the concepts 'world', 'life' and 'primal One'.

102 WP no. 617, p. 330.

103 See Z III 'On the Vision and the Riddle' no. 2, p. 178 [KGW VI.1: pp. 195–96].

104 The link between the sequentiality and the 'thingliness' of time is argued by Aristotle, *Physics* 219a–222a.

105 BGE no. 56, pp. 63–64 [KGW VI.2: pp. 72–73]. See Heidegger's discussion in *Nietzsche*, Vol. II, Harper & Row, San Francisco, 1984, pp. 63–69.

106 Z 'Prologue' no. 3, p. 42 [KGW VI.1: p. 9].

107 AC no. 43, pp. 155–56 [KGW VI.3: p. 215].

108 EH 'Thus Spoke Zarathustra' no. 6, p. 306 [KGW VI.3: p. 343].

109 WP no. 251, pp. 144–45: 'Hitherto one has always attacked Christianity not merely in a modest way but in the wrong way. As long as one has not felt Christian morality to be a capital crime against life its defenders have had it all their own way. The question of the mere "truth" of Christianity – whether in regard to the existence of its God or the historicity of the legend of its origin, not to speak of Christian astronomy and natural science – is a matter of secondary importance as long as the question of the value of Christian *morality* is not considered.'

110 D no. 440, p. 187 [KGW V.1: p. 273].
111 See e.g. AC no. 32, pp. 144–45 [VI.3: pp. 201–203].
112 Schopenhauer, *The World as Will and Representation* I, p. 409.
113 *The World as Will and Representation* II, p. 626.
114 GS no. 381, p. 346 [KGW V.2: p. 317].
115 Plato, *The Republic* 487b–497a.
116 Z III 'The Wanderer', p. 173 [KGW VI.1: p. 189].
117 That Zarathustra's experience at the end of Part Three is 'Diony-sian' is confirmed by Nietzsche himself in EH 'Thus Spoke Zarathustra' no. 6, p. 306 [KGW VI.1: p. 343]: 'Zarathustra is a dancer – how he that has the hardest, most terrible insight into reality, that has thought the "most abysmal idea", nevertheless does not consider it an objection to existence, not even to its eternal recurrence – but rather one reason more for being himself the eternal Yes to all things, "the tremendous, unbounded saying Yes and Amen" – "Into all abysses I still carry the blessings of my saying Yes" – *But this is the concept of Dionysus again*' (emphasis in original).
118 Z III 'The Homecoming', p. 202 [KGW VI.1: p. 227].
119 Z III 'Of the Great Longing', p. 239 [KGW VI.1: pp. 275–76].
120 See e.g. BGE no. 265, p. 185 [KGW VI.2: pp. 229–30] and Z III 'Of the Three Evil Things' no. 2, p. 208 [KGW VI.1: p. 234].
121 BGE no. 287, p. 196 [KGW VI.2: p. 243].
122 WP no. 1050, p. 539.
123 WP no. 1041, p. 536.
124 WP no. 485, pp. 268–69.
125 BGE no. 12, p. 25 [KGW VI.2: p. 21].
126 WP no. 108, p. 68
127 This is the way Nietzsche understands the Christian 'immortal soul'. Of course, it is not a fair representation. In Pauline theology, salvation of the soul is much more than preservation of a 'soul atom' through passive 'belief'. By contrast, it is noticeable how passive the human individual becomes in postmodernist deconstructionism, where the self can be nothing more than the outcome of anonymous structures of power/knowledge/discourse.
128 See Søren Kierkegaard, *The Sickness Unto Death*, Penguin, Harm-ondsworth, Middlesex, 1989, p. 43. Nietzsche and Kierkegaard have often been compared, e.g. Karl Jaspers, *Reason and Existence*, Farrar, Straus and Giroux, New York, 1955, pp. 19–50.
129 GS no. 335, p. 263 [KGW V.2: p. 240].
130 Diels-Kranz Fragment 101, in G. S. Kirk, J. E. Raven and M. Schofield, *The Presocratic Philosophers*, op. cit., p. 211. Nietzsche quotes this fragment with approval in PTAG no. 8, pp. 67–68 [KGW III.2: p. 329].

131 See e.g. WP no. 477, pp. 263–64.
132 GS no. 345, p. 283 [KGW V.2: p. 259].
133 *Phaedo* 62a.
134 *Phaedo* 61d.
135 AC no. 46, p. 161 [KGW VI.3: p. 221].
136 BGE no. 271, pp. 190–91 [KGW VI.2: pp. 236–37].
137 GM III no. 14, p. 125 [KGW VI.2: p. 389].
138 EH 'Why I Am So Wise' no. 8, p. 233 [KGW VI.3: pp. 273–74].
139 See Karl Jaspers, *Nietzsche und das Christentum*, Piper, Munich, 1952, pp. 45–47.
140 See William James, *The Varieties of Religious Experience*, Penguin, Harmondsworth, Middlesex, 1982, p. 290. On philosophy as purification of the soul, see Plato's *Sophist* 227d–30e.
141 In BGE 'Preface', p. 14 [KGW VI.2: p. 4] Nietzsche describes his philosophical task as 'wakefulness itself' (*Wachsein selbst*). 'Wakefulness' is a frequently encountered motif not only in the fragments of Heraclitus, but in Platonic and Neoplatonic philosophy, Gnosticism and the New Testament. It is a fundamental aspect of Nietzsche's 'existential' conception of truth.
142 EH 'Why I Am So Wise' no. 8, p. 234 [KGW VI.3: p. 274].

CHAPTER FOUR: NIETZSCHE AND HEIDEGGER
1 Heidegger, *Nietzsche* II, p. 66 (see note 3 below).
2 Heidegger, *Nietzsche* II, pp. 101–102.
3 Martin Heidegger, *Nietzsche* Vols I and II, Neske Verlag, Pfullingen, 1961. I shall refer to the English translation in four volumes by David Krell et al., *Nietzsche,* Harper & Row, New York, 1979–87.
4 A general idea of the postmodernist view on the Nietzsche–Heidegger relation can be obtained from Ernst Behler's *Derrida–Nietzsche: Nietzsche–Derrida*, Ferdinand Schöningh, Munich, 1988, and Alan Schrift's *Nietzsche and the Question of Interpretation*, Routledge, London, 1990. Valuable discussions from outside the postmodernist orbit are Stanley Rosen, *The Question of Being: A Reversal of Heidegger*, Yale University Press, New Haven and London, 1993, and Otto Pöggeler, *Martin Heidegger's Path of Thinking*, Humanities Press International, Atlantic Highlands, 1987, Ch. 6. See also Karl Löwith's review of Heidegger's *Nietzsche* volumes 'Heideggers Vorlesungen über Nietzsche' (1962), in Löwith's *Sämtliche Schriften* 8, J. B. Metzlersche, Stuttgart, 1984, pp. 242–57.
5 Jacques Derrida, *Of Grammatology*, John Hopkins University Press, Baltimore, 1974, p. 20.
6 Derrida, *Of Grammatology* (op. cit.) p. 19.

7 It is notable that, particularly in Anglo-American circles, the postmodernists of today are the revisionist epistemologists of yesterday (e.g. Richard Rorty). Apparently, perspectivism provides epistemological 'land' within the 'open sea' of Nietzsche's philosophy, a kind of 'bridge' between Feyerabend et al. and Derrida.

8 See e.g. Aristotle, *Metaphysics* 1026a.

9 See e.g. Heidegger, *Nietzsche* IV, pp. 150–58.

10 For Heidegger, 'presence' (*Anwesenheit*) is the meaning of Aristotelian *ousia* (substance), itself the foundational concept of metaphysical ontology. Heidegger's basic philosophical project can be seen as an attempt to work out an alternative to 'ousiological' ontology. See John Caputo, *Heidegger and Aquinas*, Fordham University Press, New York, 1982, and Werner Marx, *Heidegger and the Tradition*, Northwestern University Press, Evanston, 1971.

11 Heidegger opens *Being and Time*, Basil Blackwell, Oxford, 1962, p. 21, with the claim that the question of Being has been 'forgotten' (*ist in Vergessenheit gekommen*).

12 Heidegger, *Nietzsche* I, p. 9.

13 The comparative importance of 'will to power' and 'Dionysus' cannot of course be determined by simply counting the number of references to each. The particular contexts in which these motifs appear must be taken into account. In Nietzsche's late writings, the Dionysian appears at those points where he attempts to sum up his philosophical position. This is why it is so prominent in *Ecce Homo*, Nietzsche's intellectual autobiography.

14 Through a meticulous examination of the relevant portion of the *Nachlaß*, Mazzino Montinari has shown that by late 1888 Nietzsche abandons the idea of writing a work called 'The Will to Power'. See the essay 'Nietzsches Nachlaß von 1885 bis 1888 oder Textkritik und Wille Zur Macht', in Montinari's *Nietzsche Lesen*, Walter de Gruyter, Berlin, 1982.

15 Lou Andreas-Salomé, *Friedrich Nietzsche in seinen Werken*, Carl Konegan, Vienna, 1911, p. 141.

16 WP Book Three, Section II ('The Will to Power in Nature') and Book Four, Section III ('The Eternal Recurrence'), particularly nos 1062–64.

17 Heidegger, *Nietzsche* II, pp. 204–05.

18 Heidegger, *Nietzsche* I, p. 18.

19 Heidegger, *Nietzsche* I, p. 38.

20 Heidegger, *Nietzsche* I, pp. 38–39.

21 Heidegger, *Nietzsche* I, p. 42.

22 Heidegger, *Nietzsche* I, p. 52.

23 Heidegger, *Nietzsche* I, p. 63.

24 Heidegger, *Nietzsche* I, p. 72.

25 Heidegger, *Nietzsche* I, p. 140.

26 WP no. 617, p. 330.

27 Heidegger, *Nietzsche* II, p. 202. I have modified Krell's translation, which does not observe a consistent distinction between '*Sein*' and '*das Seiende*', often rendering them both simply as 'being'. Kaufmann's translation of *The Will to Power* suffers from the same fault.

28 Heidegger, *Nietzsche* II, p. 203.

29 Heidegger, *Nietzsche* II, p. 6.

30 PTAG no. 5, p. 54 [KGW III.2: pp. 318–19].

31 See Pöggeler, *Martin Heidegger's Path of Thinking*, op. cit., pp. 82–107.

32 Heidegger, *Nietzsche* IV, p. 86.

33 Heidegger, *Nietzsche* IV, p. 28: 'No matter how sharply Nietzsche pits himself time and again against Descartes, whose philosophy grounds modern metaphysics, he turns against Descartes only because the latter *still* does *not* posit man as a *subiectum* in a way that is complete and decisive enough. The representation of the *subiectum* as ego, the I, thus the "egoistic" interpretation of the *subiectum*, is still not subjectivistic enough for Nietzsche. Modern metaphysics first comes to the full and final determination of its essence in the doctrine of the Overman, the doctrine of man's absolute preeminence among beings. In that doctrine, Descartes celebrates his supreme triumph.'

34 Alexander Nehamas, *Nietzsche: Life as Literature*, Harvard University Press, Cambridge, Massachusetts, 1985, p. 16.

35 Ernst Behler, 'Nietzsche and Deconstruction', in Volker Dürr et al. (eds) *Nietzsche: Literature and Values*, University of Wisconsin Press, Madison and London, 1988, p. 16.

36 See e.g. Jacques Derrida, *Margins of Philosophy*, University of Chicago Press, Chicago, 1982, p. 135.

37 Karl Löwith, *Nietzsches Philosophie der ewigen Wiederkehr des Gleichen* (1st edition 1934), in Löwith's *Sämtliche Schriften* 6, J. B. Metzlersche Verlag, Stuttgart, 1987, pp. 111–23.

38 Karl Jaspers, *Nietzsche: An Introduction to the Understanding of his Philosophical Activity* (op. cit., 1st German edition 1936) pp. 8–13.

39 Nehamas, *Nietzsche: Life as Literature* (op. cit.) p. 20.

40 Heidegger, *Nietzsche* I, p. 28. Heidegger discusses the general idea of 'system' in philosophy in his 1936 lectures *Schelling's Treatise on the Essence of Human Freedom*, Ohio University Press, Athens, Ohio, 1985, pp. 22–33.

41 Heidegger, *Nietzsche* I, pp. 35–36. Cf. Nietzsche's claim in BGE no. 20, pp. 31–32 [KGW VI.2: p. 28] that 'the most diverse philosophers unfailingly fill out again and again a certain basic scheme of possible

philosophies....Their thinking is in fact not so much a discovering as a recognizing, a remembering, a return to a far off, primordial household of the soul.' One of the most profound discussions of the relation between the 'perennial' and 'historical' dimensions of philosophy is Henri Bergson's 1911 lecture 'Philosophical Intuition', in Bergson's *The Creative Mind*, Littlefield, Adams & Co., Totowa, New Jersey, 1965. Bergson's understanding of philosophical intuition has much in common with Nietzsche's.

42 The publication of Heidegger's early Freiburg lectures in the *Gesamtausgabe* has revealed that the ideas of *Being and Time* have their origin in a concept of 'factical life-experience'. See e.g. *Grundprobleme der Phänomenologie (1919/20)*, Vittorio Klostermann, Frankfurt am Main, 1993, and *Ontologie (Hermeneutik der Faktizität*, Vittorio Klostermann, Frankfurt am Main, 1988. It is only in the mid-1920s that Heidegger begins to speak consistently of 'Being' and 'Existence' rather than of 'factical life'.

43 It is hardly necessary to point out that this 'seeing' is not at all 'ocular'. The thinker does not form an 'image' of the *Sache* in his 'mind's eye'. In many works, Heidegger undertakes a critique of the 'ocularcentrism' of the metaphysical tradition, which equates the 'reality' of entities with their 'look' (the Platonic *eidos*).

44 GM III no. 8, p. 110 [KGW VI.2: p. 372]. Cf. Nietzsche's statement in the 'Preface' to HAH II, no. 1, p. 209 [KGW IV.3: p. 3]: 'One should speak only when one may not remain silent; and then only of that which one has overcome – everything else is chatter (*Geschwätz*), "literature", lack of breeding.'

45 Heidegger, *Nietzsche* II, pp. 207–208. For further on 'Erschweigen' and 'Erschweigung', see Heidegger's *Beiträge zur Philosophie*, Vittorio Klostermann, Frankfurt am Main, 1989, p. 79f.

46 EH 'Why I Write Such Good Books' no. 1, p. 261 [KGW VI.3: p. 298]: 'Ultimately, nobody can get more out of things, including books, than he already knows. For what one lacks access to from experience one will have no ear.' See Chapter One above, 'Truth and the limits of language', esp. note 90. Of course, this 'remembrance' is of a particular kind, which Heidegger tries to convey in his later writings through the word '*Andenken*' (commemoration) as distinct from mere '*Erinnerung*' (recollection).

47 The credibility of Derrida's 'semiotic' objection to Heidegger depends on the credibility of the former's metaphysical statement that 'everything is text', i.e. that there simply is nothing outside the total complex of signifiers. It would be absurd to think that such a statement is supported, nay even touched upon, by the linguistics of Saussure (who, incidentally, compared language to the game of chess, i.e. to something with no external referent) or anyone else.

The Saussurian considerations adduced by Derrida in his 'Différance' essay, to show that 'the signified concept is never present in and of itself, in a sufficient presence that would refer only to itself' (*Margins of Philosophy*, op. cit., p. 11) at best bear on what Heidegger calls the 'being of beings' (the 'nature of things') and on no account on Being itself. Heidegger's 'Being' is not a mere word, nor a 'thing', but a given 'phenomenon', a phenomenon, moreover, which is in no sense a 'presence'. To be engaged in semiotic and quasi-epistemological considerations about whether Being can be 'admitted' (as if it were something which might be 'posited', like black holes) is to have already capitulated to verbal-conceptual thought.

Ultimately, however, the point for Derrida and other postmodernists is a moral one: they do not like 'authority' or 'hierarchy', they detest the 'obligatory' character of the *Seinsfrage*. E.g. in 'Interpreting Signatures (Nietzsche–Heidegger): Two Questions' (in Laurence Rickels, ed., *Looking after Nietzsche*, State University of New York Press, Albany, 1990) Derrida writes (p. 9): 'When he [Heidegger] is pretending to rescue Nietzsche from this or that distortion – that of the Nazis, for example – he does so with categories which can themselves serve to distort – namely with the opposition between essential and inessential thinkers, authentic thinkers and inauthentic ones, and with the definition of the essential thinker as someone selected, chosen, marked out or, I would even say "signed".' That such categories may distort is no doubt true, but the implication that they must and do distort in Heidegger's writings (the point which Derrida wants to make) depends on the moral outrage which can be expected at such 'arrogant' distinctions. In the light of Chapter Two above, one could ask Derrida whether Nietzsche himself does not believe in 'essential' and 'inessential' thinkers, but, of course, Derrida chooses to notice only Nietzsche's 'pluralism'. Again, in the essay *'Ousia and Gramme*: Note on a Note from *Being and Time'* (in *Margins of Philosophy*, op. cit. p. 63) Derrida writes: 'Now, is not the opposition of the primordial to the derivative still metaphysical? Is not the quest for an *archia* in general, no matter with what precautions one surrounds the concept, still the "essential" operation of metaphysics? Supposing, despite powerful presumptions, that one may eliminate it from any other provenance, is there at least some Platonism in the *Verfallen*? Why determine as fall the passage from one temporality to another? And why qualify temporality as authentic – or proper (*eigentlich*) – and as inauthentic – or improper – when any ethical preoccupation has been suspended?' What concept of 'metaphysics' is Derrida referring to here? It is certainly not

Heidegger's, for Heidegger does not think of Being as an *arche*. The suggestion that Heidegger embraces metaphysical *archai* with certain 'precautions' simply begs the question. Derrida is clearly relying on his own conception of metaphysics as discursive 'closure', together with the apparent 'ethical' reprehensibility of the 'elitist' distinction between 'primordial' and 'derivative' truth. There is indeed, I would contend, 'some Platonism in the *Verfallen*', but is Platonism a refutation? How is Platonism to be understood? Is it, too, discursive closure? Is it necessarily 'metaphysical' in Heidegger's sense? I cannot pursue these questions here, but they are not pursued by Derrida either: instead 'Platonism' functions as yet another bogey word for those who abhor all hierarchy and authority.

48 On the 'mineness' of existence, see Heidegger, *Being and Time* (op. cit.) pp. 67–68.

49 Heidegger, *Nietzsche* II, p. 119.

50 Heidegger discusses Nietzsche's 'perspectivism' primarily in the 1939 lectures on 'will to power as knowledge'. Perspectivism is understood by Heidegger in terms of the 'poetizing essence of reason' (*das dichtende Wesen der Vernunft*), which Nietzsche was not the first to discover: 'The poetizing character of reason was first seen and thought through by Kant in his doctrine of the transcendental imagination. The German idealist conception of absolute reason (in Fichte, Schelling, Hegel) is thoroughly grounded in the Kantian insight into the essence of reason as a "forming" poetizing force' (*Nietzsche* III, pp. 95–96). According to Heidegger, Nietzsche misunderstands perspectivism when he sees it as fundamentally in opposition to Plato's docrine of Ideas: the Ideas and Nietzsche's perspectivism are just two alternatives within the problem of the 'schematization' of experience. For a critique of the idea of 'world picture' – which underlies much postmodernist perspectivism – see Heidegger's essay 'The Age of the World Picture', in Heidegger, *The Question Concerning Technology and Other Essays*, Harper & Row, San Francisco, 1977. In the 1937 Nietzsche lectures, Heidegger refers to the cultural impact, after the First World War, of Spengler's 'discovery' of *Weltanschauungen*: 'What a revelation it was for the mass of people who were unfamiliar with actual thinking and its rich history when two decades ago, in 1917, Oswald Spengler announced that he was the first to discover that every age and every civilization had its own world-view! Yet is was nothing more than a very deft and clever popularization of thoughts and questions on which others long before him had ruminated far more profoundly' (*Nietzsche* II, p. 101). Heidegger would undoubtedly see the postmodernists as latterday Spenglers.

51 GS no. 357, p. 308 [KGW V.2: p. 282].

52 In an article 'Geschlecht, Sexual Difference, Ontological Difference' (*Research in Phenomenology*, Vol. 13, 1983, p. 74), Derrida,
again playing to the gallery, holds it against Heidegger that he takes
'*Dasein*' as sexually neutral: 'What if "sexuality" already marked the
most original *Selbstheit*? If it were an ontological structure of
ipseity? If the *Da* of *Dasein* were already "sexual"? What if sexual
difference were already marked in the opening up of the question
of the sense of Being and of the ontological difference? And what
if, though not self-evident, neutralization were already a violent
operation?' What postmodernist feminists believe on these 'what
ifs?' need not detain us. But if Derrida and others wish to 'unmask'
the 'ruse' of Heidegger's implicit 'phallocentrism', they should do
the same for Nietzsche, who likewise takes 'human existence' as
'sexually neutral'. As for how the substantive question may be
settled, erudite discussions are beside the point: at this level we have
only 'intuition' to guide us. For Nietzsche and Heidegger at any rate,
an unhesitating rejection of concepts like 'phallocentrism' is a *sine
qua non* of philosophical seriousness.

53 On 'Ereignis', see Heidegger, *Beiträge zur Philosophie* (op. cit.). This
concept goes back to the 1919/20 Freiburg lectures *Zur Bestimmung
der Philosophie*, Vittorio Klostermann, Frankfurt am Main, 1987, p.
75.

54 See the essay 'Kants These über das Sein', in Heidegger, *Wegmarken*,
Vittorio Klostermann, Frankfurt am Main, 1978.

55 Heidegger, *Being and Time* (op. cit.) p. 284.

56 GS no. 381, p. 346 [KGW V.2: p. 317].

57 On thinking as 'thanking' see Heidegger, *What is Called Thinking?*,
Harper & Row, New York, 1968, pp. 138–47. 'For questioning is
the piety of thought' is the last sentence of Heidegger's essay 'The
Question Concerning Technology', in Heidegger, *The Question
Concerning Technology and Others Essays* (op. cit.) p. 35.

58 The *locus classicus* of Heidegger's 'alethiological' conception of truth
is *Being and Time* (op. cit.) Section 44 (pp. 256–73).

59 Heidegger, *Being and Time* (op. cit.), p. 265; HAH I, no. 34, p. 30
[KGW IV.2: p. 50].

60 For Heidegger's conception of 'falling' (*Verfallenheit*) see *Being and
Time* (op. cit) pp. 219–24.

61 Heidegger, *Being and Time* (op. cit.) p. 233.

62 Robert Solomon concludes his article 'Nietzsche, Postmodernism,
and Ressentiment: a Genealogical Hypothesis' (in Clayton Koelb,
ed. *Nietzsche as Postmodernist*, State University of New York Press,
Albany, 1990, pp. 267–93) with the apt remark 'what Nietzsche
wanted to say is not just "post" anything.'

63 In BGE no. 1, p. 15 [KGW VI.2: p. 9], speaking of the problem of the value of truth, Nietzsche says 'it has eventually come to seem to us as if this problem has never before been posed – that we have been the first to see it, to fix our eye on it, to hazard it.' But this statement is in the subjunctive: it 'seems as if', although of course the situation is otherwise. (The awkward translation by Hollingdale 'it has finally almost come to seem to us that this problem has never before been posed' does not adequately convey the subjunctive of the German '*daß es uns schließlich bedünken will, als sei das Problem noch nie bisher gestellt*'.) The 'seems as if' refers to the impact of this question on the individual who so questions: it is always 'as if' the individual were asking this question alone and for the first time in history. For Nietzsche, what is 'revolutionary' is not his own thought specifically, but philosophical thought (more accurately, philosophical existence) as such: the impact, however, is confined to the individual, to the human being who philosophizes.

64 GA XIX: p. 177.

65 See GM 'Preface' no. 1, p. 15 [KGW VI.2: p. 259].

66 Hannah Arendt, *The Life of the Mind*, two vols in one, Harcourt Brace Jovanovich, New York, 1978, p. 178. On Schopenhauerian aspects of the later Heidegger, see Hellmuth Hecker, 'Heideggger und Schopenhauer', *Schopenhauer Jahrbuch* 71 (1990), pp. 85–96.

67 Commenting on Nietzsche's dictum 'God is dead', Heidegger has this to say: 'But which God? The God of "morality", the Christian God is dead – the "Father" in whom we seek sanctuary, the "Personality" with whom we negotiate and bare our hearts, the "Judge" with whom we adjudicate, the "Paymaster" from whom we receive our virtues' reward, that God with whom we "do business"....The God who is viewed in terms of morality, this God alone is meant when Nietzsche says "God is dead"' (*Nietzsche* II, p. 66). Elsewhere in these lectures (p. 123) Heidegger states that Nietzsche's idea of eternal return attempts to show 'what kind of religion can exist in the future. The thought itself is to define the relationship to God – and to define God himself.' By contrast, the postmodernists are the first generation of Nietzsche commentators for whom the 'problem of God' is essentially irrelevant. Unlike Salomé, Steiner, Bertram, Jaspers, Löwith and Heidegger, they show little appreciation of the fact that Nietzsche wrote so much about religion in general and Christianity in particular. Because of their antipathy to 'authority' and the 'final word', they subsume the problem of God under that of politico-ideological 'delivery from oppression', while the 'death of God' is simplified into the collapse of authoritative definitions of truth.

68 Heidegger has been more influential on contemporary theology than any other philosopher. The literature on 'Heidegger and

theology' is therefore voluminous. From the philosophical side, the books by John Caputo are especially valuable: *Heidegger and Aquinas*, op. cit., and *The Mystical Element in Heidegger's Thought*, Fordham University Press, New York, 1986. See also Caputo's article 'Heidegger and Theology', in Charles B. Guignon (ed.), *The Cambridge Companion to Heidegger*, Cambridge University Press, Cambridge, 1993, pp. 270–88.

69 As Heidegger puts it, Nietzsche 'does not want to instill perfect comprehension by means of the few, cryptic things he says about his doctrine of eternal return. Rather, he wants to pave the way for a transformation of that fundamental attunement (*Grundstimmung*) by which alone his doctrine can be comprehensible and effective' (*Nietzsche* II, p. 17). This and many other comments by Heidegger are in conflict with his 'Nietzsche as metaphysician' thesis, for the 'object' of 'fundamental attunement' is always 'Being' rather than 'beings'.

70 Heidegger, *Nietzsche* II, pp. 94–95.

71 GS no. 34, p. 290 [KGW V.2: p. 265].

72 *Nietzsche* II, p. 195: 'Thus the most durable and unfailing touch-stone of genuineness and forcefulness of thought in a philosopher is the question of whether he experiences in a direct and fundamental manner the nearness of the Nothing in the being of beings. Whoever fails to experience it remains forever outside the sphere of philosophy, without hope of entry.'

Bibliography of Works Cited

Allison, David (ed.), *The New Nietzsche*, MIT Press, Cambridge, Massachusetts, 1977.

Altizer, Thomas J. J., 'Eternal recurrence and the Kingdom of God', in Allison, pp. 232–46.

Andreas-Salomé, Lou, *Friedrich Nietzsche in seinen Werken*, Konegan, Vienna, 1894.

Ansell-Pearson, Keith J., 'Nietzsche's overcoming of Kant and metaphysics: from tragedy to nihilism', *Nietzsche-Studien* 16 (1987), pp. 310–39.

Arendt, Hannah, *The Life of the Mind*, one volume edition, Harcourt Brace Jovanovich, New York, 1978.

Aristotle, *The Basic Works of Aristotle*, edited by Richard McKeon, Random House, New York, 1941.

Babich, Babette E., 'Post-Nietzschean postmodernism', in Koelb, pp. 249–66.

Baeumler, Alfred, *Die Unschuld des Werdens: Der Nachlaß*, 2 vols, Alfred Kröner Verlag, Stuttgart, 1978.

Baeumler, M. L., 'Das moderne Phänomen des Dionysischen und seine "Entdeckung" durch Nietzsche', *Nietzsche-Studien* 6 (1977), pp. 123–53.

Bauschinger, Sigrid, Susan Cocalis and Sara Lennox (eds), *Nietzsche Heute: Die Rezeption seines Werks nach 1968*, Francke Verlag, Bern and Stuttgart, 1988.

Behler, Ernst, 'Nietzsche and deconstruction', in Dürr et al., pp. 180–98.

Behler, Ernst , *Derrida–Nietzsche: Nietzsche–Derrida*, Ferdinand Schöningh, Munich, 1988.

Bergoffen, Debra B., 'Perspectivism without nihilism', in Koelb, pp. 57–71.

Bergson, Henri, *The Creative Mind*, trans. Mabelle Andison, Littlefield, Adams & Co., Totowa, New Jersey, 1965.

Bollnow, Otto, *Das Wesen der Stimmungen*, Klostermann, Frankfurt am Main, 1956.

Borsche, Tilman, 'Nietzsches Erfindung der Vorsokratiker', in Simon (1985), pp. 62–87.

Bremer, Dieter, 'Platonisches, Antiplatonisches', *Nietzsche-Studien* 8 (1979), pp. 39–103.

Caputo, John, *Heidegger and Aquinas*, Fordham University Press, New York, 1982.

Caputo, John, *The Mystical Element in Heidegger's Thought*, Fordham University Press, New York, 1986.

Caputo, 'Heidegger and theology', in Guignon, pp. 270–88.

Clark, Maudemarie, *Nietzsche on Truth and Philosophy*, Cambridge University Press, Cambridge, 1990.

Climacus, John, *The Ladder of Divine Ascent*, trans. Colm Luibheid and Norman Russell, Paulist Press, Ramsey, New Jersey, 1982.

Deleuze, Gilles, 'Nomad thought', in Allison, pp. 142–49.

Deleuze, Gilles, *Nietzsche and Philosophy*, trans. Hugh Tomlinson, Athlone, London, 1983.

Derrida, Jacques, *Of Grammatology*, trans. Chakravorty Spivak, John Hopkins University Press, Baltimore and London, 1976.

Derrida, Jacques, *Spurs. Nietzsche's Styles*, trans. Barbara Harlow (bilingual edition), University of Chicago Press, Chicago and London, 1979.

Derrida, Jacques, *Margins of Philosophy*, trans. Alan Bass, Harvester, Brighton, 1982.

Derrida, Jacques, 'Geschlecht, sexual difference, ontological difference', *Research in Phenomenology* Vol. 13 (1983), pp. 65–83.

Derrida, Jacques, 'Interpreting signatures (Nietzsche/ Heidegger): two questions', in Rickels.

Dürr, Volker, et al. (eds), *Nietzsche. Literature and Values*, University of Wisconsin Press, Madison and London, 1988.

Fink, Eugen, *Nietzches Philosophie*, Kohlhammer, Stuttgart, 1960.

Goedert, Georges, 'Nietzsche und Schopenhauer', *Nietzsche-Studien* 7 (1978), pp. 1–26.

Granier, Jean, 'Perspectivism and interpretation', in Allison, pp. 190–200.

Guignon, Charles (ed.), *The Cambridge Companion to Heidegger*, Cambridge University Press, Cambridge, 1993.

Hayman, Ronald, *Nietzsche: A Critical Life*, Weidenfeld & Nicolson, London, 1980.

Heidegger, Martin, *Being and Time*, trans. John Macquarrie and Edward Robinson, Basil Blackwell, Oxford, 1962.

Heidegger, Martin, *Nietzsche* (2 vols), Neske, Pfullingen, 1961.

Heidegger, Martin, *Nietzsche* (4 vols), trans. by D. F. Krell, J. Stambaugh and F. Capuzzi, Harper & Row, New York, 1979–87.

Heidegger, Martin, *What is Called Thinking?*, trans. John Glenn Gray, Harper Torchbooks, New York, 1968.

Heidegger, Martin, *The Question Concerning Technology and Other Essays*, trans. William Lovitt, Harper & Row, San Francisco, 1977.

Heidegger, Martin, 'Who is Nietzsche's Zarathustra', in Allison, 1977.

Heidegger, Martin, *Wegmarken*, Vittorio Klostermann, Frankfurt am Main, 1978.

Heidegger, Martin, *Basic Writings*, trans. David Krell, Routledge & Kegan Paul, London and Henley, 1978.

Heidegger, Martin, *The Metaphysical Foundations of Logic*, trans. Michael Helm, Indiana University Press, Bloomington, 1984.

Heidegger, Martin, *Schelling's Treatise on the Essence of Human Freedom*, Ohio University Press, Athens, Ohio, 1985.

Heidegger, Martin, *Zur Bestimmung der Philosophie*, Vittorio Klostermann, Frankfurt am Main, 1987.

Heidegger, Martin, *Ontologie (Hermeneutik der Faktizität)*, Vittorio Klostermann, Frankfurt am Main, 1988.

Heidegger, Martin, *Beiträge zur Philosophie*, Vittorio Klostermann, Frankfurt am Main, 1989.

Heidegger, Martin, *Grundprobleme der Phänomenologie (1919/20)*, Vittorio Klostermann, Frankfurt am Main, 1993.

Heller, Erich, *The Importance of Nietzsche*, University of Chicago Press, Chicago and London, 1988.

Hersbell, Jackson P. and Nimis, Stephen A., 'Nietzsche and Heraclitus', *Nietzsche-Studien* 8 (1979), pp. 17–38.

Higgins, Kathleen, 'Nietzsche and postmodern subjectivity', in Koelb, pp. 189–215.

James, William, *The Varieties of Religious Experience*, Penguin, Harmondsworth, Middlesex, 1982.

Janz, K. P., 'Nietzsche's Verhältnis zur Musik seiner Zeit', *Nietzsche-Studien* 7 (1978).

Jaspers, Karl, *Nietzsche und das Christentum*, Piper, Munich, 1952.

Jaspers, Karl, *Reason and Existence*, Farrar, Straus and Giroux, New York, 1955.

Jaspers, Karl, *Nietzsche. An Introduction to the Understanding of his Philosophical Activity*, trans. Charles F. Wallraff and Frederick J. Schmitz, Gateway, South Bend, Indiana, 1965 (first German edition 1936).

Kaempfert, Manfred, *Säkularisation und neue Heiligkeit*, Erich Schmidt Verlag, Berlin, 1971.

Kaufmann, Walter, *Nietzsche: Philosopher, Psychologist, Antichrist*, Princeton University Press, Princeton, 1974.

Kierkegaard, Søren, *The Sickness Unto Death*, trans. A. Hannay, Penguin, Harmondsworth, Middlesex, 1989.

Kirk, G. S., Raven, J. E. and Schofield, M., *The Presocratic Philosophers*, Cambridge University Press, Cambridge, 1983.

Koelb, Clayton (ed.), *Nietzsche as Postmodernist*, State University of New York Press, Albany, 1990.

Kofman, Sarah, 'Nietzsche und die Dunkelheit des Heraklit', in Bauschinger et al., pp. 75–104.

Köster, Peter, 'Nietzsche-Kritik und Nietzsche-Rezeption in der Theologie des 20. Jahrhunderts', *Nietzsche-Studien* 10/11 (1981–82), pp. 615–85.

Kühneweg, Uwe, 'Nietzsche und Jesus – Jesus bei Nietzsche', *Nietzsche-Studien* 15 (1986), pp. 382–97.

Louth, Andrew, *The Origins of the Christian Mystical Tradition*, Clarendon, Oxford, 1981.

Löwith, Karl, *Sämtliche Schriften*, J. B. Metzlersche Verlag, Stuttgart, 1984 ff.

Magnus, Berndt, 'Nietzsche and postmodern criticism', *Nietzsche-Studien* 18 (1989), pp. 301–16.

Mann, Thomas, *Essays: Band 3 Musik und Philosophie*, Fischer Taschenbuch Verlag, Frankfurt am Main, 1978.

Marx, Werner, *Heidegger and the Tradition*, Northwestern University Press, Evanston, 1971.

Montinari, Mazzino, *Nietzsche Lesen*, Walter de Gruyter, Berlin, 1982.

Morgenstern, Martin, 'Schopenhauers Grundlegung der Metaphysik', *Schopenhauer Jahrbuch* 69 (1988), pp. 57–66.

Nancy, Jean-Luc, '"Our Probity" – on truth in the moral sense in Nietzsche', in Rickels, pp. 67–87.

Nehamas, Alexander, *Nietzsche. Life as Literature*, Harvard University Press, Cambridge, Massachusetts, 1985.

Otto, Rudolf, The Idea of the Holy, trans. J. W. Harvey, Oxford U. P., Oxford, 1923.

Overbeck, Franz, *Über die Christlichkeit unserer heutigen Theologie*, C. G. Naumann Verlag, Leipzig, 1873.

Plato, *Theaetetus and Sophist*, trans. Harold Fowler, Loeb Library, Harvard University Press and William Heinemann, Cambridge Massachusetts and London, 1921.

Plato, *Phaedrus and Letters VII and VIII*, trans. Walter Hamilton, Penguin, Harmondsworth, Middlesex, 1973.

Plato, *The Republic*, trans. Desmond Lee, Penguin, Harmondsworth, Middlesex, 1974.

Plato, *The Last Days of Socrates*, trans. of *Euthyphro, The Apology, Crito,* and *Phaedo,* by Hugh Tredennick, Penguin, Harmondsworth, Middlesex, 1959.

Pöggeler, Otto, *Martin Heidegger's Path of Thinking*, trans. Daniel Magurshak and Sigmund Barber, Humanities Press International, Atlantic Highlands, N. J., 1987.

Pseudo-Dionysius, *The Complete Works*, trans. Colm Luibheid, Paulist Press, Mahwah, New Jersey, 1987.

Rickels, Laurence (ed.), *Looking After Nietzsche*, State University of New York Press, Albany, 1990.

Rosen, Stanley, *The Question of Being: A Reversal of Heidegger*, Yale University Press, New Haven and London, 1993.

Ross, Werner, *Der ängstliche Adler: Friedrich Nietzsches Leben*, Deutscher Taschenbuch Verlag, Munich, 1980.

Salaquarda, Jörg, 'Nietzsche und Lange', *Nietzsche-Studien* 7 (1978), pp. 236–60.

Salaquarda, Jörg, 'Zur gegenseitigen Verdrängung von Schopenhauer und Nietzsche', *Schopenhauer Jahrbuch* 65 (1984), pp. 13–30.

Salaquarda, Jörg, 'Die ungeheure Augenblick', *Nietzsche-Studien* 18 (1989), pp. 317–37.

Sallis, John, *Crossings. Nietzsche and the Space of Tragedy*, University of Chicago Press, Chicago and London, 1991.

Scheler, Max, *Das Ressentiment im Aufbau der Moralen*, Klostermann, Frankfurt am Main, 1978 (first edition 1912).

Schlecta, Karl, (ed.) *Friedrich Nietzsche Werke* (5 vols), Ullstein, Frankfurt am Main, 1984.

Schopenhauer, Arthur, *The World as Will and Representation* (2 vols), trans. E. F. J. Payne, The Falcon's Wing Press, Indian Hills, Colorado, 1958.

Schopenhauer, Arthur, *Parerga und Paralipomena I*, *Sämtliche Werke* IV, ed. Wolfgang Frhr. von Löhneysen, Suhrkamp, Stuttgart, 1986.

Schrift, Alan, *Nietzsche and the Question of Interpretation*, Routledge, London, 1990.

Simmel, Georg, *Schopenhauer and Nietzsche*, trans. by Helmut Loiskandl, Deena Weinstein and Michael Weinstein, University of Illinois Press, Urbana and Chicago, 1986.

Simon, Josef (ed.), *Nietzsche und die Philosophische Tradition* I, Königshausen & Neumann, Würzburg, 1985.

Simon, Josef, 'Die Krise des Wahrheitsbegriffs als Krise der Metaphysik', *Nietzsche-Studien* 18 (1989), pp. 242–59.

Solomon, Robert C., 'Nietzsche, postmodernism, and resentment: a genealogical hypothesis', in Koelb, pp. 267–93.

Stack, George, *Lange and Nietzsche*, Walter de Gruyter, Berlin and New York, 1983.

Thiele, Leslie Paul, *Friedrich Nietzsche and the Politics of the Soul*, Princeton University Press, Princeton, New Jersey, 1990.

Tillich, Paul, *A History of Christian Thought*, Simon & Schuster, New York, 1967.

Wallis, R. T., *Neoplatonism*, Duckworth, London, 1972.
Warren, Mark, *Nietzsche and Political Thought*, MIT Press, Cambridge, Massachusetts, 1988.

Index